# ENTERPRISE CLOUD COMPUTING
## Technology, Architecture, Applications

Cloud computing promises to revolutionize IT and business by making computing available as a utility over the internet. This book is intended primarily for practicing software architects who need to assess the impact of such a transformation. It explains the evolution of the internet into a cloud computing platform, describes emerging development paradigms and technologies, and discusses how these will change the way enterprise applications should be architected for cloud deployment.

Gautam Shroff provides a technical description of cloud computing technologies, covering cloud infrastructure and platform services, programming paradigms such as MapReduce, as well as 'do-it-yourself' hosted development tools. He also describes emerging technologies critical to cloud computing. The book also covers the fundamentals of enterprise computing, including a technical introduction to enterprise architecture, so it will interest programmers aspiring to become software architects and serve as a reference for a graduate-level course in software architecture or software engineering.

**Gautam Shroff** heads TCS' Innovation Lab in Delhi, a corporate R&D lab that conducts applied research in software architecture, natural language processing, data mining, multimedia, graphics and computer vision. Additionally he is responsible for TCS' Global Co-Innovation Network (COIN), which works with venture-backed emerging technology companies to create and take to market solutions that have disruptive innovation potential. Further, as a member of TCS' Corporate Technology Board, he is part of the process of recommending directions to existing R&D efforts, spawning new R&D efforts, sponsoring external research and proliferating the resulting technology and intellectual property across TCS' businesses.

# ENTERPRISE CLOUD COMPUTING

## TECHNOLOGY, ARCHITECTURE, APPLICATIONS

### GAUTAM SHROFF

CAMBRIDGE
UNIVERSITY PRESS

CAMBRIDGE UNIVERSITY PRESS
Cambridge, New York, Melbourne, Madrid, Cape Town, Singapore,
São Paulo, Delhi, Dubai, Tokyo, Mexico City

Cambridge University Press
The Edinburgh Building, Cambridge CB2 8RU, UK

Published in the United States of America by Cambridge University Press, New York

www.cambridge.org
Information on this title: www.cambridge.org/9780521760959

© G. Shroff 2010

First published 2010

Printed in the United Kingdom at the University Press, Cambridge

*A catalog record for this publication is available from the British Library*

ISBN 978-0-521-76095-9 Hardback
ISBN 978-0-521-13735-5 Paperback

# Contents

CONTENTS

# Preface

---

In today's world virtually all available information on any technical topic is just a few clicks away on the web. This is especially true of an emerging area such as cloud computing. So why write a book, and, who should read this book and why?

Every few years a new 'buzzword' becomes the rage of the technology world. The PC in the 80s, the internet in the 90s, service-oriented architecture in the early 2000s, and more recently 'cloud computing': By enabling computing itself to be delivered as a utility available over the internet, cloud computing could transform enterprise IT. Such a transformation could be as significant as the emergence of power utilities in the early twentieth century, as eloquently elucidated in Nicholas Carr's recent book *The Big Switch*.

Over the years large enterprises have come to rely on information technology to run their increasingly complex business operations. Each successive technology 'revolution' promises tremendous gains. It falls upon the shoulders of the *technical architects* in the IT industry to evaluate these promises and measure them against the often significant pain that is involved in adapting complex IT systems to new computing paradigms: The transition to cloud computing is no exception.

So, this book is first and foremost for technical architects, be they from IT departments or consulting organizations. The aim is to cover cloud computing **technology**, **architectures** and **applications** in detail, so as to be able to properly assess its true impact on enterprise IT.

Since cloud computing promises to fundamentally revolutionize the way enterprise IT is run, we also revisit many principles of enterprise architecture and applications. Consequently, this is also a book on the fundamentals of **enterprise computing**, and can therefore serve as a reference for a graduate-level course in software architecture or software engineering. Alternatively, software professionals interested in acquiring the 'architect' tag may also find it a useful read.

From a personal perspective this book is also an attempt to capture my experience of a decade in the IT industry after an initial career in academic computer science: The IT industry seemed ever busier dealing with constant changes in technology. At the same time, every generation of professionals, in particular the technical architects, were constantly reinventing the wheel: Even though automation techniques, such as large-scale code generation using 'model driven architecture' often actually worked in practice, these were far from the panacea that they theoretically appeared to be.

Nevertheless, the academic in me continued to ask, what after all does an enterprise application *do*, and why should it be so complex? In 2004 I wrote an *interpreter* for what appeared to me to be a perfectly reasonable 3-tier architecture on which, I thought, *any* enterprise application should run. This was the seed of what became TCS' InstantApps platform. At the same time Salesforce.com was also experimenting with an interpretive architecture that later became Force.com. While software as a service was the rage of the industry, I began using the term Dev 2.0 to describe such interpretive hosted development platforms.

In the meantime Amazon launched its elastic computing cloud, EC2. Suddenly, the entire IT infrastructure for an enterprise could be set up 'in the cloud.' 'Dev 2.0 in the Cloud' seemed the next logical step, as I speculated in a keynote at the 2008 ACM SIGSOFT FSE conference. After my talk, Heather Bergman from Cambridge University Press asked me whether I would be interested in writing a book. The idea of a book had been in my mind for more than a year then; I had envisaged a book on software architecture. But maybe a technical book on cloud computing was more the need of the hour. And thus this book was born.

In my attempt to present cloud computing in the context of enterprise computing, I have ended up covering a rather vast landscape. Part I traces the evolution of computing technology and how enterprise architecture strives to manage change with continuity. Part II introduces cloud computing platforms and the economics of cloud computing, followed by an overview of technologies essential for cloud applications in Part III. Part IV delves into the details of cloud computing and how it impacts application development. The essentials of enterprise software architecture are covered in Part V, from an overview of enterprise data models to how applications are built. We also show how the *essence* of what an enterprise application does can be abstracted using *models*. Part V concludes with an integrated picture of enterprise analytics and search, and how these tasks can be efficiently implemented on computing clouds. These are important topics that are unfamiliar to many architects; so hopefully, their unified treatment here using matrix algebra is illuminating. Finally, Part VI presents an overview of the industry ecosystem around enterprise cloud computing and concludes by speculating on the possible future of cloud computing for enterprises.

A number of people have helped bring this book to fruition: First of all, Heather Bergman who suggested that I write, helped me finalize the topic and table of contents, and led me through the book proposal process in record time. Once the first draft was written, Jeff Ullman reviewed critical parts of the book in great detail, for which I remain eternally grateful. Rob Schreiber, my PhD advisor from another lifetime, also took similar pains, even 20 years after doing the same with my PhD thesis; thanks Rob! Many of my colleagues in TCS also reviewed parts of the manuscript; in particular Ananth Krishnan, C. Anantaram, Puneet Agarwal, Geetika Sharma, Lipika Dey, Venkatachari Raghavan, Surjeet Mishra, Srinivasan Varadanarayanan and Harrick Vin. I would also like to thank David Tranah for taking over as my editor when Heather Bergman left Cambridge University Press soon after I began writing, and for shepherding the book through the publication process.

Finally, I am grateful for the continuous encouragement and support I have received over the years from TCS management, in particular F.C. Kohli, S. Ramadorai and Phiroz Vandrevala, as well as, more recently, N. Chandrasekaran. I would also like to thank E. C. Subbarao and Kesav Nori, who have been my mentors in TCS R&D, for serving as role models, influencing my ideas and motivating me to document my experience.

I have learned that while writing is enjoyable, it is also difficult: Whenever my intrinsic laziness threatened this project, my motivation was fueled by the enthusiasm of my family. With my wife, sister-in-law and mother-in-law all having studied at Cambridge University, I suspect this was also in no small measure due to the publisher I was writing for! Last but not least, I thank my wife Brinda, and kids Selena and Ahan, for tolerating my preoccupation with writing on weekends and holidays for the better part of a year.

I sincerely hope that you enjoy reading this book as much as I have enjoyed writing it.

# Abbreviations

| Term | Description |
| --- | --- |
| AJAX | Asynchronous JavaScript and XML |
| AMI | Amazon Machine Image |
| API | Application Programming Interface |
| BPMN | Business Process Modeling Notation |
| CGI | Common Gateway Interface |
| CICS | Customer Information Control System |
| CORBA | Common Object Request Broker Architecture |
| CPU | Central Processing Unit |
| CRM | Customer Relationship Management |
| CRT | Cathode Ray Tube |
| EAI | Enterprise Application Integration |
| EBS | [Amazon] Elastic Block Storage |
| EC2 | Elastic Compute Cloud |
| ECA | Event Condition Action |
| EJB | Enterprise Java Beans |
| ERP | Enterprise Resource Planning |
| GAE | Google App Engine |
| GFS | Google File System |
| GL | General Ledger |
| GML | Generalized Markup Language |
| HDFS | Hadoop Distributed File System |
| HTML | Hypertext Transport Protocol and Secure Socket Layer |
| HTTP | Hypertext Transport Protocol |
| HTTPD | Hypertext Transfer Protocol Daemon |

| Term | Description |
| --- | --- |
| IA | [TCS] InstantApps |
| IaaS | Infrastructure as a Service |
| IBM | International Business Machines |
| IDL | Interface Definition Language |
| IDMS | Integrated Database Management System |
| IDS | Integrated Data Store [Database System] |
| IIS | Internet Information Server |
| IMS | [IBM] Information Management System |
| IT | Information Technology |
| ITIL | Information Technology Infrastructure Library |
| J2EE | Java 2 Enterprise Edition |
| JAAS | Java Authentication and Authorization Service |
| JCL | Job Control Language |
| JSON | JavaScript Object Notation |
| LDAP | Lightweight Directory Access Protocol |
| MDA | Model Driven Architecture |
| MDI | Model Driven Interpreter |
| MDX | Multidimensional Expressions [Query Language] |
| MVC | Model View Controller |
| MVS | Multiple Virtual Storage [Operating System] |
| OLAP | Online analytical processing |
| OMG | Object Management Group |
| PaaS | Platform as a Service |
| PKI | Public Key Infrastructure |
| REST | Representational State Transfer |
| RMI | Remote Method Invocation |
| RPC | Remote Procedure Call |
| SaaS | Software as a Service |
| SCM | Supply Chain Management |
| SGML | Standardized Generalized Markup Language |
| SNA | Systems Network Architecture |
| SOA | Service Oriented Architecture |
| SOAP | Simple Object Access Protocol |
| SQL | Structured Query Language |
| SQS | [Amazon] Simple Queue Service |
| SVD | Singular Value Decomposition |

| Term | Description |
| --- | --- |
| TCP/IP | Transmission Control Protocol/Internet Protocol |
| TCS | Tata Consultancy Services |
| T&M | Time and Materials |
| TP Monitor | Transaction Processing Monitor |
| UML | Unified Modeling Language |
| URI | Uniform Resource Identifier |
| URL | Uniform Resource Locater |
| VM | Virtual Machine |
| VMM | Virtual Machine Monitor |
| VPC | Virtual Private Cloud |
| VPN | Virtual Private Network |
| VSAM | Virtual Storage Access Method |
| VTAM | Virtual Telecommunications Access Method |
| W3C | World Wide Web Consortium |
| WSDL | Web Services Description Language |
| WYSIWYG | What You See is What You Get |
| XHTML | Extensible Hypertext Markup Language |
| XML | Extensible Markup Language |

# PART I

# Computing platforms

Barely 50 years after the birth of enterprise computing, cloud computing promises to transform computing into a utility delivered over the internet. A historical perspective is instructive in order to properly evaluate the impact of cloud computing, as well as learn the right lessons from the past. We first trace the history of enterprise computing from the early mainframes, to client-server computing and 3-tier architectures. Next we examine how the internet evolved into a computing platform for enterprise applications, naturally leading to Software as a Service and culminating (so far) in what we are now calling cloud computing. Finally we describe how the 'enterprise architecture' function within IT departments has evolved over time, playing a critical role in managing transitions to new technologies, such as cloud computing.

# CHAPTER 1

# Enterprise computing: a retrospective

## 1.1 INTRODUCTION

By 'enterprise computing' we mean the use of computers for data processing in large organizations, also referred to as 'information systems' (IS), or even 'information technology' (IT) in general. The use of computers for enterprise data processing began in the 60s with the early mainframe computers. Over the years enterprise computing paradigms have changed dramatically with the emergence of new technology: The advent of the PC in the 80s led to the replacement of large mainframe computers by client-server systems. The rise of the internet in the 90s saw the client-server model give way to web-based enterprise applications and customer-facing e-commerce platforms.

With each of these advances, enterprise systems have dramatically improved in terms of scale and ubiquity of access. At the same time their complexity, and consequently cost, has increased as well: Trillions of dollars are spent world-wide on information technology, including hardware and software purchases as well as application development (in-house or out-sourced). It is also estimated that enterprises spend between two and ten percent of their revenues on IT.[1]

---

[1] From Gartner reports.

Now, cloud computing offers the potential for revolutionizing enterprise computing once more, this time by transforming computing itself into a utility that can be accessed over the internet. In his recent book *The Big Switch* [8], Nicholas Carr compares the possible ramifications of such a change to the creation of the electricity grid in the early twentieth century. Before the grid, industries built and ran their own power generation plants, much as enterprises deploy and manage their own computing systems today. After the grid came along, by 1930, 90 percent of electricity in the US was produced by specialized power utilities and delivered to consumers over power lines [8]. Barely 50 years had elapsed since Edison's invention of a reliable incandescent light-bulb. Will there be a similar revolution in enterprise computing, 50 years after its birth? Only time will tell.

The key elements of cloud computing, as we see it today, are: (a) computing resources packaged as a commodity and made available over the internet, (b) the ability for end-users to to rapidly provision the resources they need and (c) a pricing model that charges consumers only for those cloud resources they actually use. Further, as a result of centralization of computing, significant economies of scale can be exploited by a cloud provider and passed on to enterprise IT. Not surprisingly, much of the interest in cloud computing today is based on expectations of such cost savings. Finally, the concentration of massive clusters of computing resources within cloud providers opens up possibilities for large-scale data analysis at scales unheard of until now. In the process a number of new programming models and development tools have been developed, both to enable large-scale computations as well as dramatically improve software development productivity, and these also fall within the purview of cloud computing.

In this book we shall delve into the technical details of all the above elements of cloud computing: The major cloud platforms are covered in Chapter 5. Chapter 6 examines the potential cost savings from cloud computing. Key technologies essential for building cloud platforms are covered in Chapters 7, 8 and 9. New programming models and development paradigms are the subject of Chapters 10, 11 and 12. The impact of cloud computing on many of the essential aspects of enterprise computing, from data models to transaction processing, workflow and analytics, is examined in Chapters 13, 14, 15 and 16. Chapter 17 presents a snapshot of the cloud computing ecosystem, as it stands today. Finally we conclude, in Chapter 18, by discussing how enterprise IT is likely to adopt cloud computing in the near future, as well as speculate on the future of cloud computing itself.

However, before embarking on this journey, we first revisit the history of enterprise computing architectures in Chapters 1, 2 and 3. As we shall see, in many ways we have come full circle: We began with large centralized computers and went through phases of distributed computing architectures, saw the reemergence of a centralized paradigm along with the emergence of the internet as a computing platform, culminating (so far) in what we now call cloud computing.

## 1.2 MAINFRAME ARCHITECTURE

We can trace the history of enterprise computing to the advent of 'third-generation' computers in the 60s; these used integrated circuits as opposed to vacuum tubes, beginning with the IBM System/360 'mainframe' computer and its successors, which continue to be used to date, e.g. the IBM z-series range.

Until the 80s, most mainframes used punched cards for input and teleprinters for output; these were later replaced by CRT (cathode ray tube) terminals. A typical (post 1980) 'mainframe' architecture is depicted in Figure 1.1. A terminal-based user interface would display screens controlled by the mainframe server using the 'virtual telecommunications access method' (VTAM)

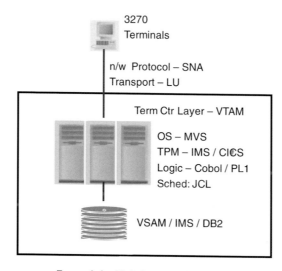

**FIGURE 1.1. Mainframe architecture**

for entering and viewing information. Terminals communicated with the mainframe using the 'systems network architecture' (SNA) protocol, instead of the ubiquitous TCP/IP protocol of today.

While these mainframe computers had limited CPU power by modern standards, their I/O bandwidth was (and is, to date) extremely generous relative to their CPU power. Consequently, mainframe applications were built using a batch architecture to minimize utilization of the CPU during data entry or retrieval. Thus, data would be written to disk as soon as it was captured and then processed by scheduled background programs, in sharp contrast to the complex business logic that gets executed during 'online' transactions on the web today. In fact, for many years, moving from a batch model to an online one was considered a major revolution in IT architecture, and large systems migration efforts were undertaken to achieve this; it is easy to see why: In a batch system, if one deposited money in a bank account it would usually not show up in the balance until the next day after the 'end of day' batch jobs had run! Further, if there was incorrect data entry, a number of corrective measures would have to be triggered, rather than the immediate data validations we are now so used to.

In the early mainframe architectures (through the mid/late 80s), application data was stored either in structured files, or in database systems based on the hierarchical or networked data model. Typical examples include the hierarchical IMS database from IBM, or the IDMS network database, managed now by Computer Associates. The relational (RDBMS) model was published and prototyped in the 70s and debuted commercially in the early 80s with IBM's SQL/DS on the VM/CMS operating system However, relational databases came into mainstream use only after the mid 80s with the advent of IBM's DB2 on the mainframe and Oracle's implementation for the emerging Unix platform. In Chapter 10 we shall see how some of the ideas from these early databases are now reemerging in new, non-relational, cloud database models.

The storage subsystem in mainframes, called 'virtual storage access mechanism' (VSAM), built in support for a variety of file access and indexing mechanisms as well as sharing of data between concurrent users using record level locking mechanisms. Early file-structure-based data storage, including networked and hierarchical databases, rarely included support for concurrency control beyond simple locking. The need for transaction control, i.e., maintaining consistency of a logical unit of work made up of multiple updates, led to the development of 'transaction-processing monitors' (TP-monitors), such as CICS (customer information control system). CICS leveraged facilities of the VSAM layer and implemented commit and roll back protocols to support atomic transactions in a multi-user environment. CICS is still in use in conjunction with DB2 relational databases on IBM z-series mainframes. At the same time, the need for speed continued to see the exploitation of so called 'direct access' methods where transaction control is left to application logic. An example is is the TPF system for the airline industry, which is still probably the fastest application-embedded TP-monitor around.

Mainframe systems also pioneered the large-scale use of *virtual machine* technology, which today forms the bedrock of cloud computing infrastructure. Mainframes running the VM family of 'hypervisors' (though the term was not used at the time; see Chapter 8) could run many independent 'guest' operating systems, such as MVS (popular through the 90s), to z-OS, and now even Linux. Further, virtual machine environments and the operating systems running on mainframes included high levels of automation, similar in many ways to those now being deployed in cloud environments, albeit at a much larger scale: Support for hardware fault tolerance included automatic migration of jobs if CPUs or memory units failed, as well as software fault tolerance, or 'recovery' facilities as pioneered in the MVS operating system. Fine-grained resource measurement, monitoring and error diagnostic capabilities were built into the mainframe architecture; such capabilities are once again becoming essential for cloud computing platforms.

Thus, we can see that far from being an academic exercise, during our excursion into mainframe history we have found many design features of the mainframe era that are now hallmarks of today's emerging cloud computing world; virtual machines, fault tolerance, non-relational databases, and last but not least, centralized computing itself. We now continue our historical tour beyond the mainframe era, continuing to look for early lessons that may stand us in good stead when we delve deeper into cloud computing architectures in later chapters.

## 1.3 CLIENT-SERVER ARCHITECTURE

The microprocessor revolution of the 80s brought PCs to business desktops as well as homes. At the same time minicomputers such as the VAX family and RISC-based systems running the Unix operating system and supporting the C programming language became available. It was now conceivable to move some data processing tasks away from expensive mainframes to exploit the seemingly powerful and inexpensive desktop CPUs. As an added benefit corporate data became available on the same desktop computers that were beginning to be used for word processing and spreadsheet applications using emerging PC-based office-productivity tools. In contrast terminals were difficult to use and typically found only in 'data processing rooms'. Moreover, relational databases, such as Oracle, became available on minicomputers, overtaking the relatively lukewarm adoption of DB2 in the mainframe world. Finally, networking using TCP/IP rapidly became a standard, meaning that networks of PCs and minicomputers could share data.

Corporate data processing rapidly moved to exploit these new technologies. Figure 1.2 shows the architecture of client-server systems. First, the 'forms' architecture for minicomputer-based data processing became popular. At first this architecture involved the use of terminals to access server-side logic in C, mirroring the mainframe architecture; later PC-based forms applications provided graphical 'GUIs' as opposed to the terminal-based character-oriented 'CUIs.' The GUI 'forms' model was the first 'client-server' architecture.

The 'forms' architecture evolved into the more general client-server architecture, wherein significant processing logic executes in a client application,

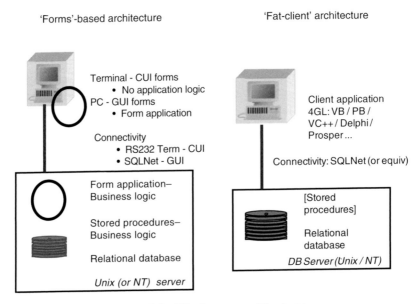

FIGURE **1.2. Client-server architectures**

such as a desktop PC: Therefore the client-server architecture is also referred to as a 'fat-client' architecture, as shown in Figure 1.2. The client application (or 'fat-client') directly makes calls (using SQL) to the relational database using networking protocols such as SQL/Net, running over a local area (or even wide area) network using TCP/IP. Business logic largely resides within the client application code, though some business logic can also be implemented within the database for faster performance, using 'stored procedures.'

The client-server architecture became hugely popular: Mainframe applications which had been evolving for more than a decade were rapidly becoming difficult to maintain, and client-server provided a refreshing and seemingly cheaper alternative to recreating these applications for the new world of desktop computers and smaller Unix-based servers. Further, by leveraging the computing power on desktop computers to perform validations and other logic, 'online' systems became possible, a big step forward for a world used to batch processing. Lastly, graphical user interfaces allowed the development of extremely rich user interfaces, which added to the feeling of being 'redeemed' from the mainframe world.

In the early to mid 90s, the client-server revolution spawned and drove the success of a host of application software products, such as SAP-R/3, the client-server version of SAP's ERP software[2] for core manufacturing process automation; which was later extended to other areas of enterprise operations. Similarly supply chain management (SCM), such as from i2, and customer relationship management (CRM), such as from Seibel, also became popular. With these products, it was conceivable, in principle, to replace large parts of the functionality deployed on mainframes by client-server systems, at a fraction of the cost.

However, the client-server architecture soon began to exhibit its limitations as its usage grew beyond small workgroup applications to the core systems of large organizations: Since processing logic on the 'client' directly accessed the database layer, client-server applications usually made many requests to the server while processing a single screen. Each such request was relatively bulky as compared to the terminal-based model where only the input and final result of a computation were transmitted. In fact, CICS and IMS even today support 'changed-data only' modes of terminal images, where only those bytes

---

[2] SAP-R2 had been around on mainframes for over a decade.

changed by a user are transmitted over the network. Such 'frugal' network architectures enabled globally distributed terminals to connect to a central mainframe even though network bandwidths were far lower than they are today. Thus, while the client-server model worked fine over a local area network, it created problems when client-server systems began to be deployed on wide area networks connecting globally distributed offices. As a result, many organizations were forced to create regional data centers, each replicating the same enterprise application, albeit with local data. This structure itself led to inefficiencies in managing global software upgrades, not to mention the additional complications posed by having to upgrade the 'client' applications on each desktop machine as well.

Finally, it also became clear over time that application maintenance was far costlier when user interface and business logic code was intermixed, as almost always became the case in the 'fat' client-side applications. Lastly, and in the long run most importantly, the client-server model *did not scale*; organizations such as banks and stock exchanges where very high volume processing was the norm could not be supported by the client-server model. Thus, the mainframe remained the only means to achieve large throughput high-performance business processing.

The client-server era leaves us with many negative lessons: the perils of distributing processing and data, the complexity of managing upgrades across many instances and versions, and the importance of a scalable computing architecture. As we shall see in later chapters, many of these challenges continue to recur as wider adoption of the new cloud computing models are envisaged.

## 1.4 3-TIER ARCHITECTURES WITH TP MONITORS

Why did client-server architectures fail to scale for high volume transaction processing? Not because the CPUs were inferior to mainframes; in fact by the late 90s, RISC CPUs had exceeded mainframes in raw processing power. However, unlike the mainframe, client-server architectures had no virtual machine layer or job control systems to control access to limited resources such as CPU and disk. Thus, as depicted in Figure 1.3, 10 000 clients machines would end up consuming 10 000 processes, database connections, and a proportional amount of memory, open files and other resources, and thereby crash the server. (The numbers in the figure represent a late 90s view of computing, when 500MB of server memory was 'too much,' but the

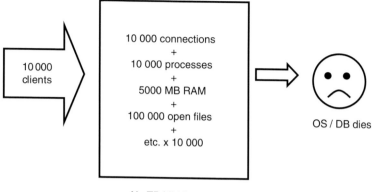

No TP Middleware

**FIGURE 1.3. Client-server fails**

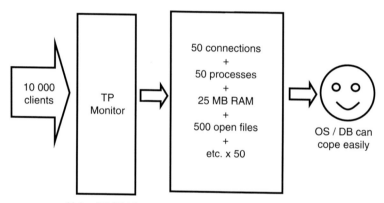

Using TP Middleware with 50 server processes

**FIGURE 1.4. 3-tier architecture scales**

principle remains the same even with the gigabytes of server memory available today.)

Transaction-processing monitors were *redeveloped* to solve this problem for midrange database servers. (Recall that the first TP monitors, such as CICS, were developed for mainframes.) These TP monitors were the first examples of 'middleware,' which sat between clients and a database server to manage access to scarce server resources, essentially by queuing client requests. Thus, as depicted in Figure 1.4, by limiting concurrent requests to a small number, say 50, the server could handle the large load while the clients only paid a small price in response time while their requests waited in the TP monitor queues. Carefully configuring the middleware enabled the average waiting time to be smaller than the processing time at the server, so that the overall degradation in response time was tolerable, and often not even noticeable.

In a TP monitor architecture, the requests being queued were 'services' implementing business logic and database operations. These were implemented as a number of Unix processes, each publishing many such services, typically as remote procedure calls. As such service-based applications began to be developed, some of the lacunae in the client-server model of application programming began to be addressed; services encoded the business logic while the client applications limited themselves to purely user interface management and behavior. Such applications turned out to be far easier to maintain than the 'fat-client' applications where UI and business logic was intermixed in the code.

The TP monitor model became known as the *3-tier* architectural model, where client, business and data layers are clearly separated and often also reside on separate machines, as depicted in Figure 1.5. This model also allowed the data layer to remain on mainframes wherever legacy systems needed to be integrated, using mainframe-based transaction-processing monitors such as CICS to publish 'data only' services to the business logic in the middle tier.

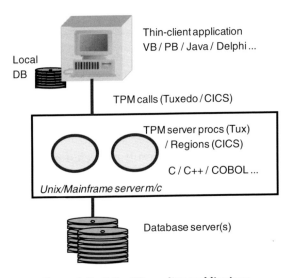

**FIGURE 1.5. 3-tier TP monitor architecture**

We note here in passing that terminal-based 'forms' architectures as well as some GUI-based client-server systems, i.e. those where business logic was confined to the database layer in stored procedures, are also structurally '3-tier' systems, but they lack the request queuing provided by the TP monitor layer and hence architecturally belong to the client-server class.

A relatively minor but important enhancement to the 3-tier model was the introduction of 'object-based' access to services, replacing flat remote procedure calls, together with the introduction of object-oriented distributed communication systems such as CORBA. In CORBA, the client application could communicate with services on the server via 'methods' on 'distributed objects,' instead of having to build in application specific message handling for passing parameters to services and receiving their responses. With the adoption of Java for building client-side applications, such features were available natively in the language through a built-in mechanism to 'serialize' objects. We mention this aspect precisely because in the internet architectures to follow, much of the complexities of web-based systems, especially 'web services,' have revolved around mechanisms to essentially recreate such facilities in an intuitive yet efficient manner.

The essential lessons from the 3-tier model are (a) clear separation of user interface and business logic and (b) load balancing using request queuing to support high transaction volumes. Both of these have become fundamental principles of enterprise software architecture design, continuing through the advent of internet-based architectures and into the emerging cloud era. The 3-tier model never disappeared, it has instead become an integral aspect of web-based computing using the internet standards that replaced the proprietary technologies of the TP monitor era.

We have discussed mainframe, client-server and 3-tier architectures. In Table 1.1 we compare essential features of each of these architectures, also highlighting the key lessons learned from the perspective of our upcoming foray into software architecture for enterprise cloud computing. In the next chapter we trace the advent of the internet and its influence on enterprise system architectures, and its evolution from a communication network into a platform for computing.

| TABLE 1.1 Comparison of Architectures | | | |
|---|---|---|---|
| | **Mainframe** | **Client-server** | **3-tier** |
| **User interface** | Terminal screens controlled by the server | 'Fat-client' applications making database requests over SQL/Net | 'Thin-client' desktop applications making service requests via RPC or CORBA |
| **Business logic** | Batch oriented processing | Online processing in client application and stored procedures in the database | Executed on a middle tier of services published by the TP monitor layer |
| **Data store** | File structures, hierarchical or network databases (later relational) | Relational databases | Relational databases |
| **Programming languages** | PL/1, Cobol | 4GLs: Visual Basic, Powerbuilder, (later Java) | 4GLs on client, 3GLs such as C and C++ on server |
| **Server operating system** | MVS, z/OS, VAX | Unix | Unix, Linux |
| **Time line** | 70s to date | 80s through late 90s | mid–late 90s |
| **Advantages (at the time)** | Reliable enterprise data processing, Virtual machine technology, Fault tolerance | Cheaper than mainframes, leveraged desktop computing power; online transactions vs. batch processing | Load balancing for scalability as compared to client-server; structuring of applications into presentation and business logic layers |

*(continued)*

| TABLE 1.1 *(continued)* | | | |
|---|---|---|---|
| | Mainframe | Client-server | 3-tier |
| Disadvantages (at the time) | Batch oriented processing | Did not scale over wide area networks or for high transaction volumes | Lack of standards |
| User/Developer friendliness: | Cryptic user interfaces and low level programming | Intuitive graphical user interfaces and high-level languages | Intuitive user interfaces but more complex distributed programming |
| Key lessons for today – especially in cloud context | Virtualization and fault tolerance | Perils of distribution | Load balancing |

# CHAPTER 2

# The internet as a platform

As is well known, the internet was born as a communication infrastructure for data sharing between large government research labs in the US, and soon grew to include academic institutions across the world. The development of the NCSA Mosaic web-browser in 1993 sparked the rapid expansion of internet use beyond these boundaries into a platform for sharing documents, using the HTTP protocol and HTML markup languages developed by Tim Berners Lee at CERN, Geneva, in 1990. Using a browser, information 'published' over the internet could be accessed anonymously by the public at large, giving rise to the 'world wide web'. The subsequent history of the commercialization of the web and the dot-com boom is also well known. In this chapter we explore how and why the internet also evolved into a platform for enterprise applications, eventually giving birth to the cloud computing paradigm.

## 2.1 INTERNET TECHNOLOGY AND WEB-ENABLED APPLICATIONS

Internet-based applications rely fundamentally on HTTP, the HyperText Transfer Protocol, and HTML, the HyperText Markup Language; both are now standards defined by the world wide web consortium (W3C). Browsers, such as Internet Explorer, and servers, such as HTTPD (HyperText Transfer Protocol Daemon) implement these standards to enable content publishing over the internet. Other technologies such as XML and SOAP are also important,

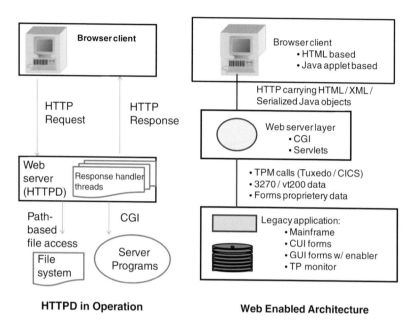

**HTTPD in Operation**                    **Web Enabled Architecture**

FIGURE **2.1.  Internet technology and web-enabled applications**

and will be covered in later chapters. Here we review the essential aspects of these underlying technologies that are critical to understanding internet-based enterprise applications and cloud computing.

As depicted to the left in Figure 2.1, a web server is a process, such as the Apache HTTPD daemon (see below), that receives HTTP requests from clients, typically web browsers. Requests are queued until assigned to a request handler thread within the web-server process. The server returns an HTTP response containing data, either retrieved directly from a file system path or as computed by a server program initiated to respond to the request. The CGI (common gateway interface) protocol is used by the web server to launch server programs and communicate with them, i.e. pass parameters and accept their results, such as data retrieved from a database. The browser client merely interprets HTML returned by the server and displays it to the user.

The widespread use of web servers was further encouraged by the creation of the *open source* HTTPD web server (written in C), and the birth of the Apache community to support it. A group of people working in enterprise IT roles, led by Brian Behlendorf, undertook this task because they feared that the HTTP protocol would become corrupted if proprietary extensions to the standard were proliferated by different vendors. The Apache web server also marked the first widespread use of open source software by enterprise IT departments.

In the initial years of the web (through the late 90s), the HTTP protocol, together with features available in HTML supporting data entry forms, presented the opportunity to develop browser-based (or 'web-enabled') interfaces to legacy systems. This became especially useful for accessing mainframe applications that otherwise could be accessed only from dedicated terminals. 'Screen scraping' programs were developed to communicate with the mainframe by emulating a terminal program and passing results back and forth to a web server via CGI, as shown to the right in Figure 2.1. In this manner mainframes as well as TP monitor or CUI-forms-based applications could be made more easily accessible to internal enterprise users. Additionally, it became possible to publish information residing in legacy systems directly to the then nascent world wide web. Further, there was the additional benefit of the browser becoming a 'universal client application,' thereby eliminating the cumbersome task of propagating upgrades to user desktops. Finally, since the internet protocol was easy to use and performed well over wide area networks, web enabling made it easy to provide geographically distributed operations access to applications running in data centers regardless of location; recall that the client-server model was particularly poor in this regard. Unfortunately, client-server systems were also the most difficult to web-enable, since they incorporated a large part (even all) of their business logic in the 'fat' client-side applications deployed on user desktops. This meant that client-server systems essentially had to be rewritten in order to web-enable their functions.

The one marked disadvantage of a web-based application was the relatively limited user interface behavior that could be created with plain HTML. While this did not pose a serious limitation when web-enabling the terminal-based interfaces of mainframes, it did result in a sacrifice of functionality in the case of client-server applications as well as 3-tier applications that provided more interactive user interfaces through client-side code. As we shall see in Chapter 7, this limitation has receded significantly in recent years with new technologies, such as AJAX, enabling 'rich internet applications' in the browser.

In view of the many potential advantages of a web-based interface, the late 90s saw a flurry of web-enabling projects wherein legacy applications were connected to the internet through a variety of mechanisms, all highly case specific and non-standard; thus, in the process another set of problems were created in the bargain.

## 2.2 WEB APPLICATION SERVERS

In a web-enabled application architecture, processing logic, including database access, took place *outside* the web server process via scripts or programs invoked by it, using CGI for interprocess communication. Each such 'CGI-script' invocation included the costly overhead of launching the required server program as a fresh operating-system process. To overcome this inefficiency, FastCGI was developed, whereby the web server could communicate with another permanently running server-side process via inter-process communication. Another alternative was to dynamically link application C code in the web server itself (as was possible with the mod_c module of the Apache HTTPD); however this latter approach was not widely publicized, and rarely used in practice.

The invention and proliferation of the Java language, designed to be portable across machine architectures with its interpreted yet efficient execution model made possible alternative approaches to execute application functionality inside the web-server process, leading to the birth of the 'application server' architecture, as illustrated on the left in Figure 2.2: In addition to serving HTTP requests from files or CGI scripts, requests could also be processed by multi-threaded execution environments, called 'containers,' embedded within the web server. The 'servlet' container, for example, first

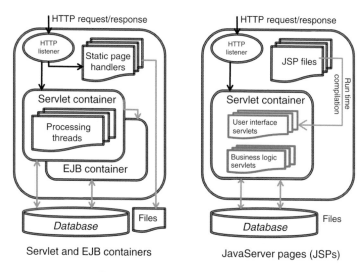

FIGURE 2.2. **Web application server**

introduced in the 'pure Java' Apache Tomcat server, allowed Java programs to execute in a multi-threaded manner within the server process as 'servlet code.' The container would also manage load balancing across incoming requests using these threads, as well as database connection pooling, in a manner similar to TP monitors. Thus, the application-server architecture also enjoyed the advantages of a 3-tier architecture, i.e., the ability to handle larger workloads as compared to the client-server model. The fact that Tomcat was a pure Java implementation of the HTTP protocol also contributed to its popularity, as it could run without recompilation on any machine that supported a Java virtual machine (JVM). Note that there is a common confusion between the HTTPD web server and Tomcat since both are servers of HTTP requests. Recall that HTTPD is written in C, and is a pure web server, while Tomcat is written in Java, and includes a servlet container, thus making it an *application server* rather than a web server.

Servlet code was used to respond to HTTP requests; because of the nature of the HTTP protocol, this code also had to manage user interface behavior, since the HTML returned from the server determined what was displayed in the browser. Recall that a major drawback of client-server systems was that they mixed-up user interface and business logic code, resulting applications that were difficult to maintain. 'Java server pages' (JSPs), also introduced in Tomcat, allowed user interface behavior to be encoded directly as Java code embedded within HTML. Such 'JSP' files are dynamically compiled into servlets, as illustrated on the right in Figure 2.2. Using JSPs enabled a clear separation of user interface and business logic to be enforced in application code, resulting in better maintainability.

While elements of the load balancing feature of TP monitors were present in servlet containers, these could not yet scale to large transaction volumes. As an attempt to bridge this gap, the 'Java 2 Enterprise Edition' (J2EE) specification was developed by Sun Microsystems in 1999, introducing a new application execution container called 'Enterprise Java Beans' (EJBs). Application code packaged as EJBs could be deployed in separate processes from the controlling web application server, thereby opening up the possibility of distributed multiprocessor execution to boost performance. The EJB container also provided a host of additional services, such as security, transactions, greater control on database connection pooling and Java-based connectors to legacy systems.

Note that strictly speaking, Tomcat was the first 'web application server,' as we have mentioned earlier; however common parlance often mistakenly refers to this as a web server, reserving the term application server only where an EJB container is provided.

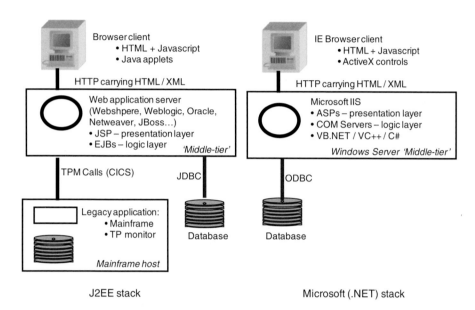

Browser client
• HTML + Javascript
• Java applets

IE Browser client
• HTML + Javascript
• ActiveX controls

HTTP carrying HTML / XML

HTTP carrying HTML / XML

Web application server
(Webshpere, Weblogic, Oracle,
Netweaver, JBoss...)
• JSP – presentation layer
• EJBs – logic layer    *'Middle-tier'*

Microsoft IIS
• ASPs – presentation layer
• COM Servers – logic layer
• VB.NET / VC++ / C#
                *Windows Server 'Middle-tier'*

TPM Calls (CICS)          JDBC          ODBC

Legacy application:
• Mainframe
• TP monitor

Database          Database

*Mainframe host*

J2EE stack                    Microsoft (.NET) stack

FIGURE **2.3. Web application server technology stacks**

Our description above has focused on the Java family of web and application servers; at the same time a competing family from Microsoft was being developed, as depicted alongside the J2EE stack in Figure 2.3. The Microsoft web/application server, IIS (Internet Information Server), runs only on the Windows operating system. However, unlike the J2EE stack, multiple language support was provided, including C, C++, and Microsoft specific languages such as C# (C 'sharp') and VB (visual basic). The application container in this case was simply Microsoft's COM environment on the Windows operating system that enabled multiple processes to execute and communicate. Recent versions of this stack are now referred to as the .NET framework.

The raison d'être of the application server, to be able to process large-scale business transactions in a purely web-oriented architecture, has to a large extent been achieved. High-performance web applications all employ horizontal scaling by distributing requests across large clusters of application servers, called 'server farms.' At the same time, deploying, load balancing and generally managing such large-scale distributed environments, which often contain hundreds or even thousands of servers, has become a major challenge. The built-in fault tolerance and manageability of the mainframes has largely been lost, driving up management costs and impacting agility. These data centers have become essentially large 'IT plants' akin to complex nuclear power plants. The complexity of these environments has been a driving factor for the large-scale interest in cloud computing architectures wherein the attendant complexities are managed in a scalable and largely automated manner.

Through the 2000s, the application server architecture has become pervasive across enterprise IT, virtually replacing all other alternatives for new application development. The only major choice to be made has been between a Java or Microsoft stack. Furthermore, a number of open source Java application servers (such as JBoss) have encouraged this trend even further. As a result, internet technology (HTTP and its siblings), which started off as a communication protocol, has come to permeate enterprise IT as the core *platform* for application development.

## 2.3 INTERNET OF SERVICES

Once applications began to be web-enabled, it became natural to open up access to some of their functionality to the general public. For example, web-based access to back-end applications meant that end-users could themselves perform tasks such as tracking courier shipments, getting quotations for services, or viewing their bank balances; soon secure payment mechanisms were also developed that enabled users to place orders and make payments online.

With web-based access to applications becoming uniformly available to users through a browser interface, the next step was programmatic access to the same applications over the internet. Simplistically, a program could of course emulate a browser without the web-enabled interface knowing the difference; besides being a cumbersome approach, this mechanism was (and is) open to abuse and malicious behavior (denial of service attacks etc.). Web services were developed initially to address this need. While we shall cover web services in detail in Chapter 7, here we review their emergence from a historical perspective.

The W3C defines a 'web service' as interoperable machine-to-machine interaction over HTTP. The HTML format for data exchange over the internet initially evolved from SGML (standardized general markup language), a descendant of IBM's GML developed in the 60s and used extensively in the mainframe world for generating reports. While hugely successfully, HTML was less suited for machine-to-machine communications as its syntax is not 'well-formed.' For example, it is *not* required to 'close' a statement such as <body> in HTML with a matching </body>. SGML on the other hand was a well-structured but complex language. In 1997 W3C published XML (extensible markup language), a simplified version of SGML, using which one could also write well-formed HTML (XHTML), thereby driving browsers to support XML in addition to HTML.

The web also provided a universal mechanism for naming and locating resources, viz. the URI. The well-known URL, or web address is an example of a URI that specifies an actual web or network location; in general the URI format can be used to name other resources or even abstractions. This, together with XML as a basis for interoperable message formats, laid the foundation for formal web service standards. The XML-RPC standard mimics remote procedure calls over HTTP with data being transferred in XML. Like RPC, XML-RPC limits itself to simple data types, such as integers, strings etc. To support complex, nested (object oriented) types, the SOAP protocol was developed, whereby the schema of the messages exchanged as input and output parameters of published 'services' was defined using an XML format called WSDL (web services description language) and communicated over HTTP as SOAP messages (another XML format). Using SOAP, applications could call the web services published by other applications over the internet.

Around the same time as the web services standards were being developed and put to pioneering use by companies such as Fed-Ex, Amazon and eBay (for placing and tracking orders and shipments via web services), there was a storm brewing inside the data center of large enterprises over how to integrate the proliferating suite of applications and architectures ranging from mainframes, client-server and TP monitor technologies to the emerging systems based on web application servers. Traditional integration techniques revolved around carefully identifying and publishing functions in each enterprise system that could be called by external applications. The semantic differences in how different systems dealt with similar data meant that integration itself was an application in its own right. For example, 'employee' in an HR system might include retirees while in another system, say payroll, retirees usually would not be included.

The emerging application server architecture that enabled users to seamlessly access legacy systems was seen as the ideal mechanism to use when building such integration layers. Software vendors built products using application servers, called 'enterprise service buses,' that abstracted aspects of the integration problem. Finally, seeing that the SOAP protocol was proving useful in connecting applications of different enterprises (B2B integration) over the internet, such integration middleware began to build in and promote SOAP and XML-based integration layers within the enterprise data center as well. The term 'service oriented architecture' (SOA) began to receive a lot of attention, most often used as a term to describe the use of SOAP and XML for application integration.

While sometimes the use of standards, such as data models using XML, forced the resolution of semantic integration issues between application data, more often than not this fundamental feature of the integration problem got lost in the details of the new technology. SOA promised interoperability between applications and savings over time: By packaging application systems as bundles of published services it would eventually become easier to evolve their usage as business needs changed. Only time will tell if this promise is redeemed; so far, a lot of effort has been spent on misguided technology-focused SOA projects with very little return.

Meanwhile, the world of services over the internet was not necessarily content with the standardization of SOAP-based interfaces. In 2000, an seemingly obscure protocol called XMLHTTPRequest was made available in the Javascript language. Javascript code running within browsers was being used to provide dynamic user interface behavior within HTML pages, such as simple type validations. Using XMLHTTPRequest, however, such 'in-browser' code could also make HTTP requests, possibly to servers other than the one that served up the main HTML page being displayed. Google was the first to make extensive use of this protocol to provide rich interactive behavior in Gmail, and more importantly for 'publishing' its Google Maps service as a 'mashup', whereby any HTML page, published by anyone, could include some Javascript code to display a Google Map. This code, provided by Google, would internally call the Google servers for data regarding the map in question. Thus came about a new approach for integrating applications, at the client side instead of between servers. The term AJAX (Asynchronous Javscript and XML) began to be used to describe this style of user interfaces. AJAX-based mashups also, in a sense, democratized application integration, and led to a proliferation of rich Javascript applications that enabled users to 'mashup' services of their choice to create their own personalized pages.

Figure 2.4 depicts both the web services and mashup architectures for integration over the internet: A mashup provides a rich client-side interface (such as a Google Map) implemented in Javascript that accesses the server over HTTP using asynchronous requests via XMLHTTPRequest. In traditional server-to-server web services, application server code accesses published services from another server via SOAP over HTTP.

Note that SOAP services use standardized XML messages to transfer data. No such requirement is there for mashups, since both the server-side and client-side (Javascript) code for accessing the service comes from the same

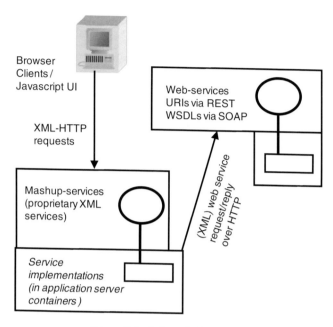

Browser
Clients /
Javascript UI

XML-HTTP
requests

Web-services
URIs via REST
WSDLs via SOAP

Mashup-services
(proprietary XML
services)

*Service
implementations
(in application server
containers)*

(XML) web service
request/reply
over HTTP

FIGURE 2.4.  **Internet of services**

provider, thereby allowing more efficient, but proprietary, formats to be used. In Chapter 7 we shall explore these mechanisms in more detail, as also an alternative to the SOAP protocol, called REST (representational state transfer), which is rapidly emerging as preferred protocol for remote data access especially in the context of cloud computing.

In the early years of web-services standards, a lot of interest was generated in UDDI (universal description, discovery and integration), whereby businesses would list the web services they published on a public UDDI registry, so that applications could automatically and dynamically discover the services they needed. The UDDI concept was also promulgated as a panacea for application integration within enterprises; a technological solution that would resolve semantic discrepancies between application services. In both these cases the optimism was misguided: The application integration problem requires resolution of semantic differences by *humans*, and so is unlikely to be solvable in such an automated manner. On the web, web services technology, especially in its broader sense to include mashups and REST interfaces, has made machine to machine interaction over the internet commonplace. At the same time the idea of a universal 'service broker' based on UDDI overlooks a fundamental aspect: Meaningful collaboration among users and providers also implies contractual obligations where human decisions, rather than mere automation, are required.

The software as a service and cloud computing paradigms bring in this contractual aspect formally, while also re-emphasizing the human element. As we shall see, this is also a lesson for the future of cloud computing. Many accounts paint a picture of cloud computing analogous to the largely anonymous electricity grid [8], enabled in part by many layers of organizational separation and contractual obligations from generation to consumption; we shall revisit these possibilities in Chapter 18.

To conclude, we note also that communication between enterprises and consumers, be it through their personal computers or mobile devices, is increasingly being driven through the web-based applications that run on the public internet and which are often hosted by independent providers. Thus it becomes increasingly apparent that not only internet technologies, but the internet itself is becoming a platform for computing. As we shall argue in Chapter 18, enterprise IT will, sooner or later, need to embrace this platform and moreover, become a part of it.

# CHAPTER 3

# Software as a service and cloud computing

## 3.1 EMERGENCE OF SOFTWARE AS A SERVICE

Even during the early days of the internet it had become evident that software products could be packaged and sold as remotely hosted 'application services.' A number of ASPs (application service providers) were born (such as Corio), for the most part offering the same software packages as enterprises used within their data centers, but in a hosted model wherein the software ran within the ASPs' data centers with users accessing it over the internet. For a variety of reasons this first wave of ASPs did not succeed. First, the internet bandwidth was simply not adequate at that time. Second, since most of the popular software products, such as ERP and CRM systems, were client-server applications, ASPs resorted to the highly inefficient practice of 'screen scraping' to enable remote access to these applications, using remote-desktop-sharing mechanisms (such as Citrix MetaFrame) that essentially transmitted screen-buffer images back and forth over the network. More importantly, the early ASPs were simply not structured to offer significant cost advantages over the traditional model; they had to pay similar license fees to the providers of packaged software while being unable to add sufficient value through economies of scale.

A notable early exception was Intuit with its successful hosted offering of QuickBooks, a desktop accounting solution. This was soon followed by the success of Salesforce.com and its hosted CRM (customer relationship management) solution. An important factor in these successes was that the applications were completely web-based and designed for sharing across multiple customers (via multi-tenancy, which we shall cover in Chapter 9). These successes spawned a new wave of hosted applications, all built from scratch using web-based architectures; these were referred to as 'software as a service' (SaaS) to differentiate them from the earlier ASPs based on legacy architectures.

From a customer perspective these SaaS solutions offered three main advantages over traditional software development by corporate IT: First, business users could subscribe to these services over the web using just a credit card; corporate IT was not involved. For users frustrated with the often cumbersome and long-drawn-out process of engaging their corporate IT departments, long lead times for project delivery, delays, mismatched requirements, etc., this came as a breath of fresh air. Second, users found that they could even make some minor customizations to their 'instances' of the SaaS solutions: In the case of Salesforce.com, for example, users could add custom fields, create new forms, as well as configure workflows, all from the same browser-based interface. In contrast, making similar modifications to leading CRM systems, such as Siebel, was a task that had to be done by corporate IT with the usual delays. Thus, business users could create a customized CRM for themselves, again with *no* involvement of corporate IT. Third, users did not have worry about product upgrades. Salesforce.com would upgrade its solution in a seamless manner to *all* users, who merely *discovered* that their application had been enhanced. Further, such upgrades seemed to take place on a far more regular basis than for applications managed by corporate IT, with upgrade frequencies of weeks rather than many months or years. In fact, a direct consequence of the popularity of Salesforce.com was the eventual demise of Siebel, the leading CRM vendor at that time, forcing it to get acquired by its largest competitor, Oracle. A point to be noted is that these perceived advantages of the SaaS model were compelling enough to override the fact that with SaaS, user data was housed within data centers controlled by the SaaS provider; in the case of CRM this included customer lists and contacts, which are clearly business sensitive and critical data.

The fact that early success of the SaaS model involved a CRM application was no accident also: In many organizations the sales process is the most autonomous and least integrated with product delivery. Once orders are generated by sales, these can be entered into the core ERP systems to drive delivery, financial processing and analytics. (We will review the nature of enterprise computing in detail in Chapter 13.) Thus, having sales data 'outside the system' was relatively easier to digest. Subsequent SaaS providers found that they had to choose their offerings carefully: HR management or customer support, for example, were well accepted as SaaS applications, whereas supply chain, or core ERP functions such as payroll and corporate financial accounting have seen far less success in a SaaS model. Lastly, analytics remains an emerging area where SaaS models might become popular in the future, especially in the context of cloud computing.

## 3.2 SUCCESSFUL SaaS ARCHITECTURES

Unlike the first-generation ASPs, both Inuit and Salesforce.com built their hosted solutions from ground up; they used completely web-based architectures as well as exploited internal cost advantages from 'multi-tenancy' and 'configurability.' These architectural features enabled these solutions to offer *sustained economic advantages* over traditional on-premise software, as we examine below.

Key elements of a successful, economically advantageous, SaaS architecture are depicted in Figure 3.1. If one considers the costs of managing a software product in the traditional manner (i.e. installed within customer premises),

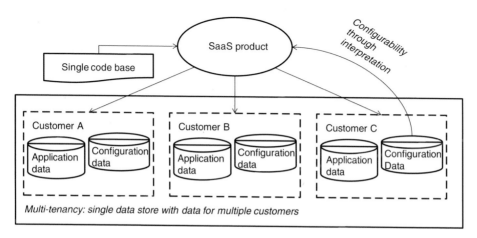

FIGURE 3.1. SaaS architecture

a large part of the costs go into managing different versions of the product and supporting upgrades to multiple customers. As a consequence, often fewer and larger upgrades are made, introducing instability in the product together with the need for releasing and managing intermediate 'patches.' On the customer side, there are corresponding costs as well: receiving and applying upgrades, testing them, and also redoing any local customizations or integrations as required.

A hosted SaaS model virtually removes these costs from the customer side, and on the provider, the 'multi-tenant' architecture brings down the costs of releasing upgrades by an order of magnitude: With multi-tenancy, the hosted SaaS application runs a single code base for *all* customers, while ensuring that the data seen by each customer is specific to them; i.e depending on who is logged in and the customer organization they belong to, an appropriate data partition is accessed. In Chapter 9 we shall examine how to implement multi-tenancy in more detail.

Thus, releasing a new version of a SaaS product amounts to a single production upgrade for all customers, who are in effect forced to upgrade, often without even being aware. Multiple versions of the product do not need to be maintained in production; further, as the costs of a new release are small, upgrades can be more frequent, smaller and therefore also more likely to be stable. Multi-tenancy is a major reason why modern SaaS offerings are able to offer a real cost advantage over in-house systems.

With traditional on-premise software, corporate IT is responsible for the development and maintenance of customizations to software products and their integration with other IT systems. It has often been documented that software maintenance costs are often two to three times greater than the costs of developing software, for some of the reasons discussed above, such as version management. The complexity of modern multi-tier architectures which require different technologies at each layer also adds to maintenance costs, as we shall argue in more detail in Chapter 12.

Thus, custom-built on-premise software is costly and time-consuming to develop and maintain, and packaged software products need extensive customizations that are often equally expensive. The SaaS platform developed by Salesforce.com introduced the ability for *end-users* to customize the functionality of their view of the product. This was a significant innovation in that it dramatically reduced the time to implement a usable CRM system; further business users could customize and begin using the platform without the overhead of going through their corporate IT. Customer specific customizations were captured as just another form of *data* rather than code, as shown in

Figure 3.1. Such data 'about the application functionality' is more appropriately called *meta-data*. The SaaS application code, which is the same for each customer (or 'tenant'), *interprets* this meta-data at runtime, thereby rendering and executing varied functionality for each customer. We examine how this is technically achieved in more detail in Chapter 14.

By enabling end-users to make certain customizations themselves in the above manner, Salesforce.com enabled customers to avoid high costs of traditional software development. Additionally, as we have already seen, multi-tenancy allowed their own internal costs to be significantly reduced, some of which were also passed on to the customer. Overall, customers experienced real cost savings in addition to the advantages of rapid deployment and independence from corporate IT.

## 3.3 DEV 2.0 PLATFORMS

The ability to render functionality by interpreting meta-data was soon expanded by Salesforce.com to cover many more application features, thereby enabling, to a certain extent, *independent* applications to be created using the same hosted SaaS platform. Later, a scripting language was added to position these features as an independent hosted development platform; today this is called Force.com and has a separate identity from the CRM product. Simultaneously other startup companies (Coghead, Zoho) as well as some large organizations (TCS[1]) had embarked on their own efforts at developing such interpretive platforms where applications could be developed 'over the web,' potentially by end-users. We use the term **Dev 2.0**[2] to describe platforms such as the above, because they aim to bring end-user participation into *application development*, much as Web 2.0 technologies, such as blogs and social networking, have brought end-user *publishing of content* to the web.

Figure 3.2 depicts the architecture of a Dev 2.0 platform; an 'application player' renders application functionality defined by meta-data, in a manner analogous to a media player playing a video file, or a word processor displaying a document. As in the word processor analogy, the Dev 2.0 platform also allows users to edit the functionality of the application, often at the same time it is being 'played.' Just as WYSIWYG word processors largely

---

[1] Tata Consultancy Services.
[2] The term Dev 2.0 was first coined by the author in [51].

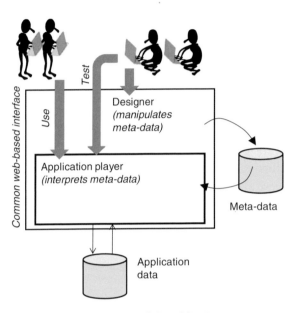

FIGURE 3.2. Dev 2.0 architecture

replaced typesetting languages which had to be compiled for formatting, Dev 2.0 aims to replace application specific code with meta-data that is rendered (and edited) in the web application player. At the same time, for large complex documents (such as this book), one prefers to use a typesetting language (in this case LaTeX); similarly Dev 2.0 is most applicable for smaller applications, rather than very large ones. In Chapter 12 we discuss more Dev 2.0 platforms, their applicability, limitations and possible future directions. We explain how Dev 2.0 platforms are designed in Chapter 14.

Dev 2.0 platforms are still a nascent technology. In the future, even custom-built applications may incorporate the idea of interpreting meta-data. So, it is possible that Dev 2.0, coupled with cloud computing will lead to new paradigms for enterprise system architecture. We shall return to this topic after first discussing the emergence of cloud computing.

## 3.4 CLOUD COMPUTING

Whereas software as a service is about packaged applications made available over the internet, cloud computing makes a lower level of infrastructure and tools available over the internet in data centers maintained by a cloud provider.

We must note that alongside the evolution of the internet, hosting services, such as for websites, have been around for years. However these *are not* by themselves 'cloud' services (we explain why in Chapter 17). To understand the additional features that account for the surge of interest in cloud computing, we first need to trace the evolution of cloud computing by the pioneers in the field, viz. Amazon and Google.

The SaaS providers such as Salesforce.com could implement their systems using web application server architectures as discussed in the previous chapter. Since these offerings usually catered to small or medium businesses, the number of users for each tenant application was relatively small, so it was relatively straightforward to provision servers as the number of tenants increased, with each server catering to many tenants. In rare cases, such as for the few large customers who had probably a few thousand users each, again a traditional application server architecture suffices, by balancing the load across many machines just as it would in the case of an on-premise deployment. Thus, the scale of usage was very similar to that of traditional enterprise software.

Amazon, the first 'cloud' provider, faced a different set of challenges as it grew from an online bookseller to an online retail hub, but solved them in a highly innovative and reusable manner, leading eventually to a new cloud computing business. First, the complexity of Amazon's application suite; to display one page featuring a book, a number of services from fairly complex applications are needed, such as reviews, recommender systems, and collaborative filtering. Next, the peaks and troughs of the seasonal retail business necessitated Amazon to continuously monitor load and automatically provision additional capacity on demand. Finally, as they became a retailer catering to the 'long tail' of small niche products, they saw the need to support their suppliers with some minimal IT, many of whom had no systematic computing systems apart from a few personal computers.

Recall the virtual machine concept which had been developed during the mainframe era. In recent years virtual machine technologies have been developed (or rather, redeveloped) for popular modern hardware architectures, such as the Intel X86 family. (Examples are VMware, Xen and KVM; the latter two being open source tools.) Using virtualization many logical operating systems can share a single physical machine resource through a hypervisor that emulates an underlying hardware model, and which is used to run different guest operating systems. This is similar, at a high level, to multi-tenant SaaS, where a single application player 'runs' different meta-data configurations. We shall cover virtualization in detail in Chapter 8.

Amazon exploited virtualization extensively, just as many large enterprises are also now doing, to *automatically* and dynamically provision hardware with those applications that were most utilized as demand fluctuated through the year. The high degree of automation they were able to achieve in this process enabled them to conceive of and launch their S3 (simple storage system) and EC2 (elastic compute cloud) whereby users could rent storage and compute power on Amazon servers. First intended for use by Amazon suppliers and partners, this was opened up to the general public as an experiment. Its popularity resulted in Amazon becoming, inadvertently, a pioneer of cloud computing.

There are key differences between the Amazon cloud and traditional hosting providers: (a) the degree of automation made available to end-users, as web services, to control the number of virtual instances running at any point in time, (b) the ability for users to package and save their own configurations of virtual machines (as Amazon machine images, or AMIs) and (c) charging per hour of actual usage as opposed to the monthly or yearly charges for traditional hosting. In addition, Amazon also made available their own system software tools, such as Amazon SQS (simple queue service) and SimpleDB (a non-relational database). These enabled many users of the cloud to build complex applications without having to rely on deploying and configuring traditional middleware and database products.

In the case of Google, on the other hand, the scale of computing power needed to support large-scale indexing of the web, the immense volume of searches, and machine-learning-based targeting of advertisements across this volume meant orders of magnitude larger computational needs as compared to even the largest enterprise. Large banks today often have tens of thousands of servers; Google, on the other hand is estimated as running over a *million* servers, as of today.

In the process of solving its computational problems, Google developed innovations in programming models for large-scale distributed processing, such as the Map Reduce model for partitioning a sequence of tasks to be performed on a very large data set and executing it in parallel across a very large set of machines. Supporting this was their 'big table' model of a data store, a *non-relational* database distributed across a very large set of physical storage with built-in redundancy and fault tolerance. Finally, supporting the massive volume of search queries necessitated building a highly scalable application server architecture designed from the beginning to execute in parallel.

Thus, when Google announced its cloud offering, the Google App Engine, it looked very different indeed from the Amazon cloud. Users could program using development libraries (initially in Python, now also in Java) and deploy their code on the App Engine. The code so deployed would be always 'running' in response to any web request to the corresponding URL. Further the application would automatically *scale* on the App Engine's large-scale distributed execution infrastructure. Thus, users did not need to do anything special to make their application scale from supporting very few to many millions of requests per day (apart from paying for higher load volumes, with a base level of 5 000 000 hits a month being free!). Data services were provided through the Google Datastore, also a non-relational distributed database. If properly exploited by application code, highly parallel distribution and querying of data would be automatic. The Google App Engine thus represents a completely new application architecture, based on automatic distributed execution and load balancing. In the Java version of the App Engine, the JVM itself is custom built by Google to support this model at the lowest level; similar modifications are also likely to be present in Google's Python interpreter, since it is well known that vanilla Python does *not* scale well to many CPUs on a normal machine. As Google has not publicized the distributed execution architecture we can only speculate about its structure.

Figure 3.3 displays the Amazon and Google cloud models side by side. In contrast to App Engine, users do need to deal with scaling issues using Amazon, and must explicitly provision a parallel architecture using the web services provided. On the other hand, they get full (root) access to virtual machines, either Linux or Windows, and are free to deploy any software they wish on them. With App Engine, users must develop fresh applications using the App Engine SDK.

Microsoft has also entered the cloud market with its Azure platform. This is along the same lines as Google's, i.e. it provides a software platform for application development rather than access to raw virtual machines. More importantly, Azure is based on the already popular Microsoft programming stack. Azure also includes the ability to describe the runtime characteristics of an application explicitly, bringing back some indirect control over application deployment to the user.

The Amazon model is an example of infrastructure as a service (IaaS) while the Google and Microsoft models are 'platform as a service' (PaaS) offerings. In Chapter 5 we shall cover each of these cloud models in detail. Now we return to our discussion of Dev 2.0 and examine what Dev 2.0 and cloud computing together may mean for large enterprises.

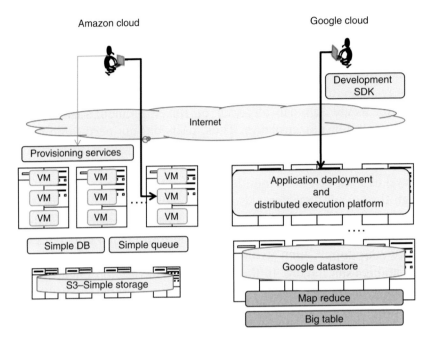

FIGURE 3.3. Cloud models

## 3.5 DEV 2.0 IN THE CLOUD FOR ENTERPRISES

The IaaS cloud model offers potentially important implications for software development processes in IT organizations, especially in the context of outsourcing and globally distributed development:

1. The issue of 'control' of server infrastructure is often a bottleneck; traditionally a server is controlled by either the 'customer' organization or the 'services provider.' In the cloud, control can be 'shared' and transferred at will, enabling efficient distributed development regardless of geographic location. Similarly for globally distributed teams; using the cloud, no team is more equal merely because they are co-located with the server infrastructure.
2. Procurement and provisioning in the cloud is orders of magnitude faster, and can be time bound; this can greatly speed project execution, user testing, analyzing production defects, etc.
3. Early performance testing is possible using 'true' replicas of the actual production environment dynamically provisioned in the cloud for a limited time, which would otherwise be too costly.

Thus, because of the high degree of control offered by the IaaS cloud model, it is likely to find many applications in large enterprises sooner than PaaS clouds.

At the same time, the question of overall cost advantages of cloud computing depends a lot on the computational profile required by an organization. It is not immediately clear why enterprises cannot replicate these models internally (after all Amazon was a retail enterprise first, and cloud provider only later), nor that replicating them will necessarily be worth the while for all enterprises. This question is addressed in more detail in Chapter 6 where we explore the economics of cloud computing.

The emergence of cloud platforms is also an opportunity to revisit the 'success' of the SaaS model. In spite of its widespread use in certain application areas and markets, 'control over data' has been the traditional inhibitor to wider adoption of SaaS in large enterprises. However, if SaaS vendors and customers share the same cloud infrastructure, SaaS applications could potentially use storage and databases that are 'controlled' by their customers, without adversely affecting performance or losing the benefits of the SaaS model. This would also enable closer integration with the internal IT systems of the end customer.

Similarly, hosted Dev 2.0 platforms could be used on 'customer-owned' data in the cloud rather than a proprietary database owned by the Dev 2.0 platform vendor. Further, many Dev 2.0 platforms (from the same or different platform vendors) could be used together while sharing the same customer-owned data in the cloud, e.g. one tool for forms-based workflows and another for analytics. We explore some of these possibilities in Chapter 12, and describe one Dev 2.0 platform (TCS InstantApps) that can work with user-controlled data in the cloud.

Finally, the new highly scalable distributed PaaS platforms such as App Engine and Azure open up new opportunities for enterprises to perform large-scale analytical tasks that are currently prohibitive: For example, if a retail chain could benefit by *occasionally* performing a highly compute intensive computation on large volumes of data (e.g. point-of-sale data), it currently might not do so since this would entail investing in a thousands of servers which would normally lie unused. However, with applications developed on scalable distributed cloud platforms, scaling would be automatic and use a large set of hardware resources only when needed. At other times, the same applications could run consuming far lower resources but still having access to (and maybe updating) the large data set as new information streamed in.

Analytics applications would need to be rebuilt to exploit the underlying non-relational but highly distributed data stores provided by these models, as we discuss in Chapter 16.

What could the future enterprise IT environment look like, when it is a mix of traditional systems, internet services as well as in-house enterprise clouds? What is the future of software development using model-based interpreters when they start operating in a cloud environment? We speculate that as IT infrastructure gets increasingly complex, all organizations, large and small, will eventually either need to implement cloud computing and Dev 2.0 technologies internally, or have to leverage such publicly available services to be efficient. They will take decisions on distributing their data across their internal 'private' clouds and external 'public' clouds. They will use a mix of traditional and SaaS applications to operate on this data. They will build these applications with traditional tools and processes, and increasingly with Dev 2.0 platforms. We envision 'Dev 2.0 in the cloud' as a potential paradigm shift for business applications and corporate IT; we shall explore such future possibilities in more detail in Chapter 18. For the remainder of this book we now go into technical details of cloud computing and related technologies as well as the needs of enterprise architecture.

# CHAPTER 4

# Enterprise architecture: role and evolution

As technology evolved from mainframes through client-server to the internet era and now to cloud computing, each large enterprise has had to continuously evaluate emerging architectures and plan the evolution of its IT environment, at the same time 'keeping the lights on' by ensuring stable IT systems to support running its business. In this process, each IT department has become characterized by a mix of technologies, as a continuous balancing act is maintained between the stability of legacy systems, demands of new business requirements and the adoption of new technologies.

The 'enterprise architecture' function within enterprise IT has evolved to manage the complexities of an ever-changing technical environment. In the process enterprise architects found it useful to maintain a description of all of an enterprise's software applications, how they fulfill business needs, how they are implemented technically and how they communicate with each other. Additionally, defining and enforcing technical standards to guide the choice of new technical platforms has become another integral part of this function. To examine how cloud computing can and will be adopted in large enterprises, we need to view this potential paradigm shift from the perspective of the enterprise architecture function.

## 4.1 ENTERPRISE DATA AND PROCESSES

Information systems, by definition, need to keep track of the core information vital to the functioning of an enterprise. We shall examine in detail what information large enterprises maintain and how these are organized as data models in Chapter 13. Information systems also manage the core business processes of an enterprise; in Chapter 15 we shall describe how these processes are modeled and enacted. Enterprise architecture views business processes and the information they access at a higher, macro level.

Enterprise architecture definition begins with a compilation of all business processes, such as 'prospect to order', 'order to cash', etc. The first step is identifying and naming each process, and identifying business events that mark its start and end. Deeper analysis includes identifying intermediate business events and human decisions made during the process, participants in the process, exceptional conditions and how these are resolved. Also documented are non-functional aspects of a process, such as how often it changes, and its expected time of completion.

Enterprise processes can often be classified as 'vertical' or 'horizontal'. Vertical processes typically operate within a single organizational function, such as sales or accounting, manage a cohesive information set pertaining to that function, and are typically supported by software packages or systems dedicated to that department. 'Prospect to order', for example, is a vertical process limited to the sales function. Horizontal processes, on the other hand, cut across functional units; 'order to cash' is a horizontal process since it spans sales, production and finance.

## 4.2 ENTERPRISE COMPONENTS

The term 'component' has traditionally been taken to mean to a 'software sub-system that has well-defined interfaces which can be used independently of its internal implementation' [50]. Structuring software into components drives modularity in software development and makes it is easier to evolve a large system by incrementally replacing its components over time.

Zachman [63] first defined a formal approach to structuring collections of software applications that need to work together to run an enterprise. Building on the Zachman framework, a 'component' view of enterprise architecture was proposed in [54], extending the component concept beyond individual software systems. In this approach, each enterprise application comprises of enterprise components, which, like software components, also have well-defined interfaces that are used by components in other applications. Defining enterprise components also aids in internally structuring application systems as software components.

The coarsest level of enterprise components are **business components**, defined as collections of high-level enterprise processes, be they vertical or horizontal. These processes are grouped by business function; horizontal processes often stand alone. At the next level of granularity, high-level enterprise processes are broken down into sequences of smaller processes, and also regrouped so as to be implemented in a set of applications. This process results in **application components**: Each application component is a set of smaller processes such that the information needs of this set is largely restricted to a cohesive set of *data*, such as 'customer data' or 'payments data.' Therefore, one or more application components can be conveniently implemented within a single enterprise application.

When implemented in software systems, application components are themselves decomposed into software components. These software components can be 'entity components,' that deal with the manipulation of enterprise data, and 'process components' that deal with the business logic and workflow needs of the application component.

Figure 4.1 illustrates this component view of enterprise architecture. High-level business processes are refined and regrouped systematically, ultimately residing in separate application systems. The set of application components define the functional architecture of each application system. Their further decomposition into process and entity software components can be directly mapped to a software implementation in a multi-tier technical architecture: Entity components define data models and process components define user interfaces, business logic and workflows. We shall return to this view in Chapter 14 where we examine how enterprise software is implemented.

It is important to note that each application system need not be custom built; rather it may be implemented using an off-the-shelf software package, and in fact this is often the case. The top-down approach using enterprise components clearly defines the process requirements being sought from such software packages while remaining flexible enough to drive the refinement process in a manner so as to exploit the functionality of available packages as much as possible. Most importantly however, this process also identifies what functionality *not* to use in some of the packaged applications, since many packages often have overlapping

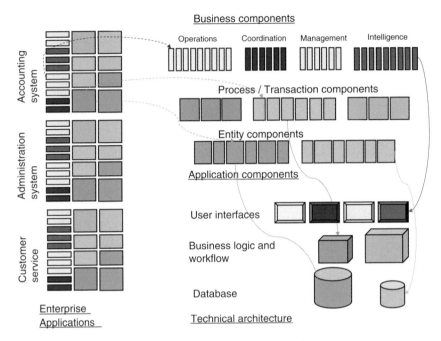

FIGURE 4.1. Enterprise components

functionality. The problems that arise from such overlaps are responsible for much of the complexity of application integration, which we cover in the next section.

## 4.3 APPLICATION INTEGRATION AND SOA

As we have seen above, enterprise applications implement processes, which may be sub-processes of larger horizontal or vertical business processes. For this reason alone it becomes obvious that enterprise applications need to communicate with each other. Additionally, the decomposition of business components into application components that are closely tied to subsets of information is never exact and applications will often need to access data that is owned by other applications. Next, while sourcing application systems via packaged solutions, it is likely that some of these will include overlapping processes or data, once again requiring some form of integration to resolve conflicts and redundancy. Finally, another driver for application integration is the often perceived need for a unified view of data residing in disparate application systems, say for end-to-end process monitoring, real-time decision support, or for data warehousing and business intelligence.

There are a number of mechanisms that applications can use to communicate with each other at different 'levels':

1. Data level integration: direct data transfer using batch programs or on-line exchange using database triggers
2. API level integration: applications publish API libraries that are used by other applications to access their data
3. Service-method-level integration: applications publish services using say, web service protocols, in an organized manner so that many different applications can use a particular service
4. User interface level integration: applications publish mashup APIs that are used to provide a common user interface to functionality from many applications
5. Workflow level integration: tasks performed in one application lead to work items being created in others, thereby driving the flow of work in a business process

We shall discuss the technology used for each level of integration, such as web services, AJAX and workflow in subsequent chapters. The choice of what integration level to use is often driven by technical considerations and limitations such as the degree of access one has to packaged software. Deployment of some enterprise applications in a cloud infrastructure rather than the enterprise data center can also play a part in determining the level of integration possible.

An EAI (enterprise application integration) strategy is usually an integral part of an enterprise architecture definition. In recent years, as web services technologies have become popular, application integration has come to become synonymous with 'service oriented architecture' (SOA), and many of the features of traditional EAI strategies have been reborn as 'SOA strategies.' Apart from detailing the mechanisms and technical standards preferred for integration, such an EAI/SOA strategy essentially provides a roadmap for evolution of an enterprise IT environment as new applications are built to replace old ones. Given the nature of enterprise IT and technology change, this cycle of evolution is a continuous activity; the EAI/SOA process maintains a bridge between the 'to be' enterprise architecture picture (which also evolves) and reality of systems as they are at any given point of time.

Let us consider a sample EAI strategy: (i) use data level integration to connect legacy systems and ERP packages (ii) develop a common data [exchange] model (iii) develop new application components using the common data model, using it to manage coexistence with legacy systems (iv) develop a unified user interface via an enterprise portal (v) replace legacy systems and application components gradually without impacting users.

To illustrate the point that EAI and SOA are quite similar apart from technology choices, let us see what such a strategy may look like under an SOA paradigm: (1) wrap legacy systems with web services and call these from other applications (2) develop an enterprise service model with well-defined schemas for data exchange (3) develop new application components that publish and use service interfaces (4) develop a common user interface using enterprise mashups (5) replace legacy systems and application components while retaining the same service interfaces without impacting users, and at a lower cost.

The point, if not already clear, is that the critical problems of application integration remain the same, i.e. resolving the semantics of data and functionality across different applications, regardless of the technical standards used for integration.

## 4.4 ENTERPRISE TECHNICAL ARCHITECTURE

So far we have not considered the issue of *where* enterprise applications and their underlying components are deployed, whether in-premise or in the cloud. To adequately highlight some of the issues that arise in making such decisions, we first need to consider another major function of enterprise architecture, namely the definition and management of standards defining the technical architecture, tools and technical components used in an enterprise.

### 4.4.1 Unformity or best of breed

Cost and simplicity is the motivation for standardizing technical components such as application servers, databases and integration tools used in an enterprise. As a common example, organizations often decide whether they want to standardize on a Java or Microsoft-based technology stack. In practice, it is often found that large organizations end up using dozens of different technical products for similar functions, especially when it comes to, say, integration technology such as EAI/SOA tools. Using a large variety of such components increases integration and maintenance efforts as well as software licensing costs. Therefore, a common enterprise architecture practice has been to attempt to limit this variety as far as possible.

This 'uniformity' approach is clearly sound when most of the integration between disparate technologies is carried out by the enterprise itself. However, with modern software architectures the internal structure of packaged components becomes increasingly invisible, and uniformity becomes less important: When packaged components are accessible using web services and web-based interfaces that follow standard communication protocols (SOAP, HTTP), their internal technology is irrelevant as far as integration mechanisms are concerned. For example, whether a network router internally uses Linux or another operating system is largely irrelevant from an enterprise architecture perspective. Similarly, it would be incongruous to object to using the Amazon cloud, which uses the Xen virtual machine, merely because one's internal standard for hypervisors happens to be VMware!

To conclude, standardization of interfaces allows relaxation of uniformity regarding product internals and even choices made by application development teams, making a 'best-of-breed' approach possible. For this reason, it is more likely that deploying some applications on Amazon, some on Google, and others internally is far more acceptable today as compared to a few years ago, at least from the technical architecture perspective.

## 4.4.2 Network and data security

Security issues arising from technology choices are also part of the enterprise architecture function. While considering the option of cloud deployment the question of security of data that will reside outside the enterprise data center is a common concern, as we have also mentioned earlier in Chapter 3. Given the fact that the sophistication of cloud data centers considerably exceeds that of most enterprise data centers, concerns on data security for purely technical or physical safety reasons are easily addressable. More important are concerns arising from regulatory restrictions on geographical data location, which are partially being addressed by some cloud vendors. Probably the most important issue with data in the cloud is not security but the ability to exchange large volumes of data: Some cloud vendors, such as Amazon, have started allowing customers to physically ship data to them for uploading on the cloud; of course, the physical security of these logistics becomes another issue to evaluate carefully.

Network security, or rather securing applications on the network, is a more serious concern when considering cloud deployment. In practice, a large number of applications developed for use within an enterprise network, or using a virtual private network (VPN) over the internet, are simply *not* secure enough. As a simple example, most Java applications use the default authentication mechanism (basic JAAS, see Chapter 14), which is not safe against eavesdropping or replay attacks as it transmits a password (albeit encrypted) over the network. Very few such applications exploit the option to plug in more secure underlying key exchange protocols (such as Kerberos), even though it is easily possible. Further, many internal applications are developed without sufficient testing for common security flaws, such as SQL injection and cross-site scripting. Thus, before moving applications to the cloud, their network security needs to be revisited and most often it will be found that this needs to be strengthened.

An important feature introduced by Amazon is the ability to offer a virtual private network for enterprises on their servers. This 'virtual private cloud' feature will certainly alleviate some security concerns and mitigate the additional effort needed to secure applications sufficiently for cloud deployment.

### 4.4.3 Implementation architectures and quick-wins

One of the aspects enterprise architects pay attention to are the 'implementation architectures' required for adopting any new technology. These include the people skills required, along with development, testing and deployment tools needed, as well as the impact on business-continuity and disaster-recovery environments. Architects need to grapple with the choice of platforms based on minimizing the *total* cost of ownership including *transition* costs to any new technology. At the same time they have to strive for maximizing the longevity of any decisions they make, while ensuring adaptability and maintainability in the long term. As a result, enterprise architects tend to be a conservative lot, and are unlikely to embrace new technology hastily, especially for mission-critical enterprise applications.

Instead, it is more likely that new technology, including cloud computing, will be first deployed in peripheral arenas far removed from core IT systems, while at the same time significantly enhancing user experience and business capabilities. For example, web-server technology was first used to create enterprise 'portal' architectures so that users could experience a single entry point to different enterprise applications, each often using disparate technologies. (Web-enabling legacy systems using 'screen-scraping' is such an example.) It is likely that cloud platforms can play a similar role for *safe*, user interface level, integration of enterprise systems with the burgeoning variety of 'mashup' applications becoming available on the web.

Another problem that enterprise architects are now grappling with is mobility: Users now expect access to enterprise applications from mobile devices. Providing a rich mobile experience requires a return to 'fatter' client applications, as well as supporting disconnected operation via intelligent asynchronous data replication. Moreover, the fact that mobile devices are *personal*, rather than enterprise owned and controlled, introduces the need for an added layer of security. Cloud-based applications serving mobile clients could potentially provide such a secure intermediate layer.

We shall re-visit both of the above 'peripheral' applications of cloud computing in Chapter 18, along with a few other potential 'quick-wins'.

## 4.5 DATA CENTER INFRASTRUCTURE: COPING WITH COMPLEXITY

We have discussed many of the architectural issues and decisions involved while considering applications for cloud deployment. But why consider cloud deployment in the first place? In the next chapter we shall look at the economics of cloud computing in more detail to examine whether or not there are savings and if so how much. Here we first outline some of the challenges being faced today by many large enterprises in managing their own increasingly complex data centers. These problems are most often the primary drivers for considering cloud computing, at least for large enterprises.

Let us consider a typical large enterprise, such as a major North American bank, for instance. If one were to do an inventory of such an enterprise's IT infrastructure and applications, what should one expect? In reality, we will likely find hundreds of thousands of desktops and tens of thousands of servers. Thousands of business applications would be running on this sprawl of hardware, in an equally complex software environment running thousands of application server and as database instances, using petabytes of storage. The variety of software infrastructure is equally complex, with dozens of different application server, database, and other middleware products and business intelligence tools. Additionally, in spite of the best efforts at application level consolidation through enterprise architecture, significant functional overlap across applications will be found at any given instance. Thus, there could often be between five and twenty-five different applications with very similar functions running in parallel for a variety of perfectly legitimate reasons. Lastly hundreds of the many thousands of applications may be legacy systems which are ten or even twenty years old, running on obsolete technology.

It is important to realize that such complexity is neither exceptional nor a result of oversight; rather it arises out of a very complex business that is *continuously evolving*. New business requirements often cannot be supported by legacy systems and demand that fresh applications be built; these need to remain in synchrony with data in legacy systems, as well as other applications. Technology is continuously evolving in the background, resulting in the variety of platforms. So, to an extent, it may seem that such complexity in inevitable and simply a fact of life.

However, an important observation is that server sprawl is also a result of the 'one application, one server' paradigm assumed by most middleware products, especially application servers. So, even if many different applications are deployed on the same middlware, if one of them requires a restart of the application server, all applications suffer. As a result, development teams often assume and insist that each new application be deployed on an independent server. The resulting server proliferation is both difficult to manage and wasteful, since rarely does each application fully utilize the capacity of its server. This has been the primary driver for the use of virtualization technology, which is also heavily exploited in cloud infrastructure platforms. Chapter 8 covers virtualization in detail, and its use to manage server sprawl.

Last but not least, the costs of such complexity most often reflect in the cost of the manpower required to manage IT infrastructure. Provisioning new servers, replacing faulty servers and monitoring the health of running servers are all largely manual activities, albeit supported by tools. An important feature of cloud infrastructure platforms is that they make many of these tasks possible to do via services (web service APIs), thereby opening up the *potential* for automation of some of this manual management activity. In fact, the cloud providers themselves exploit such automation internally to achieve significant efficiencies in their own business offerings, i.e. retail for Amazon, or search in the case of Google.

It is the promise of being able to harvest significant savings by exploiting virtualization and automation that is making cloud computing an attractive option to explore and invest in, whether using external providers or as an internal strategy within the enterprise. In subsequent chapters we shall explore in more detail the available external cloud platforms as well as technologies that they exploit.

# PART II

# Cloud platforms

Publicly available cloud computing began with the launch of Amazon's Elastic Compute Cloud, offering Infrastructure as a Service. Soon afterwards, Google launched its Google App Engine, which took a different path, offering a development Platform as a Service. In due course, Microsoft took a path similar to Google's, with its recently launched Azure platform. We first present a *user's* picture of each of these major public cloud offerings. Next we consider the economics of cloud computing, again from the perspective of an enterprise user. We examine whether, when and why using a public cloud for enterprise applications might be cheaper than deploying the same systems in-house, i.e., in a 'private' cloud.

# CHAPTER 5

# Cloud computing platforms

In this chapter we shall describe the major public cloud platforms from Amazon, Google and Microsoft, outlining the services they provide from an end-user's perspective. (While there are other providers who have similar offerings, as of this writing they are smaller. In Chapter 17 we also describe other cloud providers as well as the larger cloud computing ecosystem including cloud management applications and tools for building private clouds.)

## 5.1 INFRASTRUCTURE AS A SERVICE: AMAZON EC2

The Amazon cloud provides *infrastructure as a service* (IaaS), whereby computing infrastructure such as for servers, storage or network end points of a desired capacity are virtually provisioned in minutes through an automated web-based management console. This core IaaS service, called Elastic Compute Cloud, or EC2, is but one of a set of services that constitute the Amazon cloud platform, but the term EC2 is also often used to describe the entire cloud offering.

Figure 5.1 illustrates the services provided by the Amazon infrastructure cloud from a *user* perspective. These services are implemented on a very large network of servers, shown as dashed boxes in the figure. The Elastic Compute Cloud service provides users access to dedicated virtual machines of a desired capacity that are provisioned on these physical servers, with

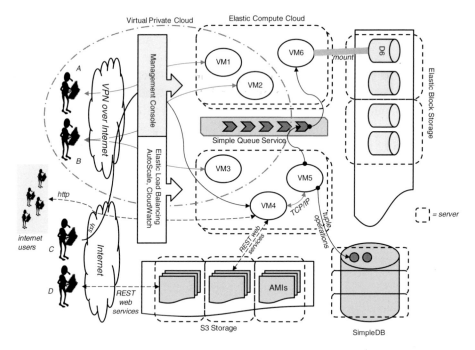

FIGURE **5.1. Amazon infrastructure cloud**

details of the actual physical server, such as its location, capacity, etc. being transparent to the end-user. Through the management console users generate PKI[1] key-pairs using which they can securely login to these virtual servers over the internet. In Figure 5.1, user C provisions the virtual server VM4 through the management console, and accesses it using ssh, for a Linux server, or via 'remote desktop' for a Windows server. Users have a choice of virtual machine images (called Amazon machine images, or AMIs) to choose from when provisioning a server. All AMIs are stored in common storage in the Amazon S3 storage service (which we shall return to below), and used to boot the desired configuration of virtual server.

The user's account is charged on an hourly basis based on actual consumption, i.e. time that the server is up. Charges vary depending on the AMI used and capacity of server chosen while provisioning. For example, a 'small' Linux server costs a few cents per cpu-hour, whereas a larger server preloaded with

---

[1] RSA keys and X.25 certificates.

licensed software, such as Windows, as well as other database or middleware products, could end up costing close to a dollar per hour.

Cloud users have root/administrator access to these servers, and therefore control them completely. For example, they can deploy applications and make them publicly accessible over the internet. Static network addresses required for such purposes can also be provisioned through the management console. Thus, VM4 is also accessible by internet users at large over HTTP. Such publicly available static IP addresses are charged on a fixed monthly basis; note that network data transfer to any server, with or without a static IP address, is charged on usage basis, at rates of a few cents per gigabyte transferred.

Users can provision and access many servers that can communicate with each other over the fast internal network within the Amazon cloud. For example, user C in Figure 5.1 has provisioned VM5 and VM6 in addition to VM4. If VM4 is a web server, VM5 may be a database server, and these two communicate over the internal cloud network using TCP/IP. Since VM5 is a database server, it needs to store and retrieve data. The Amazon SimpleDB service provides an object store where key-value pairs can be efficiently stored and retrieved. It is important to note that SimpleDB is not a relational database, and we shall describe the features provided by such key-value pair cloud databases in a later section.

Instead of using SimpleDB, virtual servers could instead use a relational database system, which may come either pre-installed as part of the AMI, or separately by users in the normal manner. However, it is important to understand that virtual servers do not have any persistent storage; so any user data on file system (i.e. whatever is not part of the AMI) is lost when the server shuts down. In order to store data persistently, such in a relational database, Elastic Block Storage needs to be mounted on a virtual server. The Elastic Block Storage service maintains persistent data across all users on a large set of physical servers. After a virtual server boots, it must attach user data from the EBS as a logical storage volume mounted as a raw device (disk). Any database service, or for that matter any application relying on persistent data, can be run once this step is performed.

In our illustration in Figure 5.1, VM6 might be an archival server where VM5 sends logs of whatever updates it makes to the SimbleDB datastore. Note that VM6 has mounted a logical volume D6, where it possibly maintains archived data. Now notice that VM5 sends data to VM6 not over TCP/IP, but using the Amazon Simple Queue Service (SQS). The SQS is a reliable persistent message queue that is useful for temporarily storing data that needs to eventually get to a processing server such as VM6, but in a manner that does not rely on VM6 always being available. Thus, VM6 may be booted say, only on a daily basis, when all it does is process the messages waiting for it in the SQS and log them in its persistent database. Usage of the SQS is charged based on data volumes and how long data resides in the queue. Thus, VM5 need not concern itself with archiving apart from logging data in the SQS, and VM6 needs to be up only when required. SQS is normally used for managing such asynchronous transfer of data between processing servers in a batch-oriented workflow.

Persistent storage in the EBS as described above can be accessed only if it is attached to a running virtual server. Further, any other servers can access this data only via the server where the EBS is attached. The Amazon S3 Storage Service provides a different storage model. Data in S3 can be files of any type, and in general any blob (binary large object). Users access and modify S3 objects via URIs, using REST web services (which we shall cover in Chapter 7). S3 objects are accessible over the internet as well as from virtual servers within the Amazon cloud. S3 is especially useful for reliably storing large collections of unstructured data that need to be accessed by many client applications. It is important to note that all data in S3 is automatically replicated at least three times for fault tolerance. The S3 storage model provides 'eventual' consistency across replicas: A write may return while data has not yet propagated to all replicas, so some clients may still read old data; eventually, however, all replicas will be updated. This consistency model and its underlying implementation architecture, which is also shared by SimpleDB, is discussed in more detail in Chapter 10.

Storage in S3 is also used for storing machine images (AMIs) that users define themselves, either from scratch by packaging OS and application files from their own physical servers, or by 'deriving' from an already available AMI. Such images can also be made available to other users, or to the public at large. Further, such sharing can be combined with the Amazon payments gateway through a DevPay agreement whereby a portion of the charges paid by users of such AMIs are credited to the AMI creator's account. Thus DevPay based sharing of AMIs in S3 has created a new software distribution channel, and many industry standard databases and middleware packages, such as from Oracle or IBM are now available in this manner. The mechanism is also secure in that 'derived' AMIs still maintain their DevPay lineage and are charged appropriately.

An important goal of any cloud service is insulating users from variable demand by automatically managing scaling up and down of the resources allocated to a cloud application. In an infrastructure cloud, such as Amazon EC2, the user needs to explicitly define an architecture that enables scalability using tools provided by Amazon to manage elasticity: Runtime performance parameters, such as CPU and I/O utilization, of a user's virtual servers can be monitored in real-time by Amazon Cloud Watch; this data can be used by Amazon Auto Scale to add (or remove) virtual servers from an application cluster and automatically provision them with predefined machine images. Finally, Elastic Load Balancing allows a group of servers to be configured into a set across which incoming requests (e.g. HTTP connections) are load balanced. The performance statistics of the load-balanced requests can also be monitored by Cloud Watch and used by Auto Scale to add or remove servers from the load balanced cluster. Using these tools users can configure a scalable architecture that can also elastically adjust its resource consumption. Note however that for a complex architecture, such as multi-tier transaction processing system, there may need to be many layers of clustering, e.g. at the web server, application server, database server etc. It remains the user's responsibility to configure a scalable cluster for each of these layers, define what performance parameters need to be monitored in Cloud Watch and set the Auto Scale parameters for each cluster.

Enterprises seeking to adopt cloud computing also need to address the security concerns of corporate IT. Network security is an important element of these concerns: An enterprise's computing resources are usually protected by firewalls, proxy servers, intrusion detection systems etc. Naturally, enterprise security requires that virtual servers running in the cloud also be protected in this manner, using the same policies and safeguards that apply to any resources in their own data centers. Amazon EC2 provides a Virtual Private Cloud service, whereby virtual servers can be connected to an enterprise's internal network using a VPN (virtual private network). For example, users A and B in Figure 5.1 access virtual servers VM1, VM2 and VM3 through a VPN running over the public internet. These servers then have private IP addresses controlled by the enterprise's network operations center. Access to and from this network to the outside world can be controlled by the same set of policies, firewalls and proxies as for other resources in the enterprise's own data center. Of course for efficiency, these firewalls, proxies etc. should ideally be replicated on virtual servers in the cloud even while maintaining the same enterprise-wide policies, just as proxy servers and firewalls are often replicated in a large enterprise network distributed across many locations.

## 5.2 PLATFORM AS A SERVICE: GOOGLE APP ENGINE

The Google cloud, called Google App Engine, is a 'platform as a service' (PaaS) offering. In contrast with the Amazon infrastructure as a service cloud, where users explicitly provision virtual machines and control them fully, including installing, compiling and running software on them, a PaaS offering hides the actual execution environment from users. Instead, a software platform is provided along with an SDK, using which users develop applications and deploy them on the cloud. The PaaS platform is responsible for executing the applications, including servicing external service requests, as well as running scheduled jobs included in the application. By making the actual execution servers transparent to the user, a PaaS platform is able to share *application* servers across users who need lower capacities, as well as automatically scale resources allocated to applications that experience heavy loads.

Figure 5.2 depicts a user view of Google App Engine. Users upload code, in either Java or Python, along with related files, which are stored on the Google File System, a very large scale fault tolerant and redundant storage system which we shall describe in detail in Chapter 10. It is important to note that an application is immediately available on the internet as soon as it is

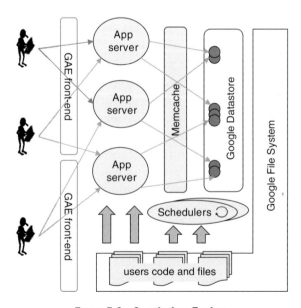

FIGURE 5.2. Google App Engine

successfully uploaded (no virtual servers need to be explicitly provisioned as in IaaS).

Resource usage for an application is metered in terms of web requests served and CPU-hours actually spent executing requests or batch jobs. Note that this is very different from the IaaS model: A PaaS application can be deployed and made globally available 24×7, but charged only when *accessed* (or if batch jobs run); in contrast, in an IaaS model merely making an application continuously available incurs the full cost of keeping at least some of the servers running all the time. Further, deploying applications in Google App Engine is free, within usage limits; thus applications can be developed and tried out free and begin to incur cost only when actually accessed by a sufficient volume of requests. The PaaS model enables Google to provide such a free service because applications do not run in dedicated virtual machines; a deployed application that is not accessed merely consumes storage for its code and data and expends no CPU cycles.

GAE applications are served by a large number of web servers in Google's data centers that execute requests from end-users across the globe. The web servers load code from the GFS into memory and serve these requests. Each request to a particular application is served by any one of GAE's web servers; there is no guarantee that the same server will serve requests to any two requests, even from the same HTTP session. Applications can also specify some functions to be executed as batch jobs which are run by a scheduler.

While this architecture is able to ensure that applications scale naturally as load increases, it also means that application code cannot easily rely on in-memory data. A *distributed* in-memory cache called Memcache is made available to partially address this issue: In particular HTTP sessions are implemented using Memcache so that even if requests from the same session go to different servers they can retrieve their session data, *most* of the time (since Memcache is not guaranteed to always retain cached data).

## 5.2.1 Google Datastore

Applications persist data in the Google Datastore, which is also (like Amazon SimpleDB) a non-relational database. The Datastore allows applications to define structured types (called 'kinds') and store their instances (called 'entities') in a distributed manner on the GFS file system. While one can view Datastore 'kinds' as table structures and entities as records, there are

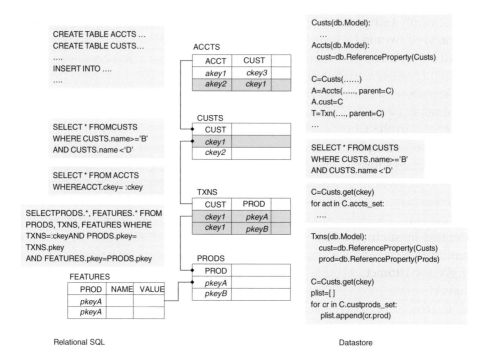

**FIGURE 5.3. Google Datastore**

important differences between a relational model and the Datastore, some of which are also illustrated in Figure 5.3.

Unlike a relational schema where all rows in a table have the same set of columns, all entities of a 'kind' need not have the same properties. Instead, additional properties can be added to any entity. This feature is particularly useful in situations where one cannot foresee all the potential properties in a model, especially those that occur occasionally for only a small subset of records. For example, a model storing 'products' of different types (shows, books, etc.) would need to allow each product to have a different set of features. In a relational model, this would probably be implemented using a separate FEATURES table, as shown on the bottom left of Figure 5.3. Using the Datastore, this table ('kind') is not required; instead, each product entity can be assigned a different set of properties at runtime.

The Datastore allows simple queries with conditions, such as the first query shown in Figure 5.3 to retrieve all customers having names in some lexicographic range. The query syntax (called GQL) is essentially the same as SQL, but with some restrictions. For example, all inequality conditions in a query must be on a single property; so a query that also filtered customers on, say, their 'type', would be illegal in GQL but allowed in SQL. The reasons for this shall be explained in more detail in Chapter 10 where we describe the internal structure of the Google Datastore.

Relationships between tables in a relational model are modeled using foreign keys. Thus, each account in the ACCTS table has a pointer *ckey* to the customer in the CUSTS table that it belongs to. Relationships are traversed via queries using foreign keys, such as retrieving all accounts for a particular customer, as shown. The Datastore provides a more object-oriented approach to relationships in persistent data. Model definitions can include references to other models; thus each entity of the Accts 'kind' includes a reference to its customer, which is an entity of the Custs 'kind.' Further, relationships defined by such references can be traversed in *both* directions, so not only can one directly access the customer of an account, but also *all* accounts of a given customer, without executing any query operation, as shown in the figure.

GQL queries *cannot* execute joins between models. Joins are critical when using SQL to efficiently retrieve data from multiple tables. For example, the query shown in the figure retrieves details of all products bought by a particular customer, for which it needs to join data from the transactions (TXNS), products (PRODS) and product features (FEATURES) tables. Even though GQL does not allow joins, its ability to traverse associations between entities often enables joins to be avoided, as shown in the figure for the above example: By storing references to customers and products in the Txns model, it is possible to retrieve all transactions for a given customer through a reverse traversal of the customer reference. The product references in each transaction then yield all products and their features (as discussed earlier, a separate Features model is not required because of schema flexibility). It is important to note that while object relationship traversal can be used as an alternative to joins, this is not always possible, and when required joins may need to be explicitly executed by application code.

The Google Datastore is a distributed object store where objects (entities) of all GAE applications are maintained using a large number of servers and the GFS distributed file system. We shall cover this distributed storage architecture in detail in Chapter 10. From a user perspective, it is important to ensure that in spite of sharing a distributed storage scheme with many other users, application data is (a) retrieved efficiently and (b) atomically updated. The Datastore provides a mechanism to group entities from different 'kinds' in a hierarchy that is used for both these purposes. Notice that in Figure 5.3

entities of the Accts and Txns 'kinds' are instantiated with a parameter 'parent' that specifies a particular customer entity, thereby linking these three entities in an 'entity group'. The Datastore ensures that all entities belonging to a particular group are stored close together in the distributed file system (we shall see how in Chapter 10). The Datastore allows processing steps to be grouped into transactions wherein updates to data are guaranteed to be atomic; however this also requires that each transaction only manipulates entities belonging to the same entity group. While this transaction model suffices for most on line applications, complex batch updates that update many unrelated entities cannot execute atomically, unlike in a relational database where there are no such restrictions.

### 5.2.2 Amazon SimpleDB

As we mentioned earlier in Section 5.1, Amazon SimpleDB is also a non-relational database, in many ways similar to the Google Datastore. SimpleDB 'domains' correspond to 'kinds', and 'items' to entities; each item can have a number of attribute-value pairs, and different items in a domain can have different sets of attributes, similar to Datastore entities. Queries on SimpleDB domains can include conditions, including inequality conditions, on any number of attributes. Further, just as in the Google Datastore, joins are not permitted. However, SimpleDB does not support object relationships as in Google Datastore, nor does it support transactions. It is important to note that all data in SimpleDB is replicated for redundancy, just as in GFS. Because of replication, SimpleDB features an 'eventual consistency' model, wherein data is guaranteed to be propagated to at least one replica and will eventually reach all replicas, albeit with some delay. This can result in perceived inconsistency, since an immediate read following a write may not always yield the result written. In the case of Google Datastore on the other hand, writes succeed only when all replicas are updated; this avoids inconsistency but also makes writes slower.

### 5.3 Microsoft Azure

Microsoft's cloud offering, called Azure, has been commercially released to the public only recently, though a community preview beta has been publicly available for longer. Thus, it is important to note that some elements of the Azure platform are likely to change in future commercial editions.

Like the Google App Engine, Azure is a PaaS offering. Developers create applications using Microsoft development tools (i.e. Visual Studio along with its supported languages, C#, Visual Basic, ASPs, etc.); an Azure extension to the standard toolset allows such applications to be developed and deployed on Microsoft's cloud, in much the same manner as developing and deploying using Google App Engine's SDK. There are also similarities with aspects of Amazon's IaaS offering, such as the use of virtualization, user control over the number of virtual servers allocated to an application and user control on elasticity. However, unlike the non-relational Google Datastore and Amazon SimpleDB, the recently released commercial edition of Azure provides *relational* storage services, albeit with certain limitations as we cover below. Azure also allows storage of arbitrary files and objects like Amazon S3 as well as a queuing service similar to Amazon SQS.

Figure 5.4 illustrates a user's view of Microsoft Azure. Application code deployed on Azure executes in a number of virtual machines (called *instances*) with each virtual machine running the Windows Server operating system. While users do not have any control on when instances boot and how long they stay up, they can specify the number of instances a particular application is likely to require. (As of this writing, each virtual server runs on a dedicated

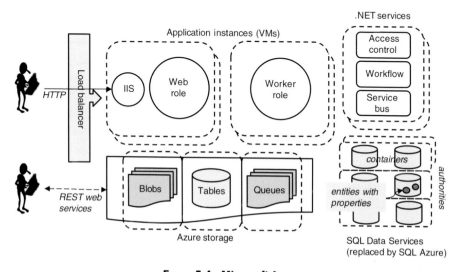

FIGURE 5.4.  **Microsoft Azure**

CPU core, though this may change in the future.) Thus, Azure provides a finer level of control on the resources to be allocated to an application as compared to Google App Engine, but not to the extent of an IaaS offering such as Amazon EC2.

Application code can be deployed on Azure as a web role or a worker role. Code in web-role instances is run through a web server (Microsoft IIS) that is included in the instance. Web roles respond to HTTP requests that are automatically load balanced across application instances. Worker role code can run as a batch process that can communicate with a web role through Azure data storage, such as queues or tables. Worker role applications cannot be accessed from an external network, but can make external HTTP requests, either to worker roles or over the internet.

Azure data storage allows storage of blobs, non-relational tables (similar to SimpleDB) as well as queues. In addition, an alternative database-storage scheme was provided by SQL Data Services in the beta edition of Azure. SQL Data Services are implemented on a number of clusters running Microsoft's SQL Server database, deployed in various Microsoft-owned data centers called *authorities*. Each authority can host a number of *containers*, which are similar to database tables. Applications access SQL Data Services at the level of containers, through a global address scheme. Each container contains entities which have properties, and like SimpleDB or Google Datastore, properties for each entity can differ in type and number. Microsoft SQL Data Services was re-branded as 'SQL Azure' in the commercial edition of Azure. The architecture of authorities, containers and tables has been replaced by a traditional relational model supported by Microsoft SQL Server. In particular this includes support for joins between tables, transactions and other features of relational database. However, as of this writing, each SQL Azure database is limited to under 10 GB in size. In case larger volumes of data need to be stored, multiple virtual database instances need to be provisioned. Further, since cross-database queries are not permitted, queries on larger data sets, including joins, need to be implemented within application code. The SQL Azure model represents a practical compromise between the limitations of non-relational models versus a traditional relational database: Full relational queries are permitted, but only on small data sets, which are likely to suffice for many of the early adopters of cloud services.

In addition to compute and storage services, Microsoft Azure also provides what are called .NET services. These include access control services that provide globally configurable and accessible security tokens, a service bus that enables globally published service end points and a configurable web-service-based workflow-orchestration service. Like SQL Data services and SQL Azure, these are all based on Microsoft's enterprise middleware products for identity management and web services, deployed in the cloud on a distributed and globally accessible platform.

As compared to Google's PaaS offering, Microsoft Azure enjoys the advantage of a large base of Microsoft applications already in use within enterprises. From what was available in the community preview of Azure and its rapid evolution in the commercial edition (such as the addition of full relational database support, at least for small applications), it is likely to become even easier to migrate existing Microsoft applications to Azure in the future. Therefore it may well be that Microsoft Azure becomes a more popular PaaS platform at least for large enterprises, as compared to Google's App Engine.

# CHAPTER 6

# Cloud computing economics

One of the reasons for the growing interest in cloud computing is the popular belief, propagated also by cloud providers, that by using public cloud offerings one can significantly reduce IT costs. In this chapter we examine the economics of cloud computing. Given that there are two varieties of cloud offerings, infrastructure clouds as well as platform clouds, we consider infrastructure costs as well as possible advantages in a development environment, including productivity. We look at cloud economics from the perspective of the user, as well as from that of the cloud provider. We also compare the economics of private and public clouds.

## 6.1 Is CLOUD INFRASTRUCTURE CHEAPER?

As of this writing, published rates for cloud infrastructure (using Amazon EC2) start from $0.10 per CPU-hour of computing, and $0.10 per GByte month of storage, for the smallest possible server configuration; larger servers cost more per hour. In our example later in this chapter we shall use the 'extra-large' server costing $0.68 per CPU-hour. We shall compare this with an actual purchase order for an equivalent server to examine whether and to what extent cloud computing is cheaper than using equivalent in-house infrastructure running within an enterprise data center.

The important driving factor for cloud economics is the way hardware capacity is planned for and purchased. From an end-user perspective cloud computing gives the illusion of a *potentially infinite* capacity with the ability to *rapidly* leverage additional capacity when needed, and pay only for what one consumes. Using a public cloud offering therefore obviates the need to plan ahead for peak load and converts fixed costs into variable costs that change with actual usage, thereby eliminating wastage. In contrast, provisioning for peak capacity is a necessity within private data centers; and without adequate scale there is limited opportunity to amortize capacity across different applications, and so most data centers operate at ridiculously low average utilizations of 5–20 percent!

## 6.1.1 IaaS economics

Let us consider, as a simple example, the 'extra-large' server on the Amazon EC2 cloud that has 8 compute units, 15 GB of memory and 1600 GB of disk. As mentioned earlier, such an instance costs $0.68 per CPU-hour. Now consider purchasing an equivalent server for in-house deployment: Based on recent experience, an x86 server with 3 quad-core CPUs (i.e. 12 processing cores), 12 GB of memory and 300 GB of disk cost $9500.

Let us compare the costs of running the in-house server for three years, or 26 260 hours, as compared with running an equivalent 'extra-large' server in Amazon EC2; Table 6.1 summarizes our calculations, as worked out in detail below: At a $9500 purchase price, the price of an in-house server is $0.36 per-hour over its life cycle; or $0.03 per core-hour. On the other hand, we find that the price of a core-hour on an EC2 server is $0.085 (0.68/8, since the large server has 8 cores), which is 2.82 times more expensive than the in-house server. Even if we discount the fact that the in-house server has 12 cores compared to the EC2 server's 8 cores, which is actually justifiable given the larger memory and disk of the EC2 server, we find the per-hour price of an 'extra-large' EC2 server to be 1.88 times the in-house server.

So it seems that the cloud server is more expensive. But now consider the fact that most servers in the data center are heavily underutilized, say only 40 percent, whereas cloud usage can be easily scaled up or down with demand and therefore enjoys a far higher utilization, say 80 percent. Factoring this in, the cost per-hour of *effective* capacity in-house becomes $0.90 (i.e., $0.36/0.4), essentially the same that for a server deployed in the cloud (i.e., $0.85 = $.68/0.8). Further, power and cooling for an in-house server over its lifetime is at least as much as the amortized base price of the server ($0.36

| **TABLE 6.1 Infrastructure cloud economics** | | |
|---|---|---|
|  | In-house server | Cloud server |
| Purchase cost | $9600 |  |
| Cost/hr (over 3 yrs) | $0.36 | $0.68 |
| Price: Cloud/In-house | 1.88 |  |
| Efficiency | 40% | 80% |
| Cost/Effective-hr | $0.90 | $0.85 |
| Power and cooling | $0.36 |  |
| Management cost | $0.10 | $0.01 |
| Total Cost/Effective-hr | $1.36 | $0.86 |
| Cost ratio: In-house/Cloud | 1.58 |  |

per-hour), and often more; so in Table 6.1 we assume that power and cooling adds an extra $0.36 per-hour for the in-house server.

Next, we consider manpower costs for infrastructure management, i.e. tasks such as taking backups, monitoring and periodic maintenance. In practice, with the kind of automation used in cloud data centers, infrastructure management costs follow a power-law[1]; so the number of servers $n$ that $p$ people can manage is proportional to $p^2$. While an in-house data center can, in principle, achieve similar efficiencies in infrastructure management as cloud data centers, it is unlikely to be able to operate at the same scale. It has been found that the manpower costs of managing a very large data center, say a few hundred thousand servers, can be as low as $0.01 per-hour per server, whereas a smaller data center with only a few thousand servers would spend $0.1 per-hour on each server.

Now, consider an enterprise that runs thousands of servers in the cloud as opposed to in-house. To a large extent, the cloud provider is *already* managing these servers, and the management costs have been built into the per-hour price of a server. So theoretically, the enterprise incurs no cost for managing cloud servers. Nevertheless, even if we assume that there is still some cost incurred on the part of an enterprise to manage cloud-based servers, it will be far less than for the servers deployed in-house. For our calculations we assume that an in-house data center comprises of thousands of servers costing $0.1 per-hour per server to manage, while the cost incurred by an enterprise to

---

[1] Private communication, using US salary costs.

manage cloud-based servers is taken as $0.01 per-hour per server, based on the power-law behavior of management costs as described above.

Table 6.1 summarizes our calculations including utilization efficiencies, power and cooling, as well as management costs. With all costs factored in, it now appears that the cloud server in EC2 has a clear cost advantage (almost factor of 1.6) over the in-house server. (A similar example has been described in [4]; however we have found some calculation errors in that example, though the conclusion therein is similar to ours here.) Note that for our analysis we have assumed a large in-house data center (thousands of servers) running at an efficiency of 40 percent. In practice, the benefits of cloud computing will be even greater for smaller data centers running at more typical efficiencies in the range of 20 percent, and where infrastructure management costs begin to outweigh server costs.

We do not go into the details of comparing storage and network costs in-house vs. the cloud. Instead we refer to [4], where it is shown that in-house storage is only 20–50 percent cheaper than on Amazon S3. When one additionally considers the fact that that cloud storage on S3 is automatically replicated at least three times, the total cost of ownership works out far cheaper in the cloud. The equation for network bandwidth is similar; network costs are simply two to three times cheaper in the cloud [4].

## 6.2 Economics of private clouds

It may appear that the economics worked out in the previous section is based on an assumption of poor utilization for an in-house data center. It is often argued that using virtualization and automatic provisioning technologies in-house it should be possible to create a private cloud where these inefficiencies would disappear and the benefits of cloud computing could be achieved on premise. The availability of open source software such as Eucalyptus (see Chapter 17), which essentially enables Amazon EC2-like automated provisioning, means that such an approach is also quite feasible. Let us analyze the economics of such private clouds in more detail and see how they compare with costs using public clouds:

Let $d_i(t)$ be the computing demand of the $i$th application running in an enterprise at time $t$, the aggregate demand $D(t) = \sum_i d_i(t)$, and the peak demand be $D_{max} = \max_t D(t)$. The relationship between $D(t)$ and $D_{max}$ can vary widely depending on the relative operational profiles of the set of applications, as illustrated in Figure 6.1. If the peaks and troughs of different

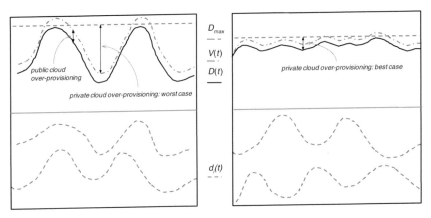

**FIGURE 6.1. Over provisioning in private clouds**

applications are highly correlated, as in the left illustration in the figure, $D(t)$ can vary widely from the peak; on the other hand if there is little or no correlation on the average, and for a large number of applications, $D(t)$ may be smooth and quite close to $D_{max}$, as shown in the right illustration in the figure.

Now let us also assume that we have managed to create a highly virtualized environment within the data center where the actual resources provisioned for use (i.e. powered up and allocated) can vary dynamically and automatically over time. More specifically, let $\delta$ be the time delay to provision extra computing resources on demand. Clearly, in cases where the provisioning rate $1/\delta$ is far smaller than the rate of change of demand $dD/dt$, there is no benefit of dynamic virtual provisioning and one may just as well provision the peak capacity $D_{max}$ at all times. We consider the case when $\delta$ is small, so that the provisioned capacity can closely track demand, as illustrated by the curve $V(t)$ in the figure. Note that because of the provisioning delay $\delta$, some excess virtual capacity always needs to be provisioned in order to ensure adequate capacity to meet demand; and this is proportional to the rate of change of demand, so the virtual capacity needed at time $t$ is

$$V(t) = D(t) + \delta \frac{dD}{dt}. \tag{6.1}$$

The total virtual capacity provisioned over a time interval $T$ is therefore

$$V = \int_T \left( D(t)dt + \delta \frac{dD}{dt} \right) = D_T + \delta(D_{max} - D_{min}), \tag{6.2}$$

where $D_T$ is the area under the demand curve $D(t)$.

Now, let us compare the costs incurred in a private cloud versus using a public cloud. For an in-house data center, the total physical capacity that needs to be purchased must meet the peak demand $D_{max}$; thus if the amortized cost per hour of this CPU purchase is $c$, this entails a cost of $cTD_{max}$. On the other hand, consider using a public cloud service whose *price* is $2c$ per CPU hour, then the cost would be $2cV$. (The factor of two comes from our earlier calculations, see Table 6.1 where the cloud server price per-hour is 1.88 times the purchase price of an in-house server amortized over three years.) We also need to factor in power costs, which are included in the cloud price but must be paid for in-house: Suppose the amortized power cost is $p$ per computing hour, then the total power cost is at least $pV$, assuming servers that are not used can be completely turned off so as to consume no power. Then, the ratio of in-house costs to that of an equivalent cloud infrastructure can be approximated as:

$$\frac{C_{private}}{C_{public}} = \frac{cD_{max}T + pV}{2cV}. \tag{6.3}$$

Further, for simplicity we shall assume that $p = c$, as has often been observed in practice [4]. Using (6.2), the expression (6.3) above works out to

$$\frac{C_{private}}{C_{public}} = \frac{1}{\frac{2D_T}{TD_{max}} + \left(1 - \frac{D_{min}}{D_{max}}\right)\frac{2\delta}{T}} + \frac{1}{2}. \tag{6.4}$$

To verify our result, note that with perfect amortization of capacity across demand $D_T = TD_{max}$ and $D_{max} = D_{min}$ and there is no difference between private and public cloud costs.

However, in practice typical transaction processing loads can vary by factors of 5 or 10 in the course of each day, and by orders of magnitude at peak times of the year. Further the demand profile for many business-facing applications in the same enterprise is likely to be similar, so in practice usually $D_{max} \gg D_{min}$ and $D_T \ll TD_{max}$, so public cloud wins as per our calculation above.

Equation (6.4) quantifies the benefits of elasticity, i.e. the ability to rapidly provision resources that one needs and pay *only* for these. Our analysis shows that even if one manages to improve utilizations in the data center through virtualization, because of critical applications that consume significant resources and need to be provisioned for peak load, the potential benefits of virtualization are rarely realized fully. In practice, over provisioning of capacity will always be required; and more so in-house because of the above reason. Figure 6.1 illustrates the degree of over provisioning needed in a private versus a public cloud.

### 6.2.1 Economics of PaaS vs. IaaS

We now compare the IaaS and PaaS cloud models from an economic perspective: The PaaS model, exemplified by the Google App Engine and Microfsoft Azure cloud offerings, can exhibit economic advantages as compared to an IaaS model for certain classes of applications. Consider a web application that needs to be available $24 \times 7$, but where the transaction volume is highly unpredictable, and can vary rapidly. Using an IaaS cloud, a minimal number of servers would need to be provisioned at all times to ensure availability of the web service.

In contrast, with a PaaS model such as Google App Engine, merely deploying the application costs nothing. Thus an application can be made $24 \times 7$ available with no cost. As usage increases beyond the free limits, charges begin to be incurred, and a well-engineered application scales automatically to meet the demand. As soon as demand drops, resources are no longer consumed and no charges are incurred. (Microsoft Azure *does* charge based on resources consumed, so the above argument does not directly apply.)

Further, since provisioning additional servers for an application takes a finite amount of time, say a few minutes, the minimum capacity provisioned in IaaS needs to account for this delay by planning and paying for excess capacity even in the cloud environment (the dotted line in Figure 6.1 corresponding to $V(t)$). With a PaaS platform such as Google App Engine, a large number of web servers catering to the platform are always running, so every user's application code is available to all servers via the distributed file system. Sudden spikes in demand are automatically routed to free web servers by the load balancer, ensuring minimal performance degradation; the only additional overhead incurred is that of loading code and data from the file system when such a web server handles a request to a new application for the first time.

Thus, for low or variable-volume web-based services PaaS is a cheaper alternative, provided one is willing to re-architect or rebuild applications for the non-standard data formats provided by these platforms (both Google App Engine as well as Microsoft Azure). For heavier, back-end applications (such as those behind web front ends, or for batch processing), IaaS is better suited.

It is possible that a combination of PaaS and IaaS may be a viable architecture in certain cases, with PaaS providing the web front end and IaaS provisioning processing power when needed.

## 6.3 SOFTWARE PRODUCTIVITY IN THE CLOUD

The infrastructure needs for developing and testing enterprise applications are different from those of a production environment, for example data security requirements are lower. At the same time the variability of demand is high, with new development servers being required for each project, many of which become redundant once the application is released to production. In this particular case, infrastructure demands from different development projects are likely to be largely uncorrelated, so virtualization is likely to succeed in improving utilizations. However, the time for provisioning and configuring a development environment can often become a significant overhead in many large organizations due to procurement and ITIL procedures.[2] For agile business environments where new development projects are initiated regularly, such delays can become an obstacle and impact IT agility. In such cases leveraging a public cloud infrastructure for development and testing can be fast, cost effective as well as low risk, thereby improving business agility by reducing delays while starting new IT projects.

Along with development and testing, designing applications for good performance requires stress testing early in the development life cycle, preferably on a production-capacity hardware configuration. This is often difficult, especially early in the development cycle, simply because of non-availability of such an environment for testing purposes. Production capacity configurations are expensive so it is not cost effective to invest in spare capacity at this scale for occasional performance testing needs. Using public cloud infrastructure a production class infrastructure can be provisioned on demand and disbanded once performance testing is complete.

Apart from agility and availability, software development using public cloud infrastructure is also often better suited to supporting globally distributed development teams. The public cloud enables such teams to rely on a 'central' build infrastructure that is easily accessible over the internet; thus no one part of the team is naturally more advantageously placed in terms of

---

[2] Procedures based on the 'information technology infrastructure library' standard.

being physically 'closer' to the build servers. It is often underestimated how important such democratization is in terms of driving team dynamics; groups physically co-located with the build environment often have higher access privileges or at least experience better network performance than others, thereby making them 'more fit' than the rest of the team for certain development tasks. Using the public cloud one eliminates such artificial barriers (at the risk of reducing everyone to the lowest common denominator of internet bandwidth!). Such teams can better leverage geographically distributed talent as well be more flexible in moving work around the world by 'following the sun' to leverage time zone differences to their advantage.

So far we have considered public IaaS clouds and how they may impact software development. PaaS clouds provide development tools using which developers can create applications; we now examine whether these also impact development productivity in some manner. It is important to reemphasize that both (Google as well as Microsoft) PaaS platforms are unique in comparison to widely used development tools: They both rely on a non-relational data model which impacts portability of applications to these platforms from other more standard ones. Also, both platforms *build in scalability* so that developers do not need to be concerned about how many servers their application will run on, how the different components of the application will execute in parallel using multiple servers or how data will be distributed. Developers are supposed to write to the platform APIs, and scaling will be managed *automatically* by the cloud.

The economic benefits of *automatic* scalability are significant: It is widely accepted in the software industry that end-to-end development productivity in 'mission critical' projects where high transaction volumes and scalability are critical is demonstrably *lower*. Moreover the difference in productivity is often a factor of two or more, as compared to smaller 'departmental' level projects where such concerns are not as important. If indeed cloud platforms are able to factor out scalability and make it a feature of the platform itself, then this itself can result in an order of magnitude improvement in productivity for large-scale systems. However, it is equally important to note that this claim that has yet to be proven given that it is still early days for cloud computing and even more so for PaaS platforms.

Finally, a certain class of cloud-based offerings, '*configurable* SaaS platforms,' allow the creation of small to medium-sized business applications with little or no programming. An example is Salesforce.com's APEX development environment, now called Force.com. We refer to these as Dev 2.0 platforms and cover them in detail in Chapter 12. While these are also software development platforms, they are are constrained to a particular class of applications, i.e. web-based transaction processing. Therefore as a class of cloud offerings these are more accurately labeled SaaS platforms for specific types of application development, unlike the more versatile PaaS platforms where a full programming language is available. Nevertheless, for this widely required class of systems, Dev 2.0 platforms also promise at least an order of magnitude improvement in development productivity, as we shall see in Chapter 12.

## 6.4 ECONOMIES OF SCALE: PUBLIC VS. PRIVATE CLOUDS

We now return to our discussion on infrastructure costs. We have argued that public cloud services can be cheaper than using similar virtualized infrastructure in-house. One needs to ask how this has become possible while also allowing for profit margins. Amortizing capacity across demand from a large number of customers enables better utilizations, but surely this alone cannot be the basis for a profitable cloud business.

From the perspective of cloud providers, the primary advantage they enjoy is scale: First, purchasing hardware, network capacity and storage is three to seven times cheaper at a scale of tens or hundreds of thousands of servers versus that at a scale of a medium-sized enterprise data center, i.e. a few thousand servers or less. Second, they have been able to amortize the cost of server administration over a larger number of servers as well as reduce it with high levels of automation, also estimated to result in a factor of seven gain. Next, the cloud providers are all leveraging significantly lower power costs (by up to a factor of three) by locating their data centers in power-producing regions, such as Idaho and Washington in the US. Finally, cloud providers are able to enjoy far higher degrees of server utilization, say 60–80 percent, as compared to smaller data centers, by multiplexing the needs of a large number of users across the available capacity.

Last but not least, it is very important to understand that the leading cloud providers, viz. Google and Amazon, developed these capabilities for other businesses (search, retail), and so, there was very little marginal investment involved in adapting this infrastructure for providing cloud services and opening up a new business model. Very few, if any, enterprises have the size to leverage such large economies of scale; and if they did it is likely that they may begin making available some of this infrastructure as yet another public cloud. After all, Amazon has for many years been a retail company first, and only now is it becoming equally known for cloud computing!

To summarize cloud computing economics, we can comfortably state that cloud infrastructure services promise significant cost reductions even as compared to privately deployed cloud infrastructure. The agility of cloud infrastructure management provides additional benefits, especially so in the context of agile development. Further, cloud development platforms promise an order of magnitude improvement in development productivity for large-scale high-performance applications, and finally Dev 2.0 platforms promise a similar order of magnitude improvement in productivity for small and medium applications, albeit so far limited to the small but important class of transaction-processing applications.

# PART III

# Cloud technologies

A few technologies have been crucial in enabling the development and use of cloud platforms. Web services allow applications to communicate easily over the internet: Composite applications are easily assembled from distributed web-based components using 'mashups.' If there is one technology that has contributed the most to cloud computing, it is virtualization. By decoupling the software platform from hardware resources, virtualization enables massive cloud data centers to function seamlessly in a fault-tolerant manner. Similarly, multi-tenancy allows the same software platform to be shared by multiple applications, and can thus be looked upon as application-level virtualization. Multi-tenancy is critical for developing software-as-a-service applications and Dev 2.0 platforms.

# CHAPTER 7

# Web services, AJAX and mashups

The internet is based on a universally accepted set of protocols, HTTP, DNS, and TCP/IP, that provide the foundation for web-based cloud computing offerings. In this chapter we examine three critical web-based technologies at the next level of granularity that have been instrumental in improving the usability of web-based applications: Web services are used to request for and access infrastructure services in the cloud; AJAX-based user interfaces allow web-based applications to be user friendly; finally mashups bring a new dimension to software as a service by enabling users to compose multiple SaaS applications into a single user interface.

## 7.1 WEB SERVICES: SOAP AND REST

We have discussed the genesis and evolution of web services briefly in Chapter 2. Here we give a brief technical overview of both SOAP/WSDL and REST-based web services, and also compare these in the context of their utility in building cloud-based offerings. For a more detailed description of web services protocols, see [30].

## 7.1.1 SOAP/WSDL Web services

SOAP/WSDL web services evolved from the need to programmatically inter-
connect web-based applications. As a result SOAP/WSDL web services are
essentially a form of remote procedure calls over HTTP, while also including support for nested structures (objects) in a manner similar to earlier
extensions of RPC, such as CORBA; we shall return to this point later.

The elements of a SOAP/WSDL web service are illustrated in Figure 7.1,
using as an example the service provided by Google for searching the web.
A client application can invoke this web service by sending a SOAP request
in XML form, as illustrated at the bottom left of the figure, to the designated service URL. The specifications of the service, including the service
URL and other parameters, are made available by the service provider (in
this case Google) as another XML file, in WSDL[1] format, as illustrated in the
rest of the figure. The WSDL file specifies the service endpoint, i.e. the URL
that responds to SOAP requests to this web service, as shown in the bottom
right of the figure. Above this are a number of *port types*, within which are
listed the *operations* (functions, methods) that are included in this service,
along with their input and output parameter types; for example the operation doGoogleSearch has input and output messages *doGoogleSearch* and
*doGoogleSearchResponse* respectively. The types of these messages are also
specified in detail in the WSDL file, as XML schemas. For example in the
case of a doGoogleSearch operation, the input messages are composed
of simple types (i.e. strings, etc.), whereas the output, i.e. search result, is a
complex type comprising of an array of results whose schema is also specified
in the WSDL (not shown in the figure). Finally, the WSDL *binding* links these
abstract set of operations with concrete transport protocols and serialization
formats.

SOAP documents, i.e. the XML messages exchanged over HTTP, comprise of a *body* (as shown in bottom left of the figure) as well as an optional
*header* that is an extensible container where message layer information can
be encoded for a variety of purposes such as security, quality of service,
transactions, etc. A number of WS-* specifications have been developed to
incorporate additional features into SOAP web services that extend and utilize the header container: For example, WS-Security for user authentication,
WS-Transactions to handle atomic transactions spanning multiple service

---

[1] WSDL: web service definition language.

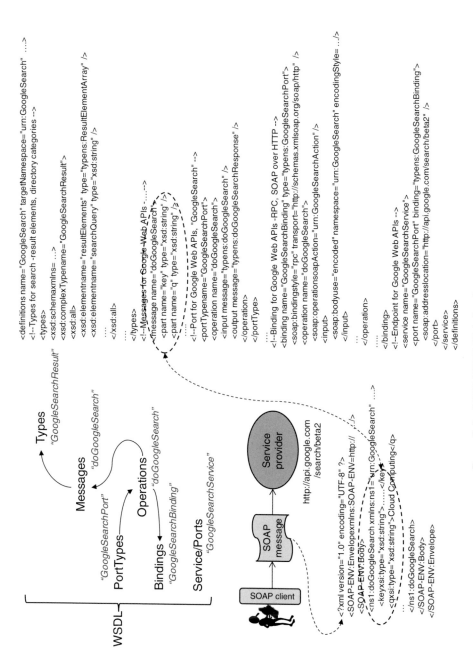

**FIGURE 7.1.** SOAP/WSDL Web Service

requests across multiple service providers, WS-Resource Framework enabling access to resource *state* behind a web service (even though each web service is inherently stateless) and WS-Addressing to allow service endpoints to be additionally addressed at the messaging level so that service requests can be routed on non-HTTP connections (such as message queues) behind an HTTP service facade, or even for purely internal application integration.

The origin of the rather complex structure used by the SOAP/WSDL approach can be traced back to the RPC (remote procedure call) standard and its later object oriented variants, such as CORBA. In the original RPC protocol (also called SUN RPC), the client-server interface would be specified by a `<..>.x` file, from which client and server stubs in C would be generated, along with libraries to handle complex data structures and data serialization across machine boundaries. In CORBA, the `.x` files became IDL descriptions using a similar overall structure; Java RMI (remote method invocation) also had a similar structure using a common Java interface class to link client and server code. SOAP/WSDL takes the same approach for enabling RPC over HTTP, with WSDL playing the role of `.x` files, IDLs or interface classes.

## 7.1.2 REST web services

Representational State Transfer (REST) was originally introduced as an architectural style for large-scale systems based on distributed *resources*, one of whose embodiments is the hypertext driven HTML-based web itself. The use of REST as a paradigm for service-based interaction between application programs began gaining popularity at about the same time as, and probably in reaction to, the SOAP/WSDL methodology that was being actively propagated by many industry players at the time, such as IBM and Microsoft.

REST web services are merely HTTP requests to URIs,[2] using exactly the four methods GET, POST, PUT and DELETE allowed by the HTTP protocol. Each URI identifies a resource, such as a record in a database. As an example, consider accessing a customer record with the REST service `http://x.y.com/customer/11998`, which returns the record in XML format. In case the record contains links (foreign keys) to related

---

[2] See Chapter 2.

records, such as the customer's accounts or address, links to these are embedded in the returned XML, such as `http://x.y.com/account/334433`. Alternatively, these links might be directly accessed via a REST service `http://x.y.com /customer/11998/accounts`. The client application merely accesses the URIs for the resources being managed in this 'RESTful' manner using simple HTTP requests to retrieve data. Further, the same mechanism can allow manipulation of these resources as well; so a customer record may be retrieved using a GET method, modified by the client program, and sent back using a PUT or a POST request to be updated on the server.

Figure 7.2 illustrates REST web services with the above example as well as two real-life examples using Yahoo! and Google, both of whom also provide a REST web service interface to their core search engine. Notice that the URLs of these search services include parameters (*appid* and *query* for Yahoo!, *ver* and *q* for Google); strictly speaking these service definitions deviate from the 'strong' REST paradigm, where resources are defined by pure URIs alone. In principle, such purity could have easily been maintained: Note that *version* is part of the URI in the Yahoo! service while it is a parameter in the case of Google, which need not have been the case; the input URL would simply need to have been processed differently. In practice however, the use of parameters in REST services has now become widespread.

Note that while the Yahoo! service returns XML, the Google Service returns JSON (JavaScript Serialized Object Notation). A JSON string is simply a piece of JavaScript code that defines a 'map'[3] data structure in that language. The advantage of using JSON is that XML parsing is avoided; instead, the response string is simply evaluated by client-side JavaScript code (e.g. `res=eval(response)`). In the case of our Google service, this would allow the results to be accessed directly from JavaScript, so that `res["responseData"]["results"][0]["url"]` returns the first result URL, etc. As far as REST is concerned, this is perfectly legal since in theory *any* allowable internet media types, such as HTML, XML, text, pdf or doc, can be exchanged via a REST service. Finally, we mention in passing that client and server authentication is easily handled in REST just as with normal HTML web pages by using SSL (i.e. HTTPS).

---

[3] A set of key-value pairs, for example {'a':1, 'b':2}.

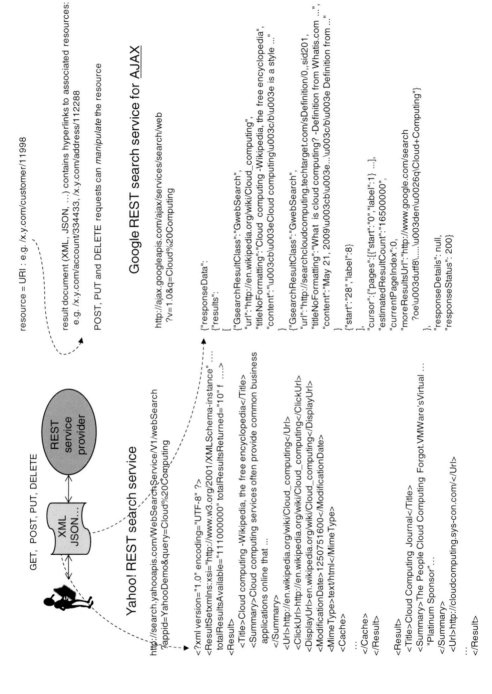

resource = URI : e.g. /x.y.com/customer/11998

result document (XML, JSON, ...) contains hyperlinks to associated resources:
e.g. /x.y.com/account/334433, /x.y.com/address/112288

POST, PUT and DELETE requests can *manipulate* the resource

GET, POST, PUT, DELETE

REST service provider

XML JSON...

## Yahoo! REST search service

http://search.yahooapis.com/WebSearchService/V1/webSearch
?appid=YahooDemo&query=Cloud%20Computing

```
<?xml version="1.0" encoding="UTF-8" ?>
<ResultSetxmlns:xsi="http://www.w3.org/2001/XMLSchema-instance" ....
totalResultsAvailable="111000000" totalResultsReturned="10" f ....>
<Result>
<Title>Cloud computing -Wikipedia, the free encyclopedia</Title>
<Summary>Cloud computing services often provide common business
applications online that ...
</Summary>
<Url>http://en.wikipedia.org/wiki/Cloud_computing</Url>
<ClickUrl>http://en.wikipedia.org/wiki/Cloud_computing</ClickUrl>
<DisplayUrl>en.wikipedia.org/wiki/Cloud_computing</DisplayUrl>
<ModificationDate>1250751600</ModificationDate>
<MimeType>text/html</MimeType>
<Cache>
...
</Cache>
</Result>

<Result>
<Title>Cloud Computing Journal</Title>
<Summary>The People Cloud Computing Forgot. VMWare's Virtual ...
"Platinum Sponsor"...
</Summary>
<Url>http://cloudcomputing.sys-con.com/</Url>
...
</Result>
```

## Google REST search service for AJAX

http://ajax.googleapis.com/ajax/services/search/web
?v=1.0&q=Cloud%20Computing

{"responseData":
{"results":

{"GsearchResultClass":"GwebSearch",
"url":"http://en.wikipedia.org/wiki/Cloud_computing",
"titleNoFormatting":"Cloud computing -Wikipedia, the free encyclopedia",
"content":"...\u003cb\u003eCloud computing\u003c/b\u003e is a style ..."

{"GsearchResultClass":"GwebSearch",
"url":"http://searchcloudcomputing.techtarget.com/sDefinition/0,,sid201,
"titleNoFormatting":"What is cloud computing? -Definition from Whatis.com ...",
"content":"May 21, 2009\u003cb\u003e....\u003c/b\u003e Definition from ..."

{"start":"28","label":8}
],
"cursor":{"pages":[{"start":"0","label":1} ...],
"estimatedResultCount":"16500000",
"currentPageIndex":0,
"moreResultsUrl":"http://www.google.com/search
?oe\u003dutf8\......\u003den\u0026q\Cloud+Computing"}
},
"responseDetails": null,
"responseStatus": 200}

FIGURE 7.2. REST web services

## 7.2 SOAP VERSUS REST

Many discussions of SOAP versus REST focus on the point that encoding services as SOAP/WSDL makes it difficult to expose the semantics of a web service in order for it to be easily and widely understood, so that many different providers can potentially offer the same service. Search is a perfect example. It is abundantly clear that the SOAP/WSDL definition of Google search does not in any way define an 'obvious' standard, and it is just as acceptable for an alternative API to be provided by other search engines. However, in the case of REST, there is the *potential* for such standardization: If for example, the REST standard for search were `http://<provider-URL>/<query-string>`, multiple providers could make this available; the response documents in XML could be self-describing by referring to provider specific name spaces where needed but adhering to a publicly specified top-level schema. We do not take a view on this aspect of the SOAP vs. REST debate, since standardization and reuse are difficult goals. As is apparent from the two very different REST APIs for web search, it is not SOAP or REST that drives standardization. Nevertheless, the relative simplicity of creating and using REST-based services as compared to the more complex SOAP/WSDL approach *is* immediately apparent from our examples. Further, REST can avoid expensive XML parsing by using alternatives such as JSON. So our view is that the case for using SOAP/WSDL needs to be explicitly made depending on the context, with REST being the option of choice from the perspective of simplicity as well as efficiency.

To examine when SOAP services may in fact be warranted, we now compare the SOAP and REST paradigms in the context of programmatic communication between applications deployed on different cloud providers, or between cloud applications and those deployed in-house. In Table 7.1 we compare these along six dimensions: The *location* where servers providing the service can reside; how *secure* the interaction is; whether *transactions* can be supported; how dependent the protocol is on HTTP *technology*; the extent of development *tools* and support required; the *efficiency* of the resulting implementations; and finally the software development *productivity* to be expected using each. We conclude from this analysis that for most requirements SOAP is an overkill; REST interfaces are simpler, more efficient and cheaper to develop and maintain. The shift from SOAP to REST especially in the cloud setting is apparent: The Google SOAP service is now deprecated, and essentially replaced by the REST API using JSON. While Amazon web services publish both SOAP as well as REST APIs, the SOAP APIs are hardly used

| TABLE 7.1 SOAP/WSDL versus REST | | | |
|---|---|---|---|
| | SOAP/WSDL | REST | Comments |
| Location | Some endpoints can be behind corporate networks on non-HTTP connects, e.g. message queues | All endpoints must be on the internet | Complex B2B scenarios require SOAP |
| Security | HTTPS which can be augmented with additional security layers | Only HTTPS | Very stringent security needs can be addressed only by SOAP |
| Efficiency | XML parsing required | XML parsing can be avoided by using JSON | REST is lighter and more efficient |
| Transactions | Can be supported | No support | Situations requiring complex multi-request / multi-party transactions need SOAP |
| Technology | Can work without HTTP, e.g. using message queues instead | Relies on HTTP | REST is for pure internet communications and cannot mix other transports |
| Tools | Sophisticated tools required (and are available) to handle client and server development | No special tools required especially if using JSON | REST is lighter and easier to use |
| Productivity | Low, due to complex tools and skills needed | High, due to simplicity | REST is faster and cheaper for developers to use |

(15 percent is a number quoted on the web). In our opinon REST web services will gradually overtake SOAP/WSDL, and it is likely that mechanisms to address more complex functionality, such as transactions, will also be developed for REST in the near future.

## 7.3 AJAX: ASYNCHRONOUS 'RICH' INTERFACES

Traditional web applications interact with their server components through a sequence of HTTP GET and POST requests, each time refreshing the HTML page in the browser. The use of client-side (i.e., in-browser) JavaScript is limited to field validations and some user interface effects such as animations, hiding or unhiding parts of the page etc. Apart from any such manipulations, between the time a server request is made and a response obtained, the browser is essentially idle. Often one server request entails retrieving data from many data sources, and even from many different servers; however requests are still routed through a single web server that acts as a gateway to these services.

We described the historical evolution of the AJAX paradigm in Chapter 2. Using AJAX JavaScript programs running in the browser can make *asynchronous* calls to the server *without* refreshing their primary HTML page. Heavy server-side processing can be broken up into smaller parts that are multiplexed with client-side processing of user actions, thereby reducing the overall response time as well as providing a 'richer' user experience. Further, client-side JavaScript can make REST service requests not only to the primary web server but also to other services on the internet, thereby enabling application integration within the browser.

From a software architecture perspective, AJAX applications no longer remain pure thin clients: Significant processing can take place on the client, thereby also exploiting the computational power of the desktop, just as was the case for client-server applications. Recall that using the client-server architecture one ran the risk of mixing user interface and business logic in application code, making such software more difficult to maintain. Similar concerns arise while using the AJAX paradigm.

Figure 7.3 illustrates how AJAX applications work; these are also called 'rich internet applications' (RIA), in comparison to traditional web applications. A base HTML page is loaded along with JavaScript code that contains the remainder of the user interface. This JavaScript program renders a 'rich' user interface that can often look like a traditional client-server application. When data is required from the server, asynchronous requests are made via REST

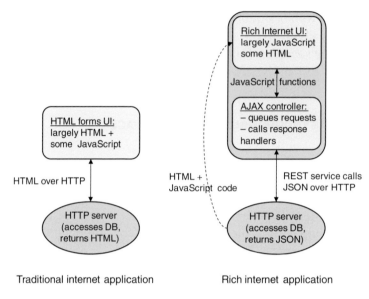

**FIGURE 7.3. Rich internet applications with AJAX**

web services, which return JSON structures that are directly used by the JavaScript code running in the browser.

Because of the nature of the HTTP protocol, a web server expects that an incoming request from a single client session will not be followed by another until the server has responded to the first request. If a client violates this protocol by sending many requests at a time, at best these will be ignored and at worst some poorly implemented servers may even crash! Therefore an AJAX controller is required to serialize the asynchronous requests being made to the server; each request is queued and sent to the server only after the previous request has returned with a response. Each response triggers a handler function which is registered with the controller when placing the request.

Using AJAX, highly interactive yet completely browser-based user interfaces become possible. Using this approach, software as a service application can begin to provide a user experience similar to thick client applications which typically run inside the enterprise, thereby making SaaS offerings more acceptable to enterprise users. Further, using AJAX, services from multiple cloud providers can be integrated within the browser, using JavaScript, instead of using more complex server-side integration mechanisms based on web services. Also, unlike server-side integration that needs to be performed by corporate IT, simple JavaScript-based integrations can often be performed by business units themselves, in much the same manner as Dev 2.0 platforms allow simple applications to be developed by end-users. This has resulted in a proliferation of *user-driven* integration of services from multiple cloud-based services and SaaS applications, often without the knowledge and participation of corporate IT.

## 7.4 MASHUPS: USER INTERFACE SERVICES

We have seen that using AJAX a JavaScript user interface can call many different web services directly. However, the presentation of data from these services within the user interface is left to the calling JavaScript program. Mashups take the level of integration one step further, by including the presentation layer for the remote service along with the service itself.

Figure 7.4 illustrates mashups, again using the Google search service that is also available as a mashup. In order to display a Google search box, a developer only needs to reference and use some JavaScript *code* that is automatically downloaded by the browser. This code provides a 'class' google that provides the AJAX API published by Google as its methods. (Strictly speaking this is a function, since JavaScript is not truly object orientated, but in colloquial usage such JavaScript functions are referred to as classes.) User code calls these methods to instantiate a search control 'object' and render it within the HTML page dynamically after the page has loaded. Notice that there is no

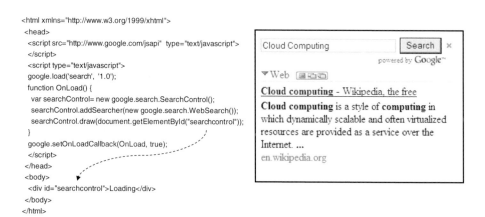

FIGURE **7.4.** **Mashup example**

AJAX controller or REST service visible to the user; all this is hidden within the API methods. Recall that the purpose of an AJAX controller was to serialize HTTP requests from a running session to a *particular* web server: There is no need for serialization across calls to different service providers, and therefore it is perfectly okay for different mashup services to provide their own AJAX controllers within their APIs.

From a user perspective, mashups make it easy to consume web services. In fact, the actual service call need not even be a REST service, and may instead involve proprietary AJAX-based interaction with the service provider. In this sense, mashups make the issue of a published service standard using REST or SOAP/WSDL irrelevant; the only thing that is published is a JavaScript library which can be downloaded at runtime and executed by a client application.

At the same time, the fact that mashups require downloading and running *foreign* code is a valid security concern especially in the enterprise scenario. JavaScript code normally cannot access resources on the client machine apart from the browser and network, so it may appear that there is no real security threat, unlike say ActiveX controls which have essentially complete access to the desktop once a user installs them. However, this may no longer remain the case in the future: For example Google Gears is a framework that enables offline operation of applications by caching data on the client desktop. This presents a potential security threat, though not as serious as ActiveX controls: For example, if a user has installed Gears for some reason, such as accessing Gmail in offline mode, another site the user accesses may ask for permission to use Gears (note that such a prompt is always shown, making Gears a bit safer), and if granted store some executables on a user's disk, and present the user with a link which runs these as a side effect. As a result of such potential security risks, enterprise adoption of mashups has been slower than warranted by the technology's advantages.

Note that Google initially published a SOAP/WSDL service but later replaced it with an AJAX mashup API, and as a by product also made available the REST web service which we discussed earlier. Another popular mashup is Google Maps. It is becoming increasingly apparent that mashup-based integration of cloud-based services is easy, popular and represents the direction being taken by the consumer web service industry. Enterprise usage of mashup technology is only a matter of time, not only in the context of cloud-based offerings, but also for integrating internal applications with cloud services, as well as amongst themselves.

## CHAPTER 8

# Virtualization technology

If one had to choose a single technology that has been most influential in enabling the cloud computing paradigm, it would have to be virtualization. As we have seen earlier in Chapter 1, virtualization is not new, and dates back to the early mainframes as a means of sharing computing resources amongst users. Today, besides underpinning cloud computing platforms, virtualization is revolutionizing the way enterprise data centers are built and managed, paving the way for enterprises to deploy 'private cloud' infrastructure within their data centers.

## 8.1 VIRTUAL MACHINE TECHNOLOGY

We begin with an overview of virtual machine technology: In general, any means by which many different users are able simultaneously to interact with a computing system while each perceiving that they have an entire 'virtual machine' to themselves, is a form of virtualization. In this general sense, a traditional multiprogramming operating system, such as Linux, is also a form of virtualization, since it allows each user process to access system resources oblivious of other processes. The abstraction provided to each process is the set of OS system calls and any hardware instructions accessible to user-level processes. Extensions, such as 'user mode Linux' [17] offer a more complete virtual abstraction where each user is not even aware of other user's processes, and can login as an administrator, i.e. 'root,' to their own seemingly

---

private operating system. 'Virtual private servers' are another such abstraction [36]. At a higher level of abstraction are virtual machines based on high-level languages, such as the Java virtual machine (JVM) which itself runs as an operating system process but provides a system-independent abstraction of the machine to an application written in the Java language. Such abstractions, which present an abstraction at the OS system call layer or higher, are called *process virtual machines*. Some cloud platforms, such as Google's App Engine and Microsoft's Azure, also provide a process virtual machine abstraction in the context of a web-based architecture.

More commonly, however, the virtual machines we usually refer to when discussing virtualization in enterprises or for infrastructure clouds such as Amazon's EC2 are *system virtual machines* that offer a complete hardware instruction set as the abstraction provided to users of different virtual machines. In this model many system virtual machine (VM) instances share the same physical hardware through a virtual machine monitor (VMM), also commonly referred to as a *hypervisor*. Each such system VM can run an independent operating system instance; thus the same physical machine can have many instances of, say Linux *and* Windows, running on it simultaneously. The system VM approach is preferred because it provides complete isolation between VMs as well as the highest possible flexibility, with each VM seeing a complete machine instruction set, against which any applications for that architecture are guaranteed to run.

It is the virtual machine monitor that enables a physical machine to be virtualized into different VMs. Where does this software itself run? A *host* VMM is implemented as a process running on a *host* operating system that has been installed on the machine in the normal manner. Multiple *guest* operating systems can be installed on different VMs that each run as operating system processes under the supervision of the VMM. A *native* VMM, on the other hand, does not require a host operating system, and runs directly on the physical machine (or more colloquially on 'bare metal'). In this sense, a native VMM can be viewed as a special type of operating system, since it supports multiprogramming across different VMs, with its 'system calls' being hardware instructions! Figure 8.1 illustrates the difference between process virtual machines, host VMMs and native VMMs. Most commonly used VMMs, such as the open source Xen hypervisor as well as products from VMware are available in both hosted as well as native versions; for example the hosted Xen (HXen) project and VMware Workstation products are hosted VMMs, whereas the more popularly used XenServer (or just Xen) and VMware ESX Server products are native VMMs.

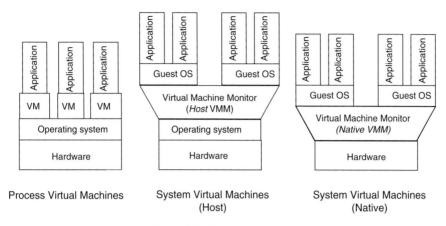

FIGURE **8.1. Virtual machines**

In the next section we shall briefly describe how system virtual machines are implemented *efficiently* and how individual virtual machines actually run.

## 8.1.1 System virtual machines

A system virtual machine monitor needs to provide each virtual machine the illusion that it has access to a complete independent hardware system through a full instruction set. In a sense, this is very similar to the need for a time-sharing operating system to provide different processes access to hardware resources in their allotted time intervals of execution. However, there are fundamental differences between the 'virtual machine' as perceived by a traditional operating system processes and a true system VM:

1. Processes under an operating system are allowed access to hardware through system calls, whereas a system VMM needs to provide a full hardware instruction set for use by each virtual machine
2. Each system virtual machine needs to be able to run a full operating system, while itself maintaining isolation with other virtual machines.

Going forward we will focus our discussion on native VMMs that run directly on the hardware, like an operating system; native VMMs are more efficient and therefore the ones used in practice within enterprises as well as cloud platforms. One way a native system VMM could work is by *emulating* instructions of the target instruction set and maintaining the state of different virtual machines at all levels of memory hierarchy (including registers etc.) *indirectly* in *memory* and switching between these as and when required, in a manner similar to how virtual memory page tables for different processes are maintained by an operating system. In cases where the target hardware instruction set and actual machine architecture are different, emulation and indirection is unavoidable, and, understandably, inefficient. However, in cases where the target instruction set is the same as that of the actual hardware on which the native VMM is running, the VMM can be implemented more efficiently.

An *efficient* native VMM attempts to run the instructions of each of is virtual machines natively on the hardware, and while doing so also maintain the state of the machine at its proper location in the memory hierarchy, in much the same manner as an operating system runs process code natively as far as possible except when required.

Let us first recall how an operating system runs a process: The process state is first loaded into memory and registers, then the program counter is reset so that process code runs from thereon. The process runs until a timer event occurs, at which point the operating system switches the process and resets the timer via a special *privileged* instruction. The key to this mechanism is the presence of privileged instructions, such as resetting the timer interrupt, which cause a *trap* (a program generated interrupt) when run in 'user' mode instead of 'system' mode. Thus, no *user* process can set the timer interrupt, since this instruction is privileged and always traps, in this case to the operating system.

Thus, it should be possible to build a VMM in exactly the same manner as an operating system, by trapping the privileged instructions and running all others natively on the hardware. Clearly the privileged instructions themselves need to be *emulated*, so that when an operating system running in a virtual machine attempts to, say, set the timer interrupt, it actually sets a *virtual* timer interrupt. Such a VMM, where only privileged instructions need to be emulated, is the most efficient native VMM possible, as formally proved in [45].

However, in reality it is not always possible to achieve this level of efficiency. There are some instruction sets (including the popular Intel IA-32, better known as x86) where some non-privileged instructions behave differently depending on whether they are called in user mode or system mode. Such instruction sets implicitly assume that there will be only one operating system (or equivalent) program that needs access to privileged instructions, a natural assumption in the absence of virtualization. However, such instructions pose a problem for virtual machines, in which the operating system is actually running in user mode rather than system mode. Thus, it is necessary for the VMM to also emulate such instructions in addition to all privileged instructions. Newer editions of the x86 family have begun to include 'hardware support' for virtualization, where such anomalous behavior can be rectified by exploiting additional hardware features, resulting in a more efficient implementation of virtualization: For example, Intel's VT-x ('Vanderpool') technology includes a new VMX mode of operation. When VMX is enabled there is a new 'root' mode of operation exclusively for use by the VMM; in non-root mode all standard modes of operation are available for the OS and applications, including a 'system' mode which is at a lower level of privilege than what the VMM enjoys. We do not discuss system virtual machines in more detail here, as the purpose of this discussion was to give some insight into the issues that are involved through a few examples; a detailed treatment can be found in [58].

## 8.1.2 Virtual machines and elastic computing

We have seen how virtual machine technology enables decoupling physical hardware from the virtual machines that run on them. Virtual machines can have different instruction sets from the physical hardware if needed. Even if the instruction sets are the same (which is needed for efficiency), the size and number of the physical resources seen by each virtual machine need not be the same as that of the physical machine, and in fact will usually be different. The VMM partitions the actual physical resources in time, such as with I/O and network devices, or space, as with storage and memory. In the case of multiple CPUs, compute power can also be partitioned in time (using traditional time slices), or in space, in which case each CPU is reserved for a subset of virtual machines.

The term 'elastic computing' has become popular when discussing cloud computing. The Amazon 'elastic' cloud computing platform makes extensive use of virtualization based on the Xen hypervisor. Reserving and booting a server instance on the Amazon EC cloud provisions and starts a virtual machine on one of Amazon's servers. The configuration of the required virtual machine can be chosen from a set of options (see Chapter 5). The user of the 'virtual instance' is unaware and oblivious to which physical server the instance has been booted on, as well as the resource characteristics of the physical machine.

An 'elastic' multi-server environment is one which is completely virtualized, with all hardware resources running under a set of *cooperating* virtual machine monitors and in which provisioning of virtual machines is largely automated and can be dynamically controlled according to demand. In general, any multi-server environment can be made 'elastic' using virtualization in much the same manner as has been done in Amazon's cloud, and this is what many enterprise virtualization projects attempt to do. The key success factors in achieving such elasticity is the degree of *automation* that can be achieved across multiple VMMs working together to maximize utilization. The *scale* of such operations is also important, which in the case of Amazon's cloud runs into tens of thousands of servers, if not more. The larger the scale, the greater the potential for amortizing demand effciently across the available capacity while also giving users an illusion of 'infinite' computing resources.

Technology to achieve elastic computing at scale is, today, largely proprietary and in the hands of the major cloud providers. Some automated provisioning technology is available in the public domain or commercially off the shelf (see Chapter 17), and is being used by many enterprises in their internal data center automation efforts. Apart from many startup companies, VMware's VirtualCentre product suite aims to provide this capability through its 'VCloud' architecture.

We shall discuss the features of an elastic data center in more detail later in this chapter; first we cover virtual machine migration, which is a pre-requisite for many of these capabilities.

### 8.1.3 Virtual machine migration

Another feature that is crucial for advanced 'elastic' infrastructure capabilities is 'in-flight' migration of virtual machines, such as provided in VMware's VMotion product. This feature, which should also be considered a key component for 'elasticity,' enables a virtual machine running on one physical machine to be suspended, its state saved and transported to or accessed from another physical machine where it is resumes execution from exactly the same state.

Virtual machine migration has been studied in the systems research community [49] as well as in related areas such as grid computing [29]. Migrating a virtual machine involves capturing and copying the entire state of the machine at a snapshot in time, including processor and memory state as well as all virtual hardware resources such as BIOS, devices or network MAC addresses. In principle, this also includes the entire disk space, including system and user directories as well as swap space used for virtual memory operating system scheduling. Clearly, the complete state of a typical server is likely to be quite large. In a closely networked multi-server environment, such as a cloud data center, one may assume that some persistent storage can be easily accessed and mounted from different servers, such as through a storage area network or simply networked file systems; thus a large part of the system disk, including user directories or software can easily be transferred to the new server, using this mechanism. Even so, the remaining state, which needs to include swap and memory apart from other hardware states, can still be gigabytes in size, so migrating this efficiently still requires some careful design.

Let us see how VMware's VMotion carries out in-flight migration of a virtual machine between physical servers: VMotion waits until the virtual machine is found to be in a stable state, after which all changes to machine state start getting logged. VMotion then copies the contents of memory, as well as disk-resident data belonging to either the guest operating system or applications, to the target server. This is the *baseline* copy; it is not the final copy because the virtual machine continues to run on the original server during this process. Next the virtual machine is suspended and the last remaining changes in memory and state since the baseline, which were being logged, are sent to the target server, where the final state is computed, following which the virtual machine is activated and resumes from its last state.

## 8.2 VIRTUALIZATION APPLICATIONS IN ENTERPRISES

A number of enterprises are engaged in virtualization projects that aim to gradually relocate operating systems and applications running directly on physical machines to virtual machines. The motivation is to exploit the additional VMM layer between hardware and systems software for introducing a number of new capabilities that can potentially ease the complexity and risk of managing large data centers. Here we outline some of the more compelling cases for using virtualization in large enterprises.

### 8.2.1 Security through virtualization

Modern data centers are all necessarily connected to the world outside via the internet and are thereby open to malicious attacks and intrusion. A number of techniques have been developed to secure these systems, such as firewalls, proxy filters, tools for logging and monitoring system activity and intrusion detection systems. Each of these security solutions can be significantly enhanced using virtualization.

For example, many intrusion detection systems (IDS) traditionally run on the network and operate by monitoring network traffic for suspicious behavior by matching against a database of known attack patterns. Alternatively, host-based systems run within each operating system instance where the behavior of each process is monitored to detect potentially suspicious activity such as repeated login attempts or accessing files that are normally not needed by user processes. Virtualization opens up the possibility of building IDS capabilities into the VMM itself, or at least at the same layer, i.e. above the network but below the operating system. The Livewire and Terra research projects are examples of such an approach [24, 25], which has the advantage of enabling greater isolation of the IDS from the monitored hosts while retaining complete visibility into the host's state. This approach also allows for complete mediation of interactions between the host software and the underlying hardware, enabling a suspect VM to be easily isolated from the rest of the data center.

Virtualization also provides the opportunity for more complete, user-group specific, low-level logging of system activities, which would be impossible or very difficult if many different user groups and applications were sharing the same operating system. This allows security incidents to be be more easily traced, and also better diagnosed by *replaying* the incident on a copy of the virtual machine.

End-user system (desktop) virtualization is another application we cover below that also has an important security dimension. Using virtual machines on the desktop or mobile phones allows users to combine personal usage of these devices with more secure enterprise usage by isolating these two worlds; so a user logs into the appropriate virtual machine (personal or enterprise), with both varieties possibly running simultaneously. Securing critical enterprise data, ensuring network isolation from intrusions and protection from viruses can be better ensured without compromising users' activities in their personal pursuits using the same devices. In fact some organizations are contemplating not even considering laptops and mobile devices as corporate resources; instead users can be given the flexibility to buy whatever devices they wish and use client-side virtual machines to access enterprise applications and data.

## 8.2.2 Desktop virtualization and application streaming

Large enterprises have tens if not hundreds of thousands of users, each having a desktop and/or one or more laptops and mobile phones that are used to connect to applications running in the enterprise's data center. Managing regular system updates, such as for security patches or virus definitions is a major system management task. Sophisticated tools, such as IBM's Tivoli are used to automate this process across a globally distributed network of users. Managing application roll-outs across such an environment is a similarly complex task, especially in the case of 'fat-client' applications such as most popular email clients and office productivity tools, as well some transaction processing or business intelligence applications.

Virtualization has been proposed as a possible means to improve the manageability of end-user devices in such large environments. Here there have been two different approaches. The first has been to deploy all end-client systems as virtual machines on central data centers which are then accessed by 'remote desktop' tools, such as Citrix Presentation Server, Windows Terminal Services (WTS), or VNC (Virtual Network Computer). At least theoretically this is an interesting solution as it (a) eases management of updates by 'centralizing' all desktops (b) allows easier recovery from crashes by simply restarting a new VM (c) enables security checks and intrusion detection to be performed centrally and (d) with all user data being central, secures it as well as enables better data sharing and potential reduction of redundant storage use. However, this approach has never really become popular, primarily because of the need for continuous network connectivity, which in spite of the advances in corporate networks and public broadband penetration, is still not ubiquitous and 'always on.' Additionally, this approach also ignores the significant computing power available on desktops, which when added up across an enterprise can be very costly to replicate in a central data center.

The second approach is called 'application streaming.' Instead of running applications on central virtual machines, application streaming envisages maintaining only virtual machine images centrally. An endpoint client, such as a desktop, runs a hypervisor that also downloads the virtual machine image from the server and launches it on the end point client. In this manner the processing power of the end point is fully exploited, a VM image can be cached for efficiency and only incrementally updated when needed, and finally user data, which can be large, need not be centrally maintained but mounted from the local disk as soon as the virtual machine boots. Such a solution is implemented, for example, in the XenApp product from Citrix (incorporating technology from Appstream, which was acquired by Citrix). Application streaming additionally allows the isolation of personal and corporate spaces for security purposes as mentioned in the previous section.

## 8.2.3 Server consolidation

The most common driver for virtualization in enterprise data centers has been to consolidate applications running on possibly tens of thousands of servers, each significantly underutilized on the average, onto a smaller number of more efficiently used resources. The motivation is both efficiency as well as reducing the complexity of managing the so-called 'server sprawl.' The ability to run multiple virtual machines on the same physical resources is also key to achieving the high utilizations in cloud data centers.

Here we explore some implications and limits of consolidation through a simplified model. Suppose we wish to consolidate applications running on $m$ physical servers of capacity $c$ onto one physical server of capacity $nc$. We assume that virtual machines are either perfectly efficient, or any inefficiency has been built into the factor $n$. We focus on a few simple questions: (i) whether the single server should have $n$ processors (or cores), or a clock speed $n$ times that of each original server; (ii) how much smaller than $m$ (the number of physical servers) can we make $n$ while retaining acceptable performance; and finally (iii) what is the impact on power consumption and whether this changes the preferred strategy.

A simple model using basic queuing theory provides some insight: A server running at an efficiency of $e$ can be thought of as a single server queuing system where, for whatever reason, either light load or inefficient software, the arrival rate of requests (instructions to be processed) is $e$ times less than that which can be served by the server. In queuing theory terminology, $e = \lambda/\mu$, where $\lambda$ is the arrival rate and $\mu$ the service rate. We define the average 'normalized response time' as the average time spent in the system $T$ normalized by average time between requests, $1/\lambda$, as $r = T\lambda$. (Note: response time is a good measure of performance for transactional workloads; however it may not be the right measure for batch processing.)

Using standard queuing theory [7] we can compute $r_o$, the normalized response time using $m$ physical servers as

$$r_o = \frac{e}{1 - e} \tag{8.1}$$

for each of the original servers. Now consider consolidating these servers into one server with $m$ processors, wherein the queue becomes one with $m$ servers working at the same rate $\mu$, servicing an arrival rate of $m\lambda$. Queuing theory yields $r_p$, normalized response time using one server with $p$ processors as

$$r_p = me + \frac{P_Q}{1 - e}. \tag{8.2}$$

(Here $P_Q$ is the 'queuing probability', which is small for light loads.[1]) If, on the other hand, we have a single server that is $m$ times faster, we once again model it as a single server queue but with service rate $m\mu$. Since $e$ remains unchanged, the normalized response time in this case ($r_c$) remains the same as $r_o$ in (8.1).

Thus we see that for light loads, i.e., underutilized servers where $e \ll 1$, the consolidation onto a multi-processor machine versus one with faster clock speed can result in significant degradation in performance, at least as measured by average normalized response time. For heavy loads, on the other hand, the second term in (8.2) dominates, and response time is poor (large) in both cases.

Now consider the case where the single server onto which we consolidate the workload is only $n$ times faster than the original servers. In this case we find that the normalized response time $r_n$ is

$$r_n = \frac{me}{n - me}. \tag{8.3}$$

Using this we can see that it is possible to use a server far less powerful than the aggregate of the $m$ original servers, as long as $n/m$ remains reasonably large as compared to $e$; and if indeed $n \gg me$ then the average normalized response time degrades only linearly by the factor of $n/m$.

Thus we see that a simple queuing theory analysis yields some natural limits to server consolidation using virtualization. The theoretical maximum benefit, in terms of a reduction in number of servers, is $n/m = e$, at which point the system becomes unresponsive. In practice it is possible to get fairly close to this, i.e. if $n/m = e(1 + \epsilon)$, then the average normalized response time becomes $1/\epsilon$. In effect, whatever the initial inefficiency, one can decide on an acceptable average normalized response time and plan the consolidation strategy accordingly.

It is instructive to bring into consideration another factor in this analysis, namely power consumption, an issue which is becoming increasingly important in data center management. Power consumption of chips is related to the voltage at which a chip operates, in particular power $P$ grows as the square of

---

[1] The formula for computing $P_Q$ can be found in [7].

the voltage, i.e. $P \propto V^2$. It is also a fact that higher clock speeds require higher voltage, with almost a linear relationship between the two. Thus, a system that runs at a clock speed $n$ times faster than a 'base' system, will consume $n^2$ the power of the base system, whereas the $n$ core system will consume only $n$ times the power. In fact this is one of the reasons for the shift to 'multi-core' CPUs, with systems having four to eight cores per CPU being commonplace as of this writing, and CPUs with dozens of cores expected to be the norm in the near future.

Revisiting our queuing model, in the case of consolidation onto an $n$ processor/core server, instead of one that is $n$ times faster, we can compute the average normalized response time, call it $r_P$, as:

$$r_P = me + \frac{P_Q}{1 - \frac{m}{n}e}. \tag{8.4}$$

Notice that the response time remains the same as $r_p$ in (8.2) for *light* loads, i.e., when $P_Q$ is small. Thus the response time still degrades by a factor of $m$, independent of $n$, as compared to the faster clock speed case (8.1). However, in the case of heavy load, where the second term dominates, there is a marked degradation in performance in the multi-processor case if $n \ll m$, as compared to the $m = n$ case, i.e. (8.2).

Thus there is a trade off, at least theoretically, between reducing power consumption by consolidating onto multi-processors or multi-core CPU systems, versus improved performance on systems with faster clock speeds but at the cost of non-linear growth in power consumption per server. In practice this trade off is less significant since there are limits on how far clock speed can be increased, for both power as well as due to fundamental physical constraints. Lastly, apart from consolidation, it is important to note that individual applications implemented using multi-threaded application servers can also exploit multi-core architectures efficiently. Therefore, both enterprise as well as cloud data centers today rely almost exclusively on multi-core, multi-processor systems.

### 8.2.4 Automating infrastructure management

An important goal of enterprise virtualization projects is to reduce data center management costs, especially people costs through greater automation. It is important to recognize that while virtualization technology provides the *ability* to automate many activities, actually designing and putting into place an automation strategy is a complex exercise that needs to be planned. Further, different levels of automation are possible, some easy to achieve through basic server consolidation, while others are more complex, requiring more sophisticated tools and technology as well as significant changes in operating procedures or even the organizational structure of the infrastructure wing of enterprise IT.

The following is a possible roadmap for automation of infrastructure management, with increasing sophistication in the use of virtualization technology at each level:

1. **Level 0 – Virtual images**: Packaging standard operating environments for different classes of application needs as virtual machines, thereby reducing the start-up time for development, testing and production deployment, also making it easier to bring on board new projects and developers. This approach is not only easy to get started with, but offers significant reduction in infrastructure management costs and saves precious development time as well.

2. **Level 1 – Integrated provisioning**: Integrated provisioning of new virtual servers along with provisioning their network and storage (SAN) resources, so that all these can be provisioned on a chosen physical server by an administrator through a single interface. Tools are available that achieve some of these capabilities (such as VMware's VirtualCenter integrated suite). In the majority of enterprises such tools are currently in the process of being explored and prototyped, with only a few enterprises having successfully deployed this level of automation on a large scale

3. **Level 2 – Elastic provisioning**: Automatically deciding the physical server on which to provision a virtual machine given its resource requirements, available capacity and projected demand; followed by bringing up the virtual machine without any administrator intervention; rather users (application project managers) are able to provision virtual servers themselves. This is the automation level provided by Amazon EC2, for example. As of this writing, and to our best knowledge, *no* large enterprise IT organization has deployed this level of automation in their internal data center at any degree of scale, though many projects are under way, using commercial products or the open source Eucalyptus tool (see Chapter 17).

4. **Level 3 – Elastic operations**: Automatically provisioning new virtual servers or migrating running virtual servers based on the need to do so, which is established through automatic monitoring of the state of all

virtual physical resources, and which can arise for a number of reasons, such as:

1. *Load balancing*, to improve response time of applications that either explicitly request for, or appear to need more resources, and depending on their business criticality.
2. *Security*, to quarantine a virtual machine that appears to have been compromised or attacked.
3. *Collocation*, to bring virtual machines that are communicating with each other physically closer together to improve performance.
4. *Fault tolerance*, to migrate applications from physical machines that have indicated possible imminent failure or need for maintenance.
5. *Fault recovery*, to provision a new instance virtual machine and launch it with the required set of applications running in order to recover from the failure of the original instance, so as to restore the corresponding business service as soon as possible.

While tools such as VMotion provide the underlying capability to migrate virtual machines 'in-flight,' as we have described in the previous section, exploiting this capability to achieve this level of automation of operations is really the *holy grail* for virtualization in enterprises, or even in infrastructure cloud platforms such as Amazon.

Virtualization projects in enterprises today are either at Level 0 or 1. Level 2 is available in Amazon EC2 in the cloud, whereas Level 3 automation has hardly ever been achieved in totality, at least with system virtual machines. Even in Amazon EC2, while monitoring and auto-scaling facilities are available, in-flight migration of virtual machines is not available, at least as of this writing.

If, however, one considers process virtual machines, such as Google App Engine, or efficient software-as-a-service providers, one can argue that to a certain extent the appearance of Level 3 is provided, since an application deployed in such a platform is essentially 'always on,' with the user not needing to be aware of any infrastructure management issues. Taking a process VM or even application virtualization (i.e. Dev 2.0) route may enable enterprises to provide pockets of services that can appear to achieve nearly Level 3 elastic automation, whereas achieving this degree of automation at a lower level of abstraction, such as system virtual machines is likely to be much harder to deploy at a large scale.

*Where to start?* An enterprise virtualization strategy needs to systematically plan which classes of applications should be moved to a virtual environment as well as whether and when the progression to increasing levels of automation should be attempted. Often the best place to start a virtualization exercise is within the IT organization itself, with the 'test and dev' environments that are used by developers in application development projects. Developers regularly require many of the capabilities enabled by virtualization, such as being able to manage project-specific sets of standard operating environments, re-create and re-start servers from a check pointed state during functional testing, or provision servers of different capacities for performance testing. As an additional benefit, having developers experience virtualization during application development also makes supporting applications in a virtualized production environment much easier. Finally, exactly the same argument holds for cloud computing as well; using a cloud data center for development is a useful first step before considering production applications in the cloud.

## 8.3 PITFALLS OF VIRTUALIZATION

As our discussion so far has revealed, virtualization is critical for cloud computing and also promises significant improvements within in-house data centers. At the same time it is important to be aware of some of the common pitfalls that come with virtualization:

1. Application deployments often replicate application server and database instances to ensure fault tolerance. Elastic provisioning results in two such replicas using virtual servers deployed on the same physical server. Thus if the physical server fails, both instances are lost, defeating the purpose of replication.
2. We have mentioned that virtualization provides another layer at which intrusions can be detected and isolated, i.e., the VMM. Conversely however, if the VMM itself is attacked, multiple virtual servers are affected. Thus some successful attacks can spread more rapidly in a virtualized environment than otherwise.
3. If the 'server sprawl' that motivated the building of a virtualized data center merely results in an equally complex 'virtual machine sprawl,' the purpose has not been served, rather the situation may become even worse than earlier. The ease with which virtual servers and server images are provisioned and created can easily result in such situations if one is not careful.
4. In principle a VMM can partition the CPU, memory and I/O bandwidth of a physical server across virtual servers. However, it cannot ensure that these resources are made available to each virtual server in a synchronized manner. Thus the fraction of hardware resources that a virtual server is actually able to utilize may be less than what has been provisioned by the VMM.

# CHAPTER 9

# Multi-tenant software

Applications have traditionally been developed for use by a single enterprise; similarly enterprise software products are also developed in a manner as to be independently deployed in the data center of each customer. The data created and accessed by such applications usually belongs to one organization. As we discussed earlier in Chapter 3, hosted SaaS platforms require a single application code to run on data of multiple customers, or 'tenants'; such behavior is referred to as multi-tenancy. In this chapter we examine different ways to achieve multi-tenancy in application software.

Before proceeding it is important to also note that virtualization, as discussed in the previous chapter, is also a mechanism to achieve multi-tenancy at the system level. In a virtualized environment, each 'tenant' could be assigned its own set of virtual machines. Here we examine alternatives for implementing multi-tenancy through application software architecture rather than at the system level using virtual machines. Thus, such multi-tenancy can also be termed *application-level* virtualization. Multi-tenancy and virtualization are both two sides of the same coin; the aim being to share resources while isolating users from each other: hardware resources in the case of system-level virtualization and software platforms in the case of multi-tenancy.

## 9.1 MULTI-ENTITY SUPPORT

Long before ASPs and SaaS, large globally distributed organizations often needed their applications to support multiple organizational units, or 'entities,' in a segregated manner. For example, consider a bank with many branches needing to transition from separate branch specific installations of its core banking software to a centralized deployment where the same software would run on data from all branches. The software designed to operate at the branch level clearly could not be used directly on data from all branches: For example branch-level users should see data related only to their branch and branch-wise accounting should consider transactions segregated by branch. If there was a need to enhance the system, say by introducing a new field, such a change would need to apply across all branches; at the same time, sometimes branch specific extensions would need to be supported as well. These requirements are almost exactly the same as for multi-tenancy! In a multi-entity scenario there are also additional needs, such as where a subset of users needed to be given access to data from all branches, or a subset of branches, depending on their position in an organizational hierarchy. Similarly, some global processing would also need to be supported, such as inter-branch reconciliation or enterprise-level analytics, without which the benefits of centralization of data might not be realized. Such advanced features could be implemented using 'data access control' as covered later in Section 9.4. We first focus on basic multi-entity support as it will lead us naturally to understand how multi-tenancy can be implemented.

Figure 9.1 depicts the changes that need to be made in an application to support basic multi-entity features, so that users only access data belonging to their own units. Each database table is appended with a column (OU_ID) which marks the organizational unit each data record belongs to. Each database query needs to be appended with a condition that ensures that data is filtered depending on the organizational unit of the currently logged-in user, which itself needs to be set in a variable, such as current_user_OU, during each transaction. An exactly similar mechanism can be used to support multi-tenancy, with OU_ID now representing the customer to whom data records belong. Note that the application runs on a single schema containing data from all organizational units; we shall refer to this as the *single schema* model.

Many early implementations of SaaS products utilized the single schema model, especially those that built their SaaS applications from scratch. One advantage of the single schema structure is that upgrading functionality of the

| Other fields | | | | | OU_ID |
|---|---|---|---|---|---|
| | | | | | North |
| | | | | | North |
| | | | | | North |
| | | | | | South |
| | | | | | South |

SELECT ... FROM T WHERE OU_ID=:current_user_OU

FIGURE 9.1. **Multi-entity implementation**

application, say by adding a field, can be done at once for all customers. At the same time, there are disadvantages: Re-engineering an existing application using the single schema approach entails significant re-structuring of application code. For a complex software product, often having millions of lines of code, this cost can be prohibitive. Further, while modifications to the data model can be done for all customers at once, it becomes difficult to support customer specific extensions, such as custom fields, using a single schema structure. Meta-data describing such customizations, as well as the data in such extra fields has to be maintained separately. Further, it remains the responsibility of the application code to interpret such meta-data for, say, displaying and handling custom fields on the screen. Additionally, any queries that require, say, filtering or sorting on these custom fields become very complex to handle. Some of these issues can be seen more clearly through the example in Figure 9.2 that depicts a multi-tenant architecture using a single schema model which also supports custom fields:

In the single schema model of Figure 9.2, a Custom Fields table stores meta-information and data values for *all* tables in the application. Mechanisms for handling custom fields in a single schema architecture are usually variants of this scheme. Consider a screen that is used to retrieve and update records in the Customer table. First the record from the main table is retrieved by name, suitably filtered by the OU attribute of the logged in user. Next, custom fields along with their values are retrieved from the Custom Fields table, for *this* particular record *and* the OU of the logged in user. For example, in OU 503, there are two custom fields as displayed on the screen, but only one in OU

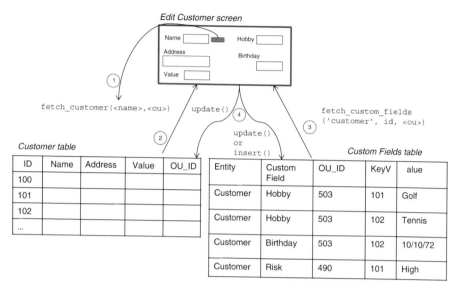

FIGURE 9.2. **Multi-tenancy using a single schema**

490, and none otherwise. Furthermore, some records may have missing values for these fields, so while saving the record care must be taken to appropriately either insert or update records in the Custom Fields table.

The above example is a simple case; more complex requirements also need to be handled, for example where a list of records is to be displayed with the ability to sort and filter on custom fields. It should be clear from this example that the single schema approach to multi-tenancy, while seemingly having the advantage of being able to upgrade the data model in one shot for all customers, has many complicating disadvantages in addition to the fact that major re-engineering of legacy applications is needed to move to this model.

## 9.2 MULTI-SCHEMA APPROACH

Instead of insisting on a single schema, it is sometimes easier to modify even an existing application to use multiple schemas, as are supported by most relational databases. In this model, the application computes which OU the logged in user belongs to, and then connects to the appropriate database schema. Such an architecture is shown in Figure 9.3

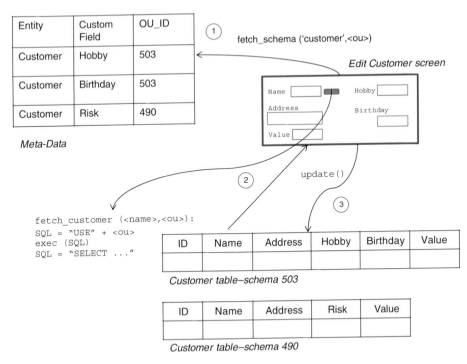

**Figure 9.3. Multi-tenancy using multiple schemas**

In the multiple schema approach a separate database schema is maintained for each customer, so each schema can implement customer-specific customizations directly. Meta-data describing customizations to the core schema is also maintained in a separate table, but unlike the Custom Fields table of Figure 9.2, this is pure meta-data and does not contain field values in individual records. As a result, the application design is simpler, and in case a legacy application needs to be re-engineered for multi-tenancy, it is likely that the modifications will be fewer and easier to accomplish.

Consider implementing the Edit Customer screen as discussed earlier using a multiple schema approach: The application renders the appropriate fields on the screen using information from the Meta-Data table. When making a database query, the application sets the database schema before issuing data manipulation (i.e. SQL) statements so as to access the appropriate schema. Note that supporting the multiple schema model involves incorporating elements of an *interpretive* architecture, very similar to the Dev 2.0 model discussed in Chapter 3, and which we shall return to in more detail in Chapters 12 and 14. Thus, it is natural that SaaS offerings based on the multiple schema model are quite naturally able to morph into Dev 2.0 platforms.

We have described a rather simple implementation to illustrate the concept of using multiple schemas for multi-tenancy. In practice, web-application servers need to have schema names configured during deployment so that they can maintain database connection pools to each schema. Therefore, another level of indirection is usually required, where customer name (i.e. OU) is mapped to the actual schema name, so that customers can be added or deleted online without bringing the system down.

In the case of a multi-entity scenario within a single organization, the number of users was relatively small, probably in the thousands at most. For a SaaS application, the number of users will be orders of magnitude larger. Thus additional factors need to be considered for a multi-tenant SaaS deployment, such as how many applications server and database instances are needed, and how a large set of users are efficiently and dynamically mapped to OUs so as to be connected to the appropriate application server and database instance.

## 9.3 MULTI-TENANCY USING CLOUD DATA STORES

As discussed in the previous chapter, cloud data stores exhibit non-relational storage models. Furthermore, each of these data stores are built to be multi-tenant from scratch since effectively a single instance of such a large-scale distributed data store caters to multiple applications created by cloud users. For example, each user of the Google App Engine can create a fixed number of applications, and each of these *appears* to have a separate data store; however the underlying distributed infrastructure is the same for *all* users of Google App Engine, as we shall describe in more detail in Chapter 10.

Here we focus on a different problem: As a *user* (application developer) of a cloud platform , how does one create one's own multi-tenant application? In the case of Amazon EC2 the answer is straightforward; since this is an infrastructure cloud it gives users direct access to (virtual) servers where one can recreate exactly the same multi-tenant architectures discussed earlier using standard application servers and database systems.

However the situation is different using a PaaS platform such as Google's App Engine with its Datastore, Amazon's SimpleDB or even Azure's data services. For example, a single App Engine application has *one* data store name space, or schema (so, if we create one 'Customer' model, then we cannot have another by the same name in the same application). Thus, it appears at first that we are constrained to use the inefficient single schema approach.

However, an interesting feature of the Google Datastore is that entities are essentially *schema-less*. Thus, it is up to the *language* API provided to define how the data store is used. In particular, the Model class in the Python API to App Engine is object-oriented as well as dynamic. As we have seen earlier in Chapter 5, the properties of all entities of a 'kind' are derived from a class-definition inheriting from the Model class. Further, as Python is a completely interpretive language, fresh classes can be defined at runtime, along with their corresponding data store 'kinds.'

Figure 9.4 shows one possible implementation of multi-tenancy using multiple schemas with Google App Engine, in Python. Separate classes are instantiated for each schema, at runtime. This approach is similar to simulating multiple schemas in a relational database by having table names that are schema dependent.

A similar strategy can be used with Amazon's SimpleDB, where *domains*, which play the role of tables in relational parlance and are the equivalent of

```
# Normal schema definition (not used)
#Class Customer(db.Model):
#   ID   = db.IntegerProperty()
#   Name = db.StringProperty()
    ... ...
# Dynamic OU specific classes for 'Customer'
for OU in OUList:
  #Gets ALL fields from meta-data
  schema=fetch_schema('Customer' OU)
  # Create OU specific class at run-time
  OUclass=type('Customer'+OU, (db.Model,), schema)
```

| ID | Name | Address | Hobby | Birthday | Value |
|----|------|---------|-------|----------|-------|
|    |      |         |       |          |       |

*Customer 503*

| ID | Name | Address | Risk | Value |
|----|------|---------|------|-------|
|    |      |         |      |       |

*Customer 490*

FIGURE 9.4. **Multi-tenancy using Google Datastore**

'kind' in the Google Datastore, can be created dynamically from any of the provided language APIs.

## 9.4 DATA ACCESS CONTROL FOR ENTERPRISE APPLICATIONS

So far we have covered the typical strategies used to achieve multi-tenancy from the perspective of enabling a single application code base, running in a single instance, to work with data of multiple customers, thereby bringing down costs of management across a potentially large number of customers.

For the most part, multi-tenancy as discussed above appears to be of use primarily in a software as a service model. There are also certain cases where multi-tenancy can be useful within the enterprise as well. We have already seen that supporting multiple entities, such as bank branches, is essentially a multi-tenancy requirement. Similar needs can arise if a workgroup level application needs to be rolled out to many independent teams, who usually do not need to share data. Customizations of the application schema may also be needed in such scenarios, to support variations in business processes. Similar requirements also arise in supporting multiple *legal* entities each of which could be operating in different regulatory environments.

As we mentioned earlier, in a multi-entity scenario a subset of users may need to be given access to data from all branches, or a subset of branches, depending on their position in an organizational unit hierarchy. More generally, access to data may need to be controlled based on the *values* of any field of a table, such as high-value transactions being visible only to some users, or special customer names being invisible without explicit permission. Such requirements are referred to as *data access control* needs, which while common, are less often handled in a reusable and generic manner. Data access control (or DAC) is a generalization of multi-tenancy in that the latter can often be implemented using DAC. In Figure 9.5 we illustrate how data access control can be implemented in a generic manner within a single schema to support fairly general rules for controlling access to records based on *field values*.

Each application table, such as Customer, is augmented with an additional field DAC_ID. The DAC Rules table lists patterns based on value ranges of arbitrary fields using which the values of the DAC_ID in each Customer record are filled through a batch process. Users are assigned privileges to access records satisfying one or more such DAC rules as specified in the User DAC Roles table. This information is expanded, via a batch process, to data

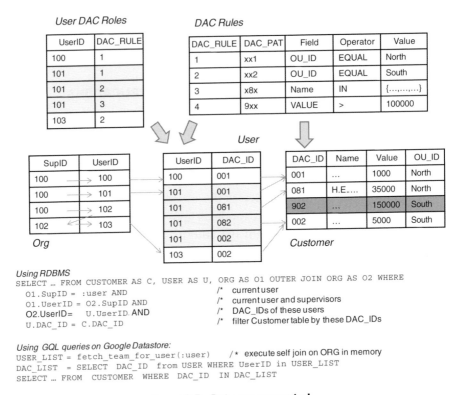

**FIGURE 9.5. Data access control**

in the User table where there is a record for each value of DAC_ID that a user can access. For example, the user 101 has access to three DAC rules, which translate to five records in the User table. This calculation involves computing the complete set of mutually exclusive and unique DAC range combinations based on the DAC Rules and thereafter which subset of these a particular user has access to based on the User DAC Roles information; note that this computation is independent of the actual DAC_ID values in the Customer or other application tables.

It is straightforward to limit access to records of the Customer table to only those a particular user is permitted, as specified in the User table using a join. In the illustration of Figure 9.5, we introduce an additional complication where users are also given access to the DAC permissions of all their direct reports, as specified in the Org table.

In a traditional relational database, SQL queries on the Customer database can be modified to support data access control by introducing a generic join, including a self-join on the Org table to find all direct reports of a user, which is then joined to the User table and the Customer table. However, in a cloud database, such as Google Datastore or Amazon's SimpleDB, *joins are not supported*. Therefore the same functionality must be implemented in code as shown in the figure: The self-join on Org is done in memory giving a list of reportees, including the user; this is used as a filter to get the permissible DAC_IDs from the User table. Finally this list is used to filter the application query on the Customer table.

It is important to note that when adding or modifying Customer records the DAC_ID needs to be recomputed based on the DAC Rules; this computation also needs to be optimized, especially if there are a large number of DAC Rules. Adding new DAC Rules or modifying existing ones will also require re-computation and updates to the DAC_ID values in the Customer table. Care also needs to be taken when filling the DAC Rules table to ensure that DAC ranges on the same field are always non-overlapping.

We thought it fit to cover data access control here, as part of our treatment of multi-tenancy, first because these requirements are closely related, but also to bring out the complexities of real enterprise applications even for incorporating a generic requirement such as data access control. Beyond the example itself the lesson to be learnt is that migrating applications to a multi-tenancy model, especially using cloud databases, is not a trivial task.

# PART IV

# Cloud development

The emergence of cloud platforms has given rise to new paradigms for dealing with distributed data in the cloud, parallel computing using very large computing clusters as well as rapid application development tools for specialized domains: Cloud-based data stores differ significantly from traditional relational databases, with different query and consistency semantics as well as performance behavior. The MapReduce programming paradigm makes large-scale analytics tasks easy to define. MapReduce implementations allow massive computing clusters to be used while tolerating faults that are inevitable at such scales. Similarly, but in a very different context, Dev 2.0 platforms allow simple business applications to be developed by end-users using always-on hosted platforms in the cloud, obviating the need for traditional development and thereby increasing business agility.

# CHAPTER 10

# Data in the cloud

Since the 80s relational database technology has been the 'default' data storage and retrieval mechanism used in the vast majority of enterprise applications. The origins of relational databases, beginning with System R [5] and Ingres [60] in the 70s, focused on introducing this new paradigm as a general purpose replacement for hierarchical and network databases, for the most common business computing tasks at the time, viz. transaction processing.

In the process of creating a planetary scale web search service, Google in particular has developed a massively parallel and fault tolerant distributed file system (GFS) along with a data organization (BigTable) and programming paradigm (MapReduce) that is markedly different from the traditional relational model. Such 'cloud data strategies' are particularly well suited for large-volume massively parallel text processing, as well as possibly other tasks, such as enterprise analytics. The public cloud computing offerings from Google (i.e. App Engine) as well as those from other vendors have made similar data models (Google's Datastore, Amazon's SimpleDB) and programming paradigms (Hadoop on Amazon's EC2) available to users as part of their cloud platforms.

At the same time there have been new advances in building specialized database organizations optimized for analytical data processing, in particular column-oriented databases such as Vertica. It is instructive to note that the BigTable-based data organization underlying cloud databases exhibits some similarities to column-oriented databases. These concurrent trends along with the ease of access to cloud platforms are witnessing a resurgence of interest in non-relational data organizations and an exploration of how these can best be leveraged for enterprise applications.

In this chapter we examine the structure of Google App Engine's Datastore and its underlying technologies, Google's distributed file system (GFS) and BigTable abstraction, as well as the open source project Hadoop's HBase and HDFS (clones of BigTable and GFS respectively). In the next chapter we cover the MapReduce parallel programming model along with additional abstractions that together present an alternative query processing model as compared to parallel and distributed relational database systems.

## 10.1 RELATIONAL DATABASES

Before we delve into cloud data structures we first review traditional relational database systems and how they store data. Users (including application programs) interact with an RDBMS via SQL; the database 'front-end' or parser transforms queries into memory and disk level operations to optimize execution time. Data records are stored on pages of contiguous disk blocks, which are managed by the disk-space-management layer.

Pages are fetched from disk into memory buffers as they are requested, in many ways similar to the file and buffer management functions of the operating system, using pre-fetching and page replacement policies. However, database systems usually do not rely on the file system layer of the OS and instead manage disk space themselves. This is primarily so that the database can have full control of when to retain a page in memory and when to release it. The database needs be able to adjust page replacement policy when needed and pre-fetch pages from disk based on expected access patterns that can be very different from file operations. Finally, the operating system files used by databases need to span multiple disks so as to handle the large storage requirements of a database, by efficiently exploiting parallel I/O systems such as RAID disk arrays or multi-processor clusters.

The storage indexing layer of the database system is responsible for locating records and their organization on disk pages. Relational records (tabular rows) are stored on disk pages and accessed through indexes on specified columns, which can be $B^+$-tree indexes, hash indexes, or bitmap indexes [46]. Normally rows are stored on pages contiguously, also called a 'row-store', and indexed using $B^+$-trees. An index can be *primary*, in which case rows of the table are physically stored in as close as possible to sorted order based on the column specified by the index. Clearly only one such primary index is possible per table; the remaining indexes are *secondary*, and maintain pointers to the actual row locations on disk.

While $B^+$-tree indexes on a row-store are optimal for write oriented workloads, such as the case in transaction processing applications, these are not the best for applications where reads dominate; in the latter case bitmap indexes, cross-table indexes and materialized views are used for efficient access to records and their attributes. Further, a row-oriented storage of records on disk may also not be optimal for read-dominated workloads, especially analytical applications. Recently column-oriented storage [61] has been proposed as a more efficient mechanism suited for analytical workloads, where an aggregation of measures columns (e.g. Sales) need to be performed based on values of dimension columns (e.g. Month). Figure 10.1 illustrates the difference between row-oriented and column-oriented storage. Notice that in a column store, projections of the table are stored sorted by dimension values, which are themselves compressed (as bitmaps, for example) for ease of comparison as well as reduced storage. Notice also that the column store needs additional 'join indexes' that map the sort orders of different projections so as to be able to recover the original row when required. When the cardinality of dimension values are small these join indexes can also be efficiently compressed

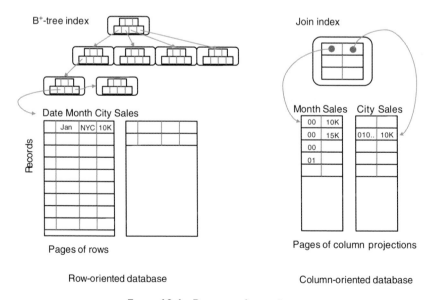

FIGURE 10.1. Row vs. column storage

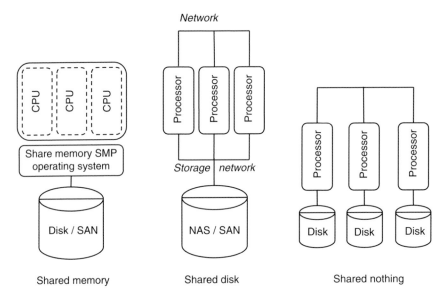

**FIGURE 10.2. Parallel database architectures**

(which we have not shown in the figure). When we cover cloud data stores later in this chapter we will see some of the similarities between their meta-data indexes and $B^+$-tree indexes, as well as between their data organization structures and column oriented databases.

Over the years database systems have evolved towards exploiting the parallel computing capabilities of multi-processor servers as well as harnessing the aggregate computing power of clusters of servers connected by a high-speed network. Figure 10.2 illustrates three parallel/distributed database architectures: The shared memory architecture is for machines with many CPUs (and with each having possibly many processing 'cores') while the memory address space is shared and managed by a symmetric multi-processing operating system that schedules processes in parallel exploiting all the processors. The shared-nothing architecture assumes a cluster of independent servers each with its own disk, connected by a network. A shared-disk architecture is somewhere in between with the cluster of servers sharing storage through high-speed network storage, such as a NAS (network attached storage) or a SAN (storage area network) interconnected via standard Ethernet, or faster Fiber Channel or Infiniband connections. Parallel database systems capable of exploiting any of these parallel architectures have existed since the 80s. These systems parallelize SQL queries to execute efficiently and exploit multiple

processors [46]. In the case of shared-nothing architectures, tables are partitioned and distributed across processing nodes with the SQL optimizer
handling distributed joins as best possible. Each of the traditional transaction-
processing databases, Oracle, DB2 and SQL Server support parallelism in
various ways, as do specialized systems designed for data warehousing such
as Vertica, Netezza and Teradata.

Traditional relational databases are designed to support high-volume transaction processing involving many, possibly concurrent, record level insertions
and updates. Supporting concurrent access while ensuring that conflicting
actions by simultaneous users do not result in inconsistency is the responsibility of the transaction management layer of the database system that ensures
'isolation' between different transactions through a variety of locking strategies. In the case of parallel and distributed architectures, locking strategies are
further complicated since they involve communication between processors
via the well-known 'two-phase' commit protocol [46].

It is important to note that the parallel database systems developed as extensions to traditional relational databases were designed either for specially
constructed parallel architectures, such as Netezza, or for closely coupled
clusters of at most a few dozen processors. At this scale, the chances of
system failure due to faults in any of the components could be sufficiently
compensated for by transferring control to a 'hot-standby' system in the case
of transaction processing or by restarting the computations in the case of
data warehousing applications. As we shall see below, a different approach is
required to exploit a parallelism at a significantly larger scale.

## 10.2 CLOUD FILE SYSTEMS: GFS AND HDFS

The Google File System (GFS) [26] is designed to manage relatively large
files using a very large distributed cluster of commodity servers connected
by a high-speed network. It is therefore designed to (a) expect and tolerate
hardware failures, even during the reading or writing of an individual file
(since files are expected to be very large) and (b) support parallel reads,
writes and appends by multiple client programs. A common use case that is
efficiently supported is that of many 'producers' appending to the same file in
parallel, which is also being simultaneously read by many parallel 'consumers'.
The reason for this particular use case being mentioned will become clearer
in the next chapter when we cover the MapReduce programming model and
its applications.

As discussed in the previous section traditional parallel databases, on the other hand, do not make similar assumptions as regards to the prevalence of failures or the expectations that failures will occur often even during large computations. As a result they also do not scale as well as data organizations built on GFS-like platforms such as the Google Datastore. The Hadoop Distributed File System (HDFS) is an open source implementation of the GFS architecture that is also available on the Amazon EC2 cloud platform; we refer to both GFS and HDFS as 'cloud file systems.'

The architecture of cloud file systems is illustrated in Figure 10.3. Large files are broken up into 'chunks' (GFS) or 'blocks' (HDFS), which are themselves large (64MB being typical). These chunks are stored on commodity (Linux) servers called Chunk Servers (GFS) or Data Nodes (HDFS); further each chunk is replicated at least three times, both on a different physical rack as well as a different network segment in anticipation of possible failures of these components apart from server failures.

When a client program ('cloud application') needs to read/write a file, it sends the full path and offset to the Master (GFS) which sends back meta-data

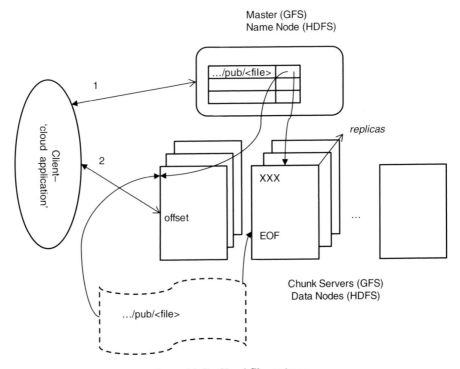

FIGURE 10.3. Cloud file systems

for one (in the case of read) or all (in the case of write) of the replicas of the chunk where this data is to be found. The client caches such meta-data so that it need not contact the Master each time. Thereafter the client directly reads data from the designated chunk server; this data is not cached since most reads are large and caching would only complicate writes.

In case of a write, in particular an append, the client sends only the data to be appended to all the chunk servers; when they all acknowledge receiving this data it informs a designated 'primary' chunk server, whose identity it receives (and also caches) from the Master. The primary chunk server appends its copy of data into the chunk at an offset of its choice; note that this may be beyond the EOF to account for multiple writers who may be appending to this file simultaneously. The primary then forwards the request to all other replicas which in turn write the data at the same offset if possible or return a failure. In case of a failure the primary rewrites the data at possibly another offset and retries the process.

The Master maintains regular contact with each chunk server through heartbeat messages and in case it detects a failure its meta-data is updated to reflect this, and if required assigns a new primary for the chunks being served by a failed chunk server. Since clients cache meta-data, occasionally they will try to connect to failed chunk servers, in which case they update their meta-data from the master and retry.

In [26] it is shown that this architecture efficiently supports multiple parallel readers and writers. It also supports writing (appending) and reading the same file by parallel sets of writers and readers while maintaining a consistent view, i.e. each reader always sees the same data regardless of the replica it happens to read from. Finally, note that computational processes (the 'client' applications above) run on the same set of servers that files are stored on. As a result, distributed programming systems, such as MapReduce, can often schedule tasks so that their data is found locally as far as possible, as illustrated by the Clustera system [16].

## 10.3 BigTable, HBase and Dynamo

BigTable [9] is a distributed *structured* storage system built on GFS; Hadoop's HBase is a similar open source system that uses HDFS. A BigTable is essentially a sparse, distributed, persistent, multidimensional sorted 'map.'[1] Data in a

---

[1] In the programming language sense, i.e. a dictionary of key-value pairs.

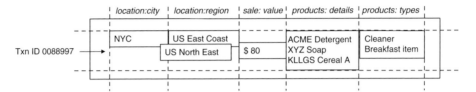

**FIGURE 10.4. Data organization in a BigTable**

BigTable is accessed by a row key, column key and a timestamp. Each column can store arbitrary name–value pairs of the form *column-family:label, string*. The set of possible column-families for a table is fixed when it is created whereas columns, i.e. labels within the column family, can be created dynamically at any time. Column families are stored close together in the distributed file system; thus the BigTable model shares elements of column-oriented databases. Further, each Bigtable cell (row, column) can contain multiple versions of the data that are stored in decreasing timestamp order. We illustrate these features below through an example.

Figure 10.4 illustrates the BigTable data structure: Each row stores information about a specific sale transaction and the row key is a transaction identifier. The 'location' column family stores columns relating to where the sale occurred, whereas the 'product' column family stores the actual products sold and their classification. Note that there are two values for region having different timestamps, possibly because of a reorganization of sales regions. Notice also that in this example the data happens to be stored in a de-normalized fashion, as compared to how one would possibly store it in a relational structure; for example the fact that XYZ Soap is a Cleaner is not maintained.

Since data in each column family is stored together, using this data organization results in efficient data access patterns depending on the nature of analysis: For example, only the *location* column family may be read for traditional data-cube based analysis of sales, whereas only the *product* column family is needed for say, market-basket analysis. Thus, the BigTable structure can be used in a manner similar to a column-oriented database.

Figure 10.5 illustrates how BigTable tables are stored on a distributed file system such as GFS or HDFS. (In the discussion below we shall use BigTable terminology; equivalent HBase terms are as shown in Figure 10.5.) Each table is split into different row ranges, called tablets. Each tablet is managed by a tablet server that stores each column family for the given row range in a separate distributed file, called an SSTable. Additionally, a single Metadata

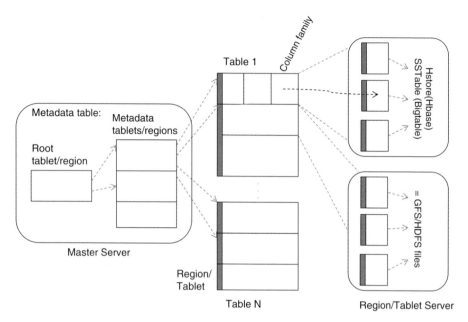

FIGURE 10.5. Google BigTable/Hadoop HDFS

table is managed by a meta-data server that is used to locate the tablets of
any user table in response to a read or write request. The Metadata table itself
can be large and is also split into tablets, with the root tablet being special in
that it points to the locations of other meta-data tablets. It is instructive to
notice how this multi-layer structure is in many ways similar to a distributed
$B^+$-tree index on the row keys of all tables.

BigTable and HBase rely on the underlying distributed file systems GFS
and HDFS respectively and therefore also inherit some of the properties of
these systems. In particular large parallel reads and inserts are efficiently supported, even simultaneously on the same table, unlike a traditional relational
database. In particular, reading all rows for a small number of column families from a large table, such as in aggregation queries, is efficient in a manner
similar to column-oriented databases. Random writes translate to data inserts
since multiple versions of each cell are maintained, but are less efficient since
cell versions are stored in descending order and such inserts require more
work than simple file appends. Similarly, the consistency properties of large
parallel inserts are stronger than that for parallel random writes, as is pointed
out in [26]. Further, writes can even fail if a few replicas are unable to write
even if other replicas are successfully updated.

We now turn to another distributed data system called Dynamo, which was developed at Amazon and underlies its SimpleDB key-value pair database. Unlike BigTable, Dynamo was designed specifically for supporting a large volume of concurrent updates, each of which could be small in size, rather than bulk reads and appends as in the case of BigTable and GFS.

Dynamo's data model is that of simple key-value pairs, and it is expected that applications read and write such data objects fairly randomly. This model is well suited for many web-based e-commerce applications that all need to support constructs such as a 'shopping cart.'

Dynamo also replicates data for fault tolerance, but uses distributed object versioning and quorum-consistency to enable writes to succeed without waiting for all replicas to be successfully updated, unlike in the case of GFS. Managing conflicts if they arise is relegated to reads which are provided enough information to enable application dependent resolution. Because of these features, Dynamo does not rely on any underlying distributed file system and instead directly manages data storage across distributed nodes.

The architecture of Dynamo is illustrated in Figure 10.6. Objects are key-value pairs with arbitrary arrays of bytes. An MD5 hash of the key is used to generate a 128-bit hash value. The range of this hash function is mapped

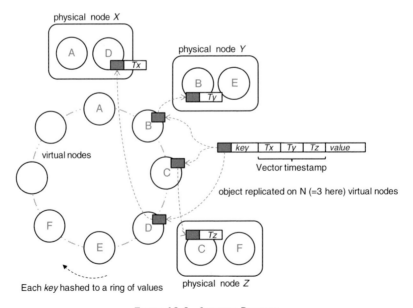

FIGURE 10.6. Amazon Dynamo

to a set of virtual nodes arranged in a ring, so each key gets mapped to one virtual node. The object is replicated at this primary virtual node as well as $N - 1$ additional virtual nodes (where $N$ is fixed for a particular Dynamo cluster). Each physical node (server) handles a number of virtual nodes at distributed positions on the ring so as to continuously distribute load evenly as nodes leave and join the cluster because of transient failures or network partitions. Notice that the Dynamo architecture is completely symmetric with each node being equal, unlike the BigTable/GFS architecture that has special master nodes at both the BigTable as well as GFS layer.

A write request on an object is first executed at one of its virtual nodes which then forwards the request to all nodes having replicas of the object. Objects are always versioned, so a write merely creates a new version of the object with its local timestamp ($T_x$ on node $X$) incremented. Thus the timestamps capture the history of object updates; versions that are superseded by later versions having a larger *vector* timestamp are discarded. For example, two sequential updates at node $X$ would create an object version with vector timestamp to [2 0 0], so an earlier version with timestamp [1 0 0] can be safely discarded. However, if the second write took place at node $Y$ before the first write had propagated to this replica, it would have a timestamp of [0 1 0]. In this case even when the first write arrives at $Y$ (and $Y$'s write arrives symmetrically at $X$), the two versions [1 0 0] and [0 1 0] would both be maintained and returned to any subsequent read to be resolved using application-dependent logic. Say this read took place at node $Z$ and was reconciled by the application which then further updated the object; the new timestamp for the object would be set to [1 1 1], and as this supersedes other versions they would be discarded once this update was propagated to all replicas. We mention in passing that such vector-timestamp-based ordering of distributed events was first conceived of by Lamport in [35].

In Dynamo write operations are allowed to return even if all replicas are not updated. However a quorum protocol is used to maintain *eventual* consistency of the replicas when a large number of concurrent reads and writes take place: Each read operation accesses $R$ replicas and each write ensures propagation to $W$ replicas; as long as $R + W > N$ the system is said to be quorum consistent [14]. Thus, if we want very efficient writes, we pay the price of having to read many replicas, and vice versa. In practice Amazon uses $N = 3$, with $R$ and $W$ being configurable depending on what is desired; for a high update frequency one uses $W = 1, R = 3$, whereas for a high-performance read store $W = 3, R = 1$ is used.

Dynamo is able to handle transient failures by passing writes intended for a failed node to another node temporarily. Such replicas are kept separately and scanned periodically with replicas being sent back to their intended node as soon as it is found to have revived. Finally, Dynamo can be implemented using different storage engines at the node level, such as Berkeley DB or even MySQL; Amazon is said to use the former in production.

## 10.4 Cloud data stores: Datastore and SimpleDB

The Google and Amazon cloud services do not directly offer BigTable and Dynamo to cloud users. Using Hadoop's HDFS and HBase, which are available as Amazon AMIs, users can set up their own BigTable-like stores on Amazon's EC2. However, as we have seen in Chapter 5, Google and Amazon both offer simple key-value pair database stores, viz. Google App Engine's Datastore and Amazon's SimpleDB. Here we describe how the Google Datastore is implemented using an underlying BigTable infrastructure, as illustrated in Figure 10.7.

All entities (objects) in a Datastore reside in one BigTable table, the Entities table having *one* column family. In addition to the single Entities table there are index tables that are used to support efficient queries.

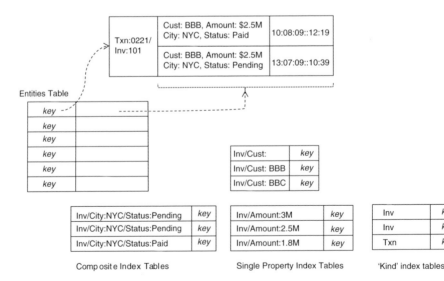

FIGURE 10.7. Google Datastore using BigTable

For the purposes of this discussion, it is useful to think of a BigTable as an array that has been horizontally partitioned (also called 'sharded') across disks, and *sorted* lexicographically by key values. In addition to single key lookup, this structure also enables highly efficient execution of *prefix* and *range* queries on key values, e.g. all keys having prefix 'Txn,' or in the range 'Amount:1M' to 'Amount:3M.' From this feature derive the key structures of entity and index tables that implement Datastore.

Recall from Chapter 5 that Datastore allows entities to be 'grouped' (entity groups) for the purposes of transactions and also efficiency. Entity keys are lexicographic by group ancestry, so if the entity Inv:101 has parent Txn:0221, then its key in the entities table would look like 'Txn:0221/Inv:101,' which is lexicographically near that of its parent 'Txn:0221.' As a result these entities end up being stored close together on disk, whereas another group, say 'Txn:9999' and 'Txn:9999/Inv:875' may be far apart from these. Notice that this is very different from a relational model where the location of records from Txn and Inv tables on disk would be unrelated to any foreign key relationships between such records.

Index tables support the variety of queries included in the Datastore API. Some indexes, such as single property indexes and 'kind' indexes are automatically created when a 'kind' is defined, whereas others such as composite indexes need to be created by developers. Index tables use values of entity attributes as keys, e.g. the index entry 'Inv/Cust:BBB' allows efficient lookup of the record with the WHERE clause 'Cust = BBB'. Similarly, the index on Amount enables efficient range queries such as 'Amount $\geq$2M AND Amount $\geq$3M'. 'Kind' indexes support queries of the form SELECT ALL Invoices, retrieving all entries of a given 'kind.' Composite indexes support more complex queries such as retrieving all invoices 'WHERE City=NYC AND Status=Pending.' In cases where composite indexes are not present (because developers did not provide them), single property indexes are used in such queries with the results being merged in memory. A query is executed by choosing indexes with highest selectivity first, which is efficient unless the selectivity of *all* of the query parameters is low (e.g. 'Status=Pending'). Notice that index operations are efficient precisely because of the efficiency of prefix and range scans in BigTable.

The entities table stores multiple versions of each entity, primarily in order to support transactions spanning updates of different entities in the same group. Only one of the versions of each entity is tagged as 'committed,' and this is updated only when a transaction succeeds on all the entities in the group; journal entries consisting of previous entity versions are used to rollback if needed.

Note that many App Engine applications are small, so it is likely that a large number of tables within the App Engine Datastore have only a single tablet; in this case the structure of BigTable allows many tablets possibly from different applications to share GFS files (SSTables), each of which may have only one or just a few chunks.

Notice also that this mapping of the Datastore API onto BigTable does *not* exploit the column-oriented storage of BigTable, since a single column family is used. Thus while BigTable (and HBase) are potentially useful in large analytical tasks for the same reason that column-oriented databases are, Datastore as an application of BigTable does not share this property. Datastore is much more suited to transactional key-value pair updates, in much the same manner as Amazon's SimpleDB is, with the difference that its consistency properties are stronger (as compared to the 'eventual' consistency of SimpleDB), at the cost of a fixed overhead even for small writes.

While it is widely speculated that SimpleDB is similarly based on an underlying Dynamo infrastructure, and its eventual consistency model substantiates this claim, there is no published information that confirms this. Nevertheless, as both Datastore and SimpleDB share many similarities, we expect that our discussion of Datastore may also shed some light on how SimpleDB might be implemented on Dynamo. While SimpleDB objects are easily mapped to Dynamo objects, indexes are probably maintained differently since Dynamo does not share any underlying sorted array structure similar to BigTable that can make queries efficient.

# CHAPTER 11

# MapReduce and extensions

The MapReduce programming model was developed at Google in the process of implementing large-scale search and text processing tasks on massive collections of web data stored using BigTable and the GFS distributed file system. The MapReduce programming model is designed for processing and generating large volumes of data via massively parallel computations utilizing tens of thousands of processors at a time. The underlying infrastructure to support this model needs to assume that processors and networks will fail, even during a particular computation, and build in support for handling such failures while ensuring progress of the computations being performed. Hadoop is an open source implementation of the MapReduce model developed at Yahoo, and presumably also used internally. Hadoop is also available on pre-packaged AMIs in the Amazon EC2 cloud platform, which has sparked interest in applying the MapReduce model for large-scale, fault-tolerant computations in other domains, including such applications in the enterprise context.

## 11.1 PARALLEL COMPUTING

Parallel computing has a long history with its origins in scientific computing in the late 60s and early 70s. Different models of parallel computing have been used based on the nature and evolution of multiprocessor computer architectures. The shared-memory model assumes that any processor can access any memory location, albeit not equally fast.[1] In the distributed-memory model each processor can address only its own memory and communicates with other processors using message passing over the network. In scientific computing applications for which these models were developed, it was assumed that data would be loaded from disk at the start of a parallel job and then written back once the computations had been completed, as scientific tasks were largely compute bound. Over time, parallel computing also began to be applied in the database arena, as we have already discussed in the previous chapter; as illustrated earlier in Figure 10.2, database systems supporting shared-memory, shared-disk and shared-nothing[2] models became available.

The premise of parallel computing is that a task that takes time $T$ should take time $T/p$ if executed on $p$ processors. In practice, inefficiencies are introduced by distributing the computations such as (a) the need for synchronization among processors, (b) overheads of communication between processors through messages or disk, and (c) any imbalance in the distribution of work to processors. Thus in practice the time $T_p$ to execute on $p$ processors is less than $T$, and the *parallel efficiency* [21] of an algorithm is defined as:

$$\epsilon = \frac{T}{p\,T_p}.$$ (11.1)

A **scalable** parallel implementation is one where: (a) the parallel efficiency remains constant as the size of data is increased along with a corresponding increase in processors and (b) the parallel efficiency increases with the size of data for a fixed number of processors.

We illustrate how parallel efficiency and scalability depends on the algorithm, as well as the nature of the problem, through an example that we shall later use to illustrate the MapReduce model. Consider a very large collection of documents, say web pages crawled from the entire internet. The problem is to determine the frequency (i.e., total number of occurrences) of each word in this collection. Thus, if there are $n$ documents and $m$ distinct words, we wish to determine $m$ frequencies, one for each word. Now we compare two approaches to compute these frequencies in parallel using $p$ processors: (a) let each processor compute the frequencies for $m/p$ words and

---

[1] Referred to as NUMA, or 'non-uniform memory access,' using a hierarchy of memory buses.
[2] The same as distributed-memory.

(b) let each processor compute the frequencies of $m$ words across $n/p$ documents, followed by all the processors summing their results. At first glance it appears that approach (a) where each processor works independently may be more efficient as compared to (b) where they need to communicate with each other to add up all the frequencies. However, a more careful analysis reveals otherwise:

We assume a distributed-memory model with a shared disk, so that each processor is able to access any document from disk in parallel with no contention. Further we assume that the time spent $c$ for reading each word in the document is the same as that of sending it to another processor via interprocessor communication. On the other hand, the time to add to a running total of frequencies is negligible as compared to the time spent on a disk read or interprocessor communication, so we ignore the time taken for arithmetic additions in our analysis. Finally, assume that each word occurs $f$ times in a document, on average. With these assumptions, the time for computing all the $m$ frequencies with a single processor is $n \times m \times f \times c$, i.e. since each word needs to be read approximately $f$ times in each document.

Using approach (a) each processor reads approximately $n \times m \times f$ words and adds them $n \times m/p \times f$ times. Ignoring the time spent in additions, the parallel efficiency can be calculated as:

$$\epsilon_a = \frac{nmfc}{pnmfc} = \frac{1}{p}. \qquad (11.2)$$

Since efficiency falls with increasing $p$ the algorithm is not scalable.

On the other hand using approach (b) each processor performs approximately $n/p \times m \times f$ reads and the same number of additions in the first phase, producing $p$ vectors of $m$ partial frequencies, which can be written to disk in parallel by each processor in time $cm$. In the second phase these vectors of partial frequencies need to be added: First each processor sends $p - 1$ sub-vectors of size $m/p$ to each of the remaining processors. Each processor then adds $p$ sub-vectors locally to compute one $p$th of the final $m$-vector of frequencies. The parallel efficiency is computed as:

$$\epsilon_b = \frac{nmfc}{p\left(\dfrac{n}{p}mfc + +cm + p\dfrac{m}{p}c\right)} = \frac{nf}{nf + 2p} = \frac{1}{1 + \dfrac{2p}{nf}}. \qquad (11.3)$$

Since in practice $p \ll nf$ the efficiency of approach (b) is higher than that of approach (a), and can even be close to one: For example, with $n = 10\,000$

documents and $f = 10$, the condition (11.3) works out to $p \ll 50\,000$, so method (b) is efficient ($\epsilon_b \approx 0.9$) even with thousands of processors. The reason is that in the first approach each processor is reading many words that it need not read, resulting in wasted work, whereas in the second approach every read is useful in that it results in a computation that contributes to the final answer. Algorithm (b) is also *scalable*, since $\epsilon_b$ remains constant as $p$ and $n$ both increase, and approaches one as $n$ increases for a fixed $p$.

## 11.2 THE MAPREDUCE MODEL

Traditional parallel computing algorithms were developed for systems with a small number of processors, dozens rather than thousands. So it was safe to assume that processors would not fail during a computation. At significantly larger scales this assumption breaks down, as was experienced at Google in the course of having to carry out many large-scale computations similar to the one in our word counting example. The MapReduce [12] parallel programming abstraction was developed in response to these needs, so that it could be used by many different parallel applications while leveraging a common underlying fault-tolerant implementation that was transparent to application developers.

Figure 11.1 illustrates MapReduce using the word counting example where we needed to count the occurrences of each word in a collection of documents. MapReduce proceeds in two phases, a distributed 'map' operation followed by a distributed 'reduce' operation; at each phase a configurable number of $M$ 'mapper' processors and $R$ 'reducer' processors are assigned to work on the problem (we have used $M = 3$ and $R = 2$ in the illustration). The computation is coordinated by a single master process (not shown in the figure).

A MapReduce implementation of the word counting task proceeds as follows: In the map phase each mapper reads approximately 1/Mth of the input (in this case documents), from the global file system, using locations given to it by the master. Each mapper then performs a 'map' operation to compute word frequencies for its subset of documents. These frequencies are *sorted* by the words they represent and written to the *local* file system of the mapper. At the next phase reducers are each assigned a subset of words; in our illustration the first reducer is assigned w1 and w2 while the second one handles w3 and w4. In fact during the map phase itself each mapper writes one file per reducer, based on the words assigned to each reducer, and keeps the master informed of these file locations. The master in turn informs the reducers where the partial counts for their words have been stored on the local files of

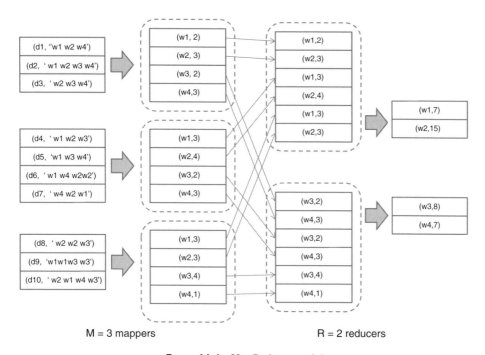

M = 3 mappers                                    R = 2 reducers

FIGURE **11.1.  MapReduce model**

respective mappers; the reducers then make remote procedure call requests
to the mappers to fetch these. Each reducer performs a 'reduce' operation that
sums up the frequencies for each word, which are finally written back to the
GFS file system.

The MapReduce programming model generalizes the computational structure of the above example. Each map operation consists of transforming one
set of key-value pairs to another:

$$\textbf{Map:} \quad (k_1, v_1) \rightarrow [(k_2, v_2)]. \tag{11.4}$$

In our example each map operation takes a document indexed by its id and
emits a list if word-count pairs indexed by word-id:

$$(d_k, [w_1 \ldots w_n]) \rightarrow [(w_i, c_i)].$$

The reduce operation groups the results of the map step using the same key
$k_2$ and performs a function $f$ on the list of values that correspond to each

key value:

$$\text{Reduce:} \quad (k_2, [v_2]) \rightarrow (k_2, f([v_2])). \tag{11.5}$$

In our example each reduce operation sums the frequency counts for each word:

$$(w_i, [c_i]) \rightarrow \left( w_i, \sum_i c_i \right).$$

The implementation also generalizes. Each mapper is assigned an input-key range (set of values for $k_1$) on which map operations need to be performed. The mapper writes results of its map operations to its local disk in $R$ partitions, each corresponding to the output-key range (values of $k_2$) assigned to a particular reducer, and informs the master of these locations. Next each reducer fetches these pairs from the respective mappers and performs reduce operations for each key $k_2$ assigned to it.

If a processor fails during the execution, the master detects this through regular heartbeat communications it maintains with each worker, wherein updates are also exchanged regarding the status of tasks assigned to workers. If a mapper fails, then the master reassigns the key-range designated to it to another working node for re-execution. Note that re-execution is required even if the mapper had completed some of its map operations, because the results were written to local disk rather than the GFS. On the other hand if a reducer fails only its remaining tasks (values $k_2$) are reassigned to another node, since the completed tasks would already have been written to the GFS. Finally, heartbeat failure detection can be fooled by a wounded task that has a heartbeat but is making no progress: Therefore, the master also tracks the overall progress of the computation and if results from the last few processors in either phase are excessively delayed, these tasks are duplicated and assigned to processors who have already completed their work. The master declares the task completed when any one of the duplicate workers complete.

Such a fault-tolerant implementation of the MapReduce model has been implemented and is widely used within Google; more importantly from an enterprise perspective, it is also available as an open source implementation through the Hadoop project along with the HDFS distributed file system.

The MapReduce model is widely applicable to a number of parallel computations, including database-oriented tasks which we cover later. Finally we describe one more example, that of indexing a large collection of documents, or, for that matter any data including database records: The map task consists of emitting a word-document/record id pair for each word:

$$(d_k, [w_1 \ldots w_n]) \rightarrow [(w_i, d_k)].$$

The reduce step groups the pairs by word and creates an index entry for each word:

$$[(w_i, d_k)] \rightarrow (w_i, [d_{i_1} \ldots d_{i_m}]).$$

Indexing large collections is not only important in web search, but also a critical aspect of handling structured data; so it is important to know that it can be executed efficiently in parallel using MapReduce. Traditional parallel databases focus on rapid query execution against data warehouses that are updated infrequently; as a result these systems often do not parallelize index creation sufficiently well.

## 11.3 PARALLEL EFFICIENCY OF MAPREDUCE

As we have seen earlier, parallel efficiency is impacted by overheads such as synchronization and communication costs, or load imbalance. The MapReduce master process is able to balance load efficiently if the number of map and reduce operations are significantly larger than the number of processors. For large data sets this is usually the case (since an individual map or reduce operation usually deals with a single document or record). However, communication costs in the distributed file system can be significant, especially when the volume of data being read, written and transferred between processors is large.

For the purposes of our analysis we assume a general computational task, on a volume of data $D$, which takes $wD$ time on a uniprocessor, including the time spent reading data from disk, performing computations, and writing it back to disk (i.e. we assume that computational complexity is linear in the size of data). Let $c$ be the time spent reading one unit of data (such as a word) from disk. Further, let us assume that our computational task can be decomposed into map and reduce stages as follows: First $c_m D$ computations are performed in the map stage, producing $\sigma D$ data as output. Next the reduce stage performs $c_r \sigma D$ computations on the output of the map stage, producing $\sigma \mu D$ data as the final result. Finally, we assume that our decomposition into a map and reduce stages introduces no additional overheads when run on a single processor, such as having to write intermediate results to disk, and so

$$wD = cD + c_m D + c_r \sigma D + c\sigma \mu D. \tag{11.6}$$

Now consider running the decomposed computation on $P$ processors that serve as both mappers and reducers in respective phases of a MapReduce-based parallel implementation. As compared to the single processor case, the additional overhead in a parallel MapReduce implementation is between the map and reduce phases where each mapper writes to its local disk followed by each reducer remotely reading from the local disk of each mapper. For the purposes of our analysis we shall assume that the time spent reading a word from a remote disk is also $c$, i.e. the same as for a local read.

Each mapper produces approximately $\sigma D/P$ data that is written to a local disk (unlike in the uniprocessor case), which takes $c\sigma D/P$ time. Next, after the map phase, each reducer needs to read its partition of data from each of the $P$ mappers, with approximately one $P$th of the data at each mapper by each reducer, i.e. $\sigma D/P^2$. The entire exchange can be executed in $P$ steps, with each reducer $r$ reading from mapper $r + i$ mod $r$ in step $i$. Thus the transfer time is $c\sigma D/P^2 \times P = c\sigma D/P$. The total overhead in the parallel implementation because of intermediate disk writes and reads is therefore $2c\sigma D/P$. We can now compute the parallel efficiency of the MapReduce implementation as:

$$\epsilon_{MR} = \frac{wD}{P\left(\dfrac{wD}{P} + 2c\dfrac{\sigma D}{P}\right)} = \frac{1}{1 + \dfrac{2c}{w}\sigma}. \tag{11.7}$$

Let us validate (11.7) above for our parallel word counting example discussed in Section 11.1: The volume of data is $D = nmf$. We ignore the time spent in adding word counts, so $c_r = c_m = 0$. We also did not include the (small) time $cm$ for writing the final result to disk. So $wD = wnmf = cnmf$, or $w = c$. The map phase produces $mP$ partial counts, so $\sigma = mP/nmf = p/nf$. Using (11.7) and $c = w$ we reproduce (11.3) as computed earlier.

It is important to note how $\epsilon_{MR}$ depends on $\sigma$, the 'compression' in data achieved in the map phase, and its relation to the number of processors $p$. To illustrate this dependence, let us recall the definition (11.4) of a map operation, as applied to the word counting problem, i.e. $(d_k, \text{'}w_1 \ldots w_n]) \rightarrow [(w_i, c_i)]$. Each map operation takes a document as input and emits a partial count for each word in *that* document alone, rather than a partial sum across all the documents it sees. In this case the output of the map phase is of size $mn$ (an $m$-vector of counts for each document). So, $\sigma = mn/nmf = 1/f$ and the parallel efficiency is $\frac{1}{1+\frac{2}{f}}$, independent of data size or number of processors, which is *not* scalable.

A strict implementation of MapReduce as per the definitions (11.4) and (11.5) does not allow for partial reduction across all input values seen by a particular reducer, which is what enabled the parallel implementation of Section 11.1 to be highly efficient and scalable. Therefore, in practice the map phase usually includes a *combine* operation in addition to the map, defined as follows:

$$\text{Combine:} \quad (k_2, [v_2]) \rightarrow (k_2, f_c([v_2])). \qquad (11.8)$$

The function $f_c$ is similar to the function $f$ in the reduce operation but is applied only across documents processed by each mapper, rather than globally. The equivalence of a MapReduce implementation with and without a combiner step relies on the reduce function $f$ being commutative and associative, i.e. $f(v_1, v_2, v_3) = f(v_3, f(v_1, v2))$.

Finally, recall our definition of a *scalable* parallel implementation: A MapReduce implementation is scalable if we are able to achieve an efficiency that approaches one as data volume $D$ grows, and remains constant as $D$ and $P$ both increase. Using combiners is crucial to achieving scalability in practical MapReduce implementations by achieving a high degree of data 'compression' in the map phase, so that $\sigma$ is proportional to $P/D$, which in turn results in scalability due to (11.7).

## 11.4 RELATIONAL OPERATIONS USING MAPREDUCE

Enterprise applications rely on structured data processing, which over the years has become virtually synonymous with the relational data model and SQL. Traditional parallel databases have become fairly sophisticated in automatically generating parallel execution plans for SQL statements. At the same time these systems lack the scale and fault-tolerance properties of MapReduce implementations, naturally motivating the quest to execute SQL statements on large data sets using the MapReduce model.

Parallel joins in particular are well studied, and so it is instructive to examine how a relational join could be executed in parallel using MapReduce. Figure 11.2 illustrates such an example: Point of sale transactions taking

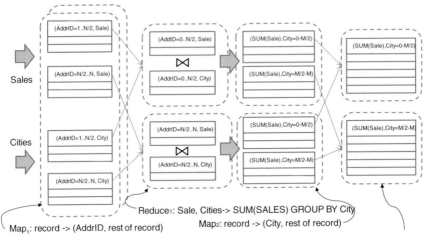

FIGURE 11.2. Join using MapReduce

place at stores (identified by addresses) are stored in a Sales table. A Cities table captures the addresses that fall within each city. In order to compute the gross sales by city these two tables need to be joined using SQL as shown in the figure.

The MapReduce implementation works as follows: In the map step, each mapper reads a (random) subset of records from each input table Sales and Cities, and segregates each of these by address, i.e. the reduce key $k_2$ is 'address.' Next each reducer fetches Sales and Cities data for its assigned range of address values from each mapper, and then performs a local join operation including the aggregation of sale value and grouping by city. Note that since addresses are randomly assigned to reducers, sales aggregates for any particular city will still be distributed across reducers. A second map-reduce step is needed to group the results by city and compute the final sales aggregates.

Note that while the parallel MapReduce implementation looks very similar to a traditional parallel sort-merge join, as can be found in most database textbooks [46], parallel SQL implementations usually distribute the smaller table, Cities in this case, to all processors. As a result, local joins and aggregations can be performed in the first map phase itself, followed by a reduce phase using city as the key, thus obviating the need for two phases of data exchange.

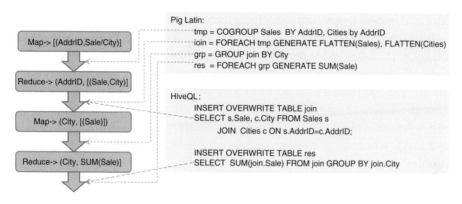

SQL:SELECT SUM(Sale), City from Sales, Cities WHERE Sales.AddrID=Cities.AddrIDGROUP BY City

FIGURE **11.3. Pig Latin and HiveQL**

Naturally there have been efforts at automatically translating SQL-like statements to a map-reduce framework. Two notable examples are Pig Latin [42] developed at Yahoo!, and Hive [62] developed and used at Facebook. Both of these are open source tools available as part of the Hadoop project, and both leverage the Hadoop distributed file system HDFS.

Figure 11.3 illustrates how the above SQL query can be represented using the Pig Latin language as well as the HiveQL dialect of SQL. Pig Latin has features of an imperative language, wherein a programmer specifies a sequence of transformations that each read and write large distributed files. The Pig Latin compiler generates MapReduce phases by treating each GROUP (or COGROUP) statement as defining a map-reduce boundary, and pushing remaining statements on either side into the map or reduce steps. HiveQL, on the other hand, shares SQL's declarative syntax. Once again though, as in Pig Latin, each JOIN and GROUP operation define a map-reduce boundary. As depicted in the figure, the Pig Latin as well as HiveQL representations of our SQL query translate into two MapReduce phases similar to our example of Figure 11.2.

Pig Latin is ideal for executing sequences of large-scale data transformations using MapReduce. In the enterprise context it is well suited for the tasks involved in loading information into a data warehouse. HiveQL, being more declarative and closer to SQL, is a good candidate for formulating analytical queries on a large distributed data warehouse.

There has been considerable interest in comparing the performance of MapReduce-based implementations of SQL queries with that of traditional parallel databases, especially specialized column-oriented databases tuned for analytical queries [44, 59]. In general, as of this writing, parallel databases are still faster than available open source implementations of MapReduce (such as Hadoop), for smaller data sizes using fewer processes where fault tolerance is less critical. MapReduce-based implementations, on the other hand, are able to handle orders of magnitude larger data using massively parallel clusters in a fault-tolerant manner. Thus, MapReduce is better suited to 'extract-transform-load' tasks, where large volumes of data need to be processed (especially using complex operations not easily expressed in SQL) and the results loaded into a database or other form of permanent structured storage [59]. MapReduce is also preferable over traditional databases if data needs to be processed only once and then discarded: As an example, the time required to load some large data sets into a database is 50 times greater than the time to both read *and* perform the required analysis using MapReduce [13]. On the contrary, if data needs to be stored for a long time, so that queries can be performed against it regularly, a traditional database wins over MapReduce, at least as of this writing.

HadoopDB [2] is an attempt at combining the advantages of MapReduce and relational databases by using databases locally within nodes while using MapReduce to coordinate parallel execution. Another example is SQL/MR [22] from Aster Data that enhances a set of distributed SQL-compliant databases with MapReduce programming constructs. Needless to say, relational processing using MapReduce is an active research area and many improvements to the available state of the art are to be expected in the near future. As an example of a possible improvement, neither Pig Latin nor Hive currently (as of this writing) leverage HBase's BigTable model and instead work directly with the file system. Using the opportunities for column-oriented storage in HBase, it should be possible to introduce optimizations similar to those used by specialized column oriented parallel databases, as has also been suggested in [13].

## 11.5 ENTERPRISE BATCH PROCESSING USING MAPREDUCE

In the enterprise context there is considerable interest in leveraging the MapReduce model for high-throughput batch processing, analysis on data warehouses as well as predictive analytics. We have already illustrated how analytical SQL queries can be handled using MapReduce, and we shall cover predictive analytics applications in more detail in Chapter 16.

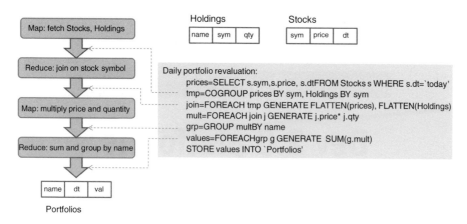

Holdings

| name | sym | qty |
|------|-----|-----|

Stocks

| sym | price | dt |
|-----|-------|----|

Map: fetch Stocks, Holdings

Reduce: join on stock symbol

Map: multiply price and quantity

Reduce: sum and group by name

Daily portfolio revaluation:
prices=SELECT s.sym,s.price, s.dtFROM Stocks s WHERE s.dt=`today'
tmp=COGROUP prices BY sym, Holdings BY sym
join=FOREACH tmp GENERATE FLATTEN(prices), FLATTEN(Holdings)
mult=FOREACH join j GENERATE j.price* j.qty
grp=GROUP multBY name
values=FOREACHgrp g GENERATE  SUM(g.mult)
STORE values INTO `Portfolios'

| name | dt | val |
|------|----|-----|

Portfolios

FIGURE **11.4.  Batch processing using MapReduce**

High-throughput batch processing operations on transactional data, usually performed as 'end-of-day' processing, often need to access and compute using large data sets. These operations are also naturally time bound, having to complete before transactional operations can resume fully. The time window required for daily batch processing often constrains the online availability of a transaction processing system. Exploiting parallel computing leveraging cloud technology presents an opportunity to accelerate batch processing.

As an example, illustrated in Figure 11.4, consider an investment bank that needs to revalue the portfolios of all its customers with the latest prices as received from the stock exchange at the end of a trading day. Each customer's Holdings (the quantity of each stock held by the customer) needs to be joined with prices from the latest Stock feed, the quantity of stock held by each customer must be multiplied by stock price, and the result grouped by customer name and appended to a set of Portfolio valuation files/tables time-stamped by the current date. Figure 11.4 depicts a Pig Latin program for such a batch process. This eventually translates to two MapReduce phases as shown. It is important to note that we append to the Portfolio file rather than update an existing table; this is because MapReduce leverages the distributed file system where storage is cheap and bulk record appends are far more efficient than updates of existing records.

The challenge in deploying public cloud-based batch processing is the cost of data transfer: Thus until transactional data is itself stored in the cloud MapReduce-based parallel batch processing can best be leveraged within enterprises using open source tools such as Hadoop.

# CHAPTER 12

# Dev 2.0 platforms

The cloud development paradigms covered so far have focused on *scale*, i.e. how data and computations can be organized in a very large distributed environment where hardware and network failures are to be expected as a matter of course rather than as exceptions. As we pointed out during our discussion on cloud economics in Chapter 6, PaaS clouds additionally offer the promise of improving *development* productivity while also catering for large volumes.

We now turn our attention to enterprise applications that may not necessarily require large volume computing, but which nevertheless account for a very large fraction of software development efforts: These are the numerous inter-organizational workflow and transaction-processing applications that enterprise IT departments spend significant development and maintenance efforts on. The computational requirements of this class of applications are typically an order of magnitude less than that of mission-critical transaction-processing or large-scale analytics applications. At the same time these constitute an important class of applications because of the sheer number of such systems being used. In Chapter 13 we shall examine in more detail the functionalities typically covered by such applications within the overall context of enterprise software needs.

Technically this class of applications can be described as 'forms-based transaction-processing and workflow systems using a relational database,' restricted also by scale; so we exclude those where very high transaction and data volumes need to be supported. It has long been recognized that such medium-scale 'office automation' systems share many common features, and over the years there have been numerous attempts to develop common abstractions to model such systems so that they can be more efficiently built, and we shall recount such earlier efforts in Section 12.3.

More recently we have also seen the emergence and growing popularity of software as a service (SaaS) offerings. *Some* SaaS providers, having rediscovered the commonalities of office automation systems, have begun to include highly *configurable* forms-based workflow as part of their hosted SaaS offerings. Further, the configurable features provided in many of these systems are so powerful that they enable, within limits, fully functional applications to be developed from scratch, over the web, with little or no programming. Thus, in a sense, the 'product' these SaaS providers offer is an 'empty' office automation application that instead of pre-built functionality enables users to configure (not program) the functionality they require. Users can immediately begin using such an application once configured, since it is in any case already hosted on the internet as a multi-tenant SaaS platform.

We believe this **confluence of software as a service and end-user configurable application frameworks for vanilla office automation tasks** represents a potential paradigm shift for a large class of enterprise IT development. We call this paradigm '**Dev 2.0**' [51]: Non-programmers can now use Dev 2.0 platforms to create a limited class of business applications, in much the same manner as ordinary (read-only) users of the internet were empowered to publish content using Web 2.0 tools, such as blogs and wikis. In this chapter we shall describe some Dev 2.0 platforms and compare their features. We shall also examine and speculate on the advantages of Dev 2.0, where it may impact enterprise IT and most importantly its limits. However, we shall reserve our discussion on the technical details of *how* Dev 2.0 platforms are architected to Chapter 14.

## 12.1 SALESFORCE.COM'S FORCE.COM PLATFORM

Salesforce.com was one of the first successful software as a service offerings, with its hosted, multi-tenant, customer relationship management (CRM) product. The hosted model enabled highly mobile sales people to have access to CRM data over the internet, which was one of the reasons for its popularity. However, a more important factor that contributed to the success of Salesforce.com's CRM product was its *configurability*. Right from the beginning, end-users could easily add custom fields to any of the screens provided by the core CRM product; such fields would automatically be included in the database, but only for the customer who had added them. Further, this process could be performed from a web-browser whilst *using* the CRM product, as a configuration setting. No programming or separate development tool was required. Similarly, simple custom workflows could be added; these resulted in tasks being placed in users' work-lists based on creation or modification of data satisfying certain conditions: For example a supervisor could be notified whenever an opportunity with value greater than some threshold was registered by any sales person. Configurability allowed end-users to tailor the CRM system to their needs without requiring the assistance of developers. The hosted platform enabled them to begin using the application in the field without the involvement, or even knowledge, of their enterprise IT department!

As such usage became established, users naturally began to require data in the Salesforce.com CRM system to integrate with data within their enterprise systems. To enable this, Salesforce.com began providing access to the hosted CRM product using SOAP/WSDL web services, using which programmers could develop such integration solutions. Once programmers began to get involved with the hosted CRM, they became users of the platform and began to create additional functionality over and above that of CRM using the configurability features provided by Salesforce.com; for example 'order management' was once such natural and popular extension to CRM. Recognizing that such add-on applications created by programmers would require platform features beyond the basic configurability provided to end-users, Salesforce.com added a server-side programming language, called APEX.

At this point, the hosted product began to look like considerably more than a CRM product; rather it had all the elements of an application development platform, but for the specific class of web-based transaction processing applications. Salesforce.com re-branded this new platform, first as Sforce.com and now simply as Force.com. It also created an online application sharing forum, called AppExchange, where third-party developers could create applications using the Force.com platform and resell them to end-users of the hosted platform, such as users of the CRM product.

While we will not go into details of the Force.com platform, we illustrate its use with a simple example as outlined in Figure 12.1: Consider an Employee Services application that stores Employee records with their names and leave balance, i.e., the number of days of leave they have not utilized. The application allows Leave Request records to be created via a screen, wherein the employee for whom the leave is being requested can be chosen via a picklist. Furthermore, a simple calculation needs to be performed while creating a new Leave Request that rejects the request (i.e., saves it with a 'rejected' status)

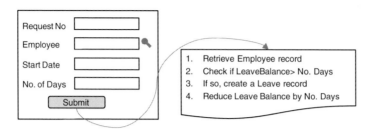

FIGURE **12.1. Leave Request example**

if the employee does not have enough leave balance. If however the leave balance is sufficient, its value is decremented by the quantity of leave applied for, and the request is approved (i.e., saved in 'approved' status).

This simple example includes features that cover many needs of basic forms-based office automation: Forms with fields of different types (including dates), the ability to link a field from one form to that of another, such as the picklist to look up employees, as well as forms for creating, searching and editing records. While this feature set is far from complete, it suffices to illustrate the idea of Dev 2.0, i.e., a reasonably complex forms-based application can be *assembled* rather than programmed, from a simple browser interface as opposed to a programming environment. Dev 2.0 platforms enable such configurability in an end-user friendly manner. Many also include more complex features such as forms with data from multiple tables, the ability to configure the 'look and feel' of the user interface, as well as definition and execution of workflows. (We shall cover workflow in more detail in Chapter 15; in Chapter 14 we shall describe *how* Dev 2.0 platforms achieve such end-user configurability.) When it comes to calculations such as computing and decrementing the leave balance, Salesforce.com requires programming using its APEX language, and this is one area where Dev 2.0 platforms differ: Some do not allow such computations, while others enable some simple computations also to be achieved in an end-user friendly manner.

Some of the steps involved in creating the Leave Request form using Force.com, such as adding a field, are shown in Figure 12.2. This involves a number of steps during which various details of the field need to be entered; however these can all be performed while *using* the application, and no separate development environment is needed. In particular, a linkage between the Leave Request form and the Employee table is automatically created simply by defining the Employee field in Leave Request as a lookup of the Employee object during one the steps of field creation.

FIGURE **12.2. Adding fields in Force.com**

Figure 12.3 depicts the leave request form created in Force.com via the above steps, as well as the APEX code required to execute the server-sided computations required when a new Leave Request record is created. This code defines a 'trigger' on the Leave Request object, so that it executes as soon as such a record is inserted. The code is able to access the database using SQL, and can update records in any table. By uploading such code that runs against triggers, fairly general computations can be performed. However, APEX development is a programmer, rather than end-user activity; in fact it is usually done from a development environment such as Eclipse. At this point the Force.com platform ceases to be an end-user configurable tool and becomes a hosted *development* platform for programmers.

## 12.2 TCS INSTANTAPPS ON AMAZON CLOUD

The Dev 2.0 platform offered by Force.com is based on the software as a service model in which computation and data reside on software and storage running on servers belonging to and managed by the SaaS provider, in this

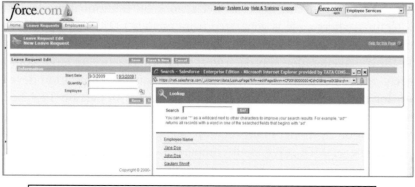

```
Trigger leaveTriggeron LeaveRequest(after insert){
    for (LeaveRequest lvrq : Trigger.new){
        ename = lvrq.Employee;
        Employee emp= [select * from Employee where EmployeeName=:ename]
        if (emp.LeaveBalance >= lvrq.Quantity){
            emp.LeaveBalance -= lvrq.Quantity;
            lvrq.Status = `Approved';
            update emp;
            update lvrq;
        } else {
            lvrq.Status = `Rejected';
            update lvrq;
        } } }
```

FIGURE 12.3. Leave Request in Force.com with APEX code

case Salesforce.com. Users, be they developers or end-users of applications, merely use the functionalities provided by the platform over the internet. In particular, end-users have limited visibility or access to the database where application data resides. Further, ensuring performance of their applications in response to increasing load is entirely left to the provider of the SaaS platform: Users neither need, nor have the ability, to manage allocated resources in anticipation of fluctuations in demand. Other Dev 2.0 platforms, which we shall briefly outline in the next section, also share a similar approach. Here we describe a different approach taken by a Dev 2.0 platform called InstantApps developed by the author's research group in TCS[1] R&D.

---

[1] Tata Consultancy Services, www.tcs.com

A precursor to InstantApps has been work on traditional model-driven architecture, where code is generated from models [32]. This experience of using code generators in enterprise software projects led to a realization that while the code-generation approach worked well in practice for large, complex projects, it had its limitations when applied to smaller application development, for reasons we shall elaborate in more detail in Section 12.4 below. InstantApps also takes a model-driven-architecture approach, but replaces code generation by model interpretation, an approach we term *model-driven interpretation*, or MDI. (We shall compare the MDA and MDI approaches in more detail in Chapter 14.) Further, instead of traditional 'modeling' using notations such as UML, InstantApps incorporates an end-user-focused WYSIWYG[2] design environment. Finally, the model interpretation approach naturally leads to a multi-tenant platform. We shall cover some of the Dev 2.0 features of InstantApps below; but first we examine its deployment model that differs significantly from other Dev 2.0 tools.

InstantApps is *not* a hosted SaaS platform such as Force.com or other Dev 2.0 tools. Instead, it is made available on the Amazon EC2 platform as an AMI image, just as many other development tools are packaged. At the same time the deployment model shares many of the characteristics of a SaaS product, including a mechanism whereby users are able, and also forced, to get regular upgrades, similar to a SaaS model where upgrades are done in a manner invisible to the end-user.

Figure 12.4 illustrates how InstantApps is deployed and used on the Amazon infrastructure cloud as compared to traditional SaaS-based Dev 2.0 products. Users provision EC2 servers using the appropriate InstantApps AMIs. The InstantApps Designer AMI includes features that allow applications to be built and customized; the InstantApps Player AMI only allows applications to run against production data. Data is stored in permanent elastic block storage (EBS) that needs to be attached to InstantApps AMI-based servers after they boot. In this manner, production data, as well as control on the size and number of servers to boot, remains in control of the user. (Along with this also comes the responsibility for ensuring sufficient resources to meet demand.) In particular, users can access their production data using SQL or connect other applications to their data. Since the servers and storage are all in their Amazon EC2 account, the data is effectively in 'control' of the user, as opposed to a SaaS-based Dev 2.0 platform where production

[2] 'what you see is what you get'.

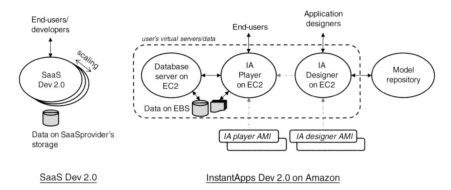

End-users/
developers

scaling

SaaS
Dev 2.0

Data on SaaSprovider's
storage

*user's virtual servers/data*

End-users

Application
designers

Database
server on
EC2

IA
Player
on EC2

IA
Designer
on EC2

Model
repository

Data on EBS

IA player AMI

IA designer AMI

SaaS Dev 2.0

InstantApps Dev 2.0 on Amazon

FIGURE **12.4. InstantApps on Amazon EC2**

data is less directly accessible to users, and is in effect controlled by the SaaS provider.

The InstantApps Designer connects to one of the Model Repository servers (common for all InstantApps users and managed by TCS); the application meta-data is populated in this repository as designers create their applications. Additionally, newer versions of InstantApps are notified through this connection, and users are asked to reboot their servers with the latest InstantApps AMIs when such upgrades take place, which can be quite often, just as in a SaaS model.

Once application design is complete, the application meta-data is transferred to the InstantApps Player as a binary file. This process is repeated each time modifications are made to the application through the Designer. Note that the InstantApps Player does not connect to a Model Repository, and therefore can continue to run without upgrading to newer versions; though such upgrades are required as soon as users wish to deploy in production any changes made to application functionality through the InstantApps Designer. In this manner, production servers can be insulated from upgrades unless actually required. Thus, the InstantApps deployment model in the cloud enjoys some of the benefits of both SaaS as well as traditional installed software products where upgrades are concerned.

We now describe WYSIWYG design of an application, such as Leave Request, using InstantApps. Starting with a blank application, a new form can be created with a single mouse click by entering a form name; an empty form is instantly created, with a blank field. Another mouse click on this blank field prompts us to enter a fieldname and type, as shown in Figure 12.5, and a fully functional new field immediately appears on the screen; this field is included

**FIGURE 12.5.  InstantApps designer**

in the database and in all layers in between. These steps are repeated to add several fields and other forms, such as the Employee form. Pages for create, search, result, edit and delete functionality are available as soon as a form is created, and can be linked from menu items as desired. An intuitive copy–paste mechanism is provided, whereby the Employee form can be 'copied' and pasted on the Leave Request form to create the picklist-based lookup of Employees in the Leave Request form. Similar copy–paste actions can create forms on multiple tables, as well as enable navigation from a button to a target form (one simply copies and pastes the target form onto the desired button). Details of the WYSIWYG features of InstantApps can be found in [53, 52].

Recall that in order to implement server-side computations, Force.com required APEX code to be written and uploaded to the hosted platform. InstantApps allows server-side code in Java to be linked to user interfaces, so a new language is not needed. More importantly, InstantApps also provides a visual modeling notation for server-side computations, called 'logic maps'. Figure 12.6 illustrates the Leave Request computation in such a logic map. The logic map contains create, search, update, compute and decision nodes, each of which are associated with forms in the application. The create, search and update nodes perform functions similar to the create, search and update pages that are created with each form, albeit on the server. The type of object flowing along each edge in the logic map depends on the form associated with the node it originates from. For example, the logic map in Figure 12.6 is called on the Leave Request form, so a Leave Request object flows into this network, denoted by edges labeled L. Once such an object flows into a Search Employees node, the output from this node is an Employee object matching the one specified in the Leave Request object's Employee field. Decision nodes check if conditions are satisfied, and computation nodes modify the

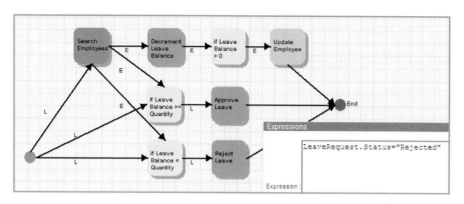

FIGURE 12.6. Logic maps in InstantApps

objects flowing in the network. Update nodes are needed to modify database records other than that on which the logic map is being triggered, such as Employee. In this manner, simple server-side computations can be defined without the need for programming. We shall cover logic maps in more detail in Chapter 14, in particular highlighting their relationship to the MapReduce model of cloud programming.

Finally, InstantApps, like other Dev 2.0 platforms including Force.com, incorporates a lightweight workflow implementation, which we shall cover briefly in Chapter 15. InstantApps also allows users to change the look and feel of the user interface, with more complex changes requiring programming, typically in JavaScript. InstantApps additionally allows its forms to be displayed as mashups within other applications, through a JavaScript mashup API, using which virtually any complex user interface can be developed, albeit by adroit developers [52].

## 12.3 MORE DEV 2.0 PLATFORMS AND RELATED EFFORTS

Forms development platforms have a long history, and some of these also use an interpretive approach: The FADS system [47] represents early work in this area, and is actually an interpretive system similar in many ways to modern Dev 2.0 platforms, but built for a VAX VMS platform! A similar approach was later reused in the academic PICASSO framework [48] and in the ABF (application by forms) tool of the INGRES database platform. These represent what we call 'first-generation' forms interpreters, as compared to the interpretive, multi-tenant architectures of Dev 2.0 platforms. (Various form 'painters' have also been included in 4GL languages, such as [37], but these are different in that they either generate code or executables rather than interpret specifications.)

In recent years many web-hosted Dev 2.0 platforms similar to Force.com have become available from startup companies. Some of these have either been acquired by larger companies, such as Jotspot by Google, Nsite by SAP, or have shut down, such as Coghead. At the same time others have risen to take their place: As of this writing some of the available web-based Dev 2.0 platforms include Bungee Labs, TrackVia, Caspio, TeamDesk, Zoho Creator, QuickBase, Qrimp, Wolf, OutSystems, PerfectForms, Cordys, Iceberg, WorkXpress and WorkLight. Each of these platforms is based on an interpretive and multi-tenant architecture, and allows creation of simple forms-based workflows. Many also allow scripting of server-side business logic in a manner similar to Force.com's APEX. Visual design of processing logic similar to that in InstantApps was available in Coghead, and will surely become available in other platforms in the future.

Other visual editors and interpretive runtimes for user interfaces have also been proposed in literature and commercially: WebRB [1] is an XML language for describing web applications that manipulate relational databases, which lends itself to visual representation and editing using a graphical editor. Similar to WebRB, Statesoft [31], is a commercial product that uses state-charts to model user interface interactions.

## 12.4 ADVANTAGES, APPLICABILITY AND LIMITS OF DEV 2.0

Dev 2.0 platforms represent a potential paradigm shift for development of small to medium enterprise applications, and can lead to significant improvements in development productivity for this class of applications. Their availability as cloud offerings further eases their adoption by end-users, circumventing possible objections from corporate IT. At the same time there are limitations to what kinds of applications are amenable to the Dev 2.0 paradigm, as well how far one can take the interpretive approach.

We first examine why web-based applications are difficult to build. The complexity of forms-based application development is compounded in a distributed web-based architecture that forces a multi-tier architectural style and influences the software process, especially downstream (coding and test). Each tier requires different technology, for example creating HTML pages,

JavaScript code, server-side Java code and database queries. Consequently it is the norm (rather than exception) to have multiple developers involved in the development of each functional feature. This necessitates a technical integration phase, whereby functional elements are tested end-to-end across all tiers. Multi-tier layering also results in a relatively large set of configurable items (pieces of code) per functional feature, which complicates assembling, compiling and building a running system as a precursor to each iteration of functional system testing.

Automation can help with the issues described above, provided one can control development and change at the level of functional features. Code generation from domain-specific languages or models has often been used for greater control. In a code-generation approach, code generators produce code for each layer from a common model. After generation and compilation this code needs to be deployed, integrated, and the system has to be reinitialized and restarted to deploy a change in functionality. If the code generators in each layer are known to be (a) correct and (b) produce code that correctly inter-operates with code generated in other layers, the unit and integration testing phases can be eliminated. However, the deployment, reinitializing and restarting steps cannot be eliminated.

The interpretive Dev 2.0 architecture represents an alternative approach. While code generation does shorten the development cycle, Dev 2.0 does better: The 'design and immediately play' approach of Dev 2.0 allows functional changes to be made from within a running application, so they can be tested as soon as the change is made. Each developer can immediately see the changes made by other developers. Thus, we have continuous integration with a single, unified application model being interpreted by all the layers in the runtime. Changes are implemented without changing running code, avoiding the build and deploy process so that system testing can be done at any level of granularity. Thus, in the multi-tier web-based setting, the interpretive approach offers significantly greater benefits in practice, provided it can be implemented efficiently.

The availability of WYSIWYG application development in platforms such as InstantApps brings with it all the traditional advantages of rapid prototyping platforms, including reduction in cycle times and reduction in defects due to better requirements elicitation. Because of these features, such Dev 2.0 platforms are particularly well suited for agile development methodologies such as extreme programming [6]. In addition, complications due to multi-tier architectures are ameliorated, enabling a compressed development cycle that avoids many technical steps, as described above and in more detail in [53].

All these benefits are multiplied by the fact that Dev 2.0 platforms enable significant application features to be created by end-users, as opposed to developers. A cloud-based deployment model enables access without any infrastructure investments. Finally, the often-cited concern regarding data ownership are mitigated by the hybrid cloud deployment model used by InstantApps.

Having said all this, the Dev 2.0 model has its limitations. First, the extent to which a pure model interpretation approach can suffice to capture the functionality needed by even small enterprise applications is, in our experience, inherently limited. This limits the features in applications that can be created by end-users using a WYSIWYG designer to a fairly useful but still restricted subset. Two major areas where the model-based approach remains essentially incomplete are (i) processing logic and (ii) user interfaces, i.e., 'look and feel' as well as complex behavior.

As we have already seen, most Dev 2.0 platforms require coding to implement processing logic, albeit in a scripting language (which is often proprietary). Visual logic designers, such as offered in InstantApps and earlier in Coghead, remain limited in the functionality they can model; for example it is not possible to implement file I/O, or complex string processing using such models as they are today. Next, note that the user interfaces of applications built using Dev 2.0 tools follow some predetermined patterns. Changing these patterns in a fundamental way is either impossible or, once again, requires coding in either JavaScript or some other proprietary language; so this level of customization too remains out of control of the end-user.

Our experience with Dev 2.0 leads us to believe that these limitations are in some way inherent. Therefore the Dev 2.0 paradigm is better viewed as a mechanism for co-development between end-users and programmers, such as in agile methodologies, rather than as an end-user development paradigm. However, used in this manner, the Dev 2.0 paradigm is truly powerful and can significantly improve software development productivity.

Finally, we have yet to see very complex applications created using Dev 2.0, such as those involving hundreds of tables and thousands of screens. The apparent simplicity of the WYSIWYG approach can in fact lead to greater complexity when the amount of functionality to be built increases by an order of magnitude. As an analogy, a WYSIWYG word processor works fine for small articles, but for a book (such as this one), LaTeX, akin to programming in this context, is more appropriate. We do however believe that this is an arena where further research is likely to be fruitful and Dev 2.0 platforms that support complex systems being developed by dozens if not hundreds of designers will become possible in the future. Naturally, these advances will have to be in tandem with increasing the scalability of Dev 2.0 platforms to tens of thousands of concurrent users for a single application; a class of systems which current Dev 2.0 platforms do not cater to either.

# PART V

# Software architecture

In this part of the book we review the fundamentals of enterprise software architecture: The information needs of many large enterprises are similar, a fact that has been exploited by packaged ERP, CRM and SCM products. Understanding how enterprise information is modeled assists in making choices regarding the applications an enterprise needs, i.e., whether to buy packaged products or build custom solutions, as well as whether to deploy systems in-house or in the cloud. Software architecture principles are the key to building custom enterprise applications efficiently. Abstracting architecture patterns leads to re-use, and eventually to Dev 2.0 platforms that enable simple applications to be built without any programming. Modeling business processes and executing them using workflow engines is also a mature example of how abstraction can lead to re-use. Finally, decision support and knowledge management are becoming increasingly crucial functions of enterprise applications. Therefore, we present an overview of search and analytics techniques using a unified, and hopefully illuminating, matrix algebra formulation.

# CHAPTER 13

# Enterprise software: ERP, SCM, CRM

So far we have traced the evolution of enterprise architectures from the early mainframes to the emerging paradigms of software as a service and cloud computing, and have examined these primarily from a technical perspective. We now turn our focus to enterprise applications and the functions they perform in the context of a large organization. In particular we study the information maintained in cross-enterprise applications such as enterprise resource planning (ERP), supply chain management (SCM) and customer relationship management (CRM).

## 13.1 ANATOMY OF A LARGE ENTERPRISE

Our first step will be to abstract the anatomy of an large corporation independent of the particular industry it may be a part of. In fact this picture is also applicable for enterprises that may not be corporations, such as governments or educational institutions, and it is only for ease of exposition that we focus on corporations. Further, since the cross-industry abstraction of enterprise software originated as MRP ('manufacturing requirements planning'), we begin by considering the manufacturing industry.

So, what does a manufacturing corporation do? It plans what products to build, when, and in what quantities. It then executes sales and marketing of its products, coordinates manufacturing across plants and suppliers, and distributes the product to customers and supports them after they have bought the product. These processes are common across discrete manufacturing (easily identifiable products such as computers or cars), as well as process industries (undifferentiated products, such as salt or oil). These basic activities are also common to other industries apart from manufacturing, such as services (financial, consulting, travel or health care). In order to generalize our discussion to non-manufacturing industries we merely need to interpret 'product' more generally, so that an insurance policy, a consulting project, or a hospital stay are also treated as 'products.'

Enterprise applications first and foremost need to keep track of information related to operations of the enterprise; after all that is why they are called 'information' systems. The core processes that take place in the enterprise are then managed by creating and manipulating this information. Figure 13.1 is our representation of a very high level 'core data model' for an enterprise.

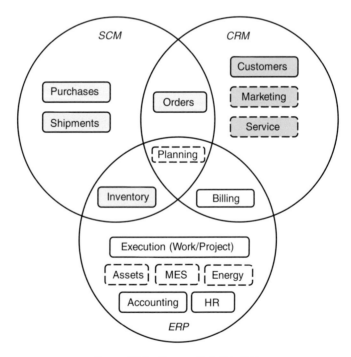

**Figure 13.1. Core enterprise data**

An enterprise has **customers**, whom it reaches out to through **marketing** and sales campaigns. These customers place **orders** for **products**. The organization then delivers products from an **inventory** and sends them to its customers via **shipments**. Note that products are stocked as inventory if the business model of the organization is to 'make for stock.' There can be alternative models such as 'make to order,' or even 'design to order,' especially when one includes non-manufacturing industries.

Manufacturing a product takes place by executing a process, or more generally through some **work** effort. The cost of such work needs to be tracked along with other material inputs required. Such material inputs also need to be **purchased**. Finally, customers are **billed**, and after-sales **services** are supplied. Incoming revenue together with the costs incurred need to be **accounted** to compute the profit made by the corporation. In addition, the people (**human resources**) in the organization need to be managed, as well as the material **assets** owned and **energy** consumed.

All the above information needs are equally applicable, albeit with appropriately adjusted semantics, for manufacturing as well as other industries. In the specific case of manufacturing industries, the micro level execution of operations in the plant has recently become the focus of detailed information tracking, analysis and optimization through 'manufacturing execution systems', or **MES**. Last but not the least, the strategic value provided by the corporation is in **planning** and coordinating all these activities through budgets and plans. For a more detailed and colloquial exposition of information systems for manufacturing industries, see [33].

Common cross-industry applications first emerged as MRP systems for manufacturing. Later these went beyond pure manufacturing to cover accounting, sales and supplies, and began to be referred to as ERP, or 'enterprise resource planning' systems. Eventually, the customer and supplier functions became increasingly complex and began to take on separate identities: Attracting customers, through sales and marketing, and servicing them afterwards are now handled by 'customer relationship management' (CRM) systems. Similarly, 'supply chain management' (SCM) systems deal with taking sales orders, issuing purchase orders, controlling the inventory of raw and finished goods, and shipping them to customers. Most of what remains falls within the purview of a core **ERP** system: This includes financial accounting, dealing with costing of all work, assets and other inputs, billing and counting incoming revenue, planning all operations, as well as managing employees.

As is seen from Figure 13.1, there are overlaps in the high-level segregation of functions across systems, such as between order management and billing that both have close interactions with CRM, while usually being grouped under SCM and ERP respectively. When dealing with packaged enterprise software, or for that matter SaaS offerings for SCM, CRM or ERP, it is important to recognize that different products may include or exclude such overlapping functions. This can lead to redundancy or require extensions and customizations to product offerings. There are also many cases where packaged solutions may not be applicable, as well as very specific processes that need custom-built software, as we shall cover in the next chapter. Here we first explore enterprise data models in some more depth so as to understand what kind of information models enterprise applications, packaged or custom, need to support. In the next few sections we examine some of the information models of Figure 13.1 in more detail. We use UML[1] class models to describe these information models; for an introduction to UML and object-oriented modeling see [20]. A complete exposition of such enterprise models, albeit as traditional data models rather than in object-oriented form, can be found in [55]. Finally, it is important to note that the models we present below are only *indicative* of how enterprise concepts could be modeled; in practice actual models can be far more complex and may also differ significantly from those illustrated here.

## 13.2 PARTNERS: PEOPLE AND ORGANIZATIONS

Corporations need to deal with other organizations, such as their customers or suppliers. They also need to deal with people in these organizations as well as with individuals as consumers of their products. Early information systems kept track of customers, suppliers and people separately, often in different applications. As a result important facts could often be overlooked during normal operations; for example a consumer complainant who happened to be a senior executive of a major corporate customer would not be treated specially by a call-center employee. Opportunities for cross-sell and up-sell to existing customers were also lost.

The current practice is to unify customer, supplier and people models wherever possible. This involves representing both organizations and people

---

[1] Unified Modeling Language.

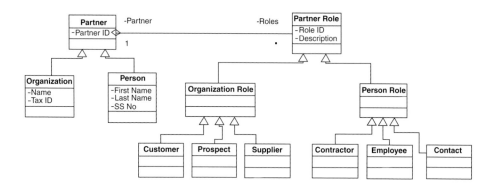

PARTNER TABLE

| Partner ID | First Name | Last Name |
|---|---|---|
| 1001 | | ABC Inc |
| 2003 | John | Doe |
| 1040 | | XYZ Supplies |
| 1699 | | EZ Software |

PARTNER–ROLE TABLE

| Partner ID | Role ID | Description |
|---|---|---|
| 1001 | 1 | Customer |
| 2003 | 5 | Employee |
| 2003 | 6 | Contact |
| 1699 | 1 | Customer |
| 1699 | 2 | Prospect |

FIGURE **13.2.** **Partner model**

as 'partners,' who play different, and possibly multiple roles. A simple partner model is illustrated in Figure 13.2, as a UML class diagram. We see that a **partner** can be an **organization** or a **person**; this relationship is therefore modeled in UML as a *generalization*, using class inheritance. Partners can play one or more **partner roles**, and this relationship is modeled as an *aggregation*. Partner role is also sub-classed into different actual roles, such as customer, supplier, or employee, via a role hierarchy. A *partial* representation of aspects of this class model in terms of relational tables, as shown in Figure 13.2, is to have a PARTNER table and a PARTNER-ROLE table, with partner ID being a foreign key representing a one-to-many relationship between these tables. Note that for the sake of simplicity we have not shown how the role hierarchy could be implemented in relational form and its impact on the PARTNER-ROLE table. There are many steps involved in translating a logical class model into a relational representation, including different options for translating class inheritance to relational tables; see [55] for more details of this process.

Communications with partners, as modeled in Figure 13.3, take place using established **contact mechanisms**, which can be postal or electronic. As before,

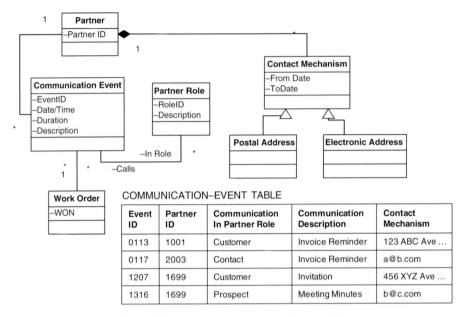

COMMUNICATION–EVENT TABLE

| Event ID | Partner ID | Communication In Partner Role | Communication Description | Contact Mechanism |
|---|---|---|---|---|
| 0113 | 1001 | Customer | Invoice Reminder | 123 ABC Ave ... |
| 0117 | 2003 | Contact | Invoice Reminder | a@b.com |
| 1207 | 1699 | Customer | Invitation | 456 XYZ Ave ... |
| 1316 | 1699 | Prospect | Meeting Minutes | b@c.com |

FIGURE **13.3. Partner communications model**

a *partial* relational representation of this model is also illustrated, where there is a one-to-many relationship between the **partner** and **communication event** classes captured through the inclusion of `Partner-ID` as a foreign key in the `COMMUNICATION-EVENT` table. Further, the many-to-many relationship between **communication event** and **partner role** is *de-normalized* and captured by an attribute `Communication-In-Partner-Role` in this table. Usually communications are also associated with other parts of the enterprise model, such as with 'work order' (which we shall cover later) for charging any costs incurred to effect the communication.

We have simplified the partner model considerably. In a real enterprise this model is often highly complex, incorporating concepts such as the internal structure of organizations, their employee hierarchies, the history of communications captured as threads, and many more concepts. Further, as we have discussed earlier in Chapter 10, the relational representation of an object model is not necessarily optimal when using a cloud database. For this reason and also since the models we explore in the sections to follow are more complex than the simple partner model, we shall describe them as class models only and refrain from illustrating any relational representations.

## 13.3 PRODUCTS

An organization produces as well as uses **products**; these can be **goods** or **services**, as depicted in the model of Figure 13.4. Often many products are produced or consumed by an organization and it becomes important to classify them in many ways, such as by model, grade, segment or other **product category**. Product categories may contain or be contained within other categories; for example 'paper' and 'pencil' are both in the 'office supplies' category. Note how such a many-to-many relationship is modeled as an *association class* in UML. In a normalized relational data model this would translate to a 'link table' with both `product-ID` and `category-ID` as foreign keys pointing to the `PRODUCT` and `PRODUCT-CATEGORY` tables.

A product may have one or more **product features**. How product is priced can depend on **price components** associated with these features, with the product itself, or with other **order attributes**, such as the value or type (e.g. retail vs. bulk) of an order.

Figure 13.4 models actual instances of products and their supply. Instances of physical goods, as opposed to services (which we shall cover later), are maintained as **inventory items**, which are stored in a storage **facility** such as a warehouse or production plant. Inventory items that are not produced by the enterprise itself need to be purchased from some supplier **organizations**. The **product suppliers** for such products along with their ratings, preferences and

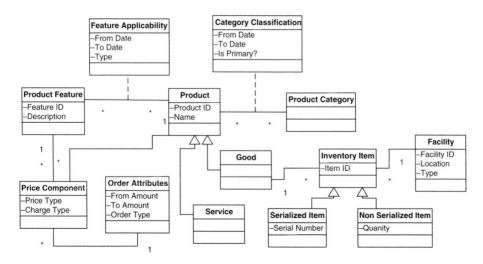

FIGURE **13.4. Product model**

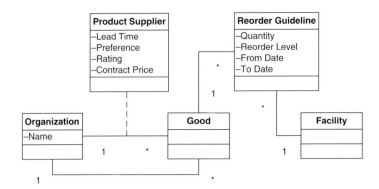

FIGURE **13.5. Product supply model**

contract rates are tracked. Additionally, information on which products any particular supplier is capable of producing is also captured. Finally, policies on how much inventory is to be maintained are defined by **reorder guidelines** for each product.

## 13.4 ORDERS: SALES AND PURCHASES

A corporation conducts business by accepting sales orders and then shipping goods or delivering services against these orders. In addition, it places orders for products that it may require, i.e. procurements. Largely similar aspects need to be tracked for both types of orders, such as who placed the order, where and when it is to be delivered, for what price and against what quotation, how the order was placed and who approved it.

Figure 13.6 illustrates a unified model for sales and purchase **orders**. Each order is composed of a number of **order items**. Each order item can be for a **product** or a **product feature**. Each order involves a number of partners playing different roles, such as who placed the order, who is to be billed, and to whom each order item is to be shipped. Further, orders are placed through a contact mechanism of the partner concerned, and each order item also captures the contact mechanism by which it needs to be shipped. When **shipments** are made to fulfill orders, they contain a number of **shipment items**. It is important to note that an order item may end up getting supplied by multiple shipments, or conversely one shipment item may fulfill many order items in possibly different orders. Therefore, order items and shipment

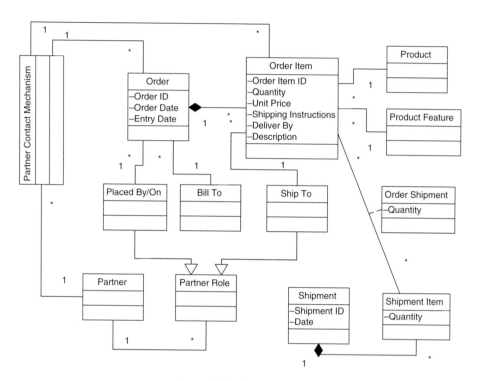

**FIGURE 13.6.  Order model**

items are linked by a class association **order shipment** that tracks the quantity
in a particular shipment item against a particular order item.

The order model of Figure 13.6 is usually handled by a supply chain application. However, getting from a customer request to a sales order is the purview
of the sales process usually handled by a CRM application. The corresponding
process for purchases is normally part of the procurement component of SCM.
In either case, before an order is placed, a **request** is usually received from
a customer, or placed on one or more suppliers. Figure 13.7 depicts a quote
model that tracks requests to orders via quotations and agreements: A request
may contain many **request items**. The receiving organization responds with
a **quote**, containing **quote items**, each of which is for some goods and/or
services that the organization can supply, for a quoted price. Once the quote
is exchanged, negotiations take place leading to an **agreement** (or contract)
being drawn up between the two organizations. The agreement lays out the
pricing arrangement comprising of a number of **agreement items** corresponding to price components for the products requested, to include any discounts

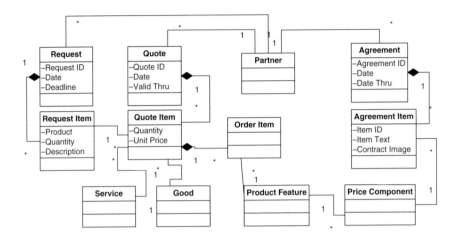

FIGURE 13.7. Quote model

and terms negotiated. Orders are then placed against the quote, based on the same price components contained in the agreement items.

## 13.5 EXECUTION: TRACKING WORK

In addition to supplying goods, corporations also provide services that involve expending some work efforts by their employees, which may be directly or indirectly billed. Additionally, designing and manufacturing products, research and development, and all such internal efforts have associated costs that need to be tracked. The model in Figure 13.8 tracks **work orders**; these may be created in response to incoming **sales orders**, or **internal requirements**. Note that we have used multiple inheritance to describe the fact that work orders may arise in two different ways. This also means that each sales order or internal requirement is in fact also a work order, in other words our model does not distinguish between these concepts. Work orders are often also called 'projects' and have explicit names. Thus our model ensures that as soon as an order is received (or some internal requirement approved), a project to ensure its completion is also begun.

Work orders are fulfilled by expending **effort**, which captures the details of the planned and actual efforts. Efforts can be broken down into sub-efforts as captured by the **effort breakdown** class. Note that a work order can be fulfilled by many efforts, likewise, the model also allows for an effort to contribute

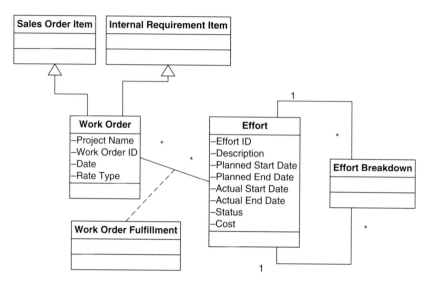

FIGURE **13.8. Work model**

to multiple work orders. However, in practice an effort is usually associated with a single work order for simplicity.

Our work model captures the essential aspects of effort tracking, such as how a requirement results in work orders for which a complex series of efforts may be planned and executed. However, it leaves out other expenses associated with fulfillment of a work order, such as the use of physical assets, consumable items and expenditure on travel. Further, internal requirements that arise out of planning can be quite complex, as they may arise for a number of reasons to which linkages may need to be maintained, such as anticipated sales, scheduled maintenance, sales and marketing efforts, or research and development.

Effort is spent by people working on assigned tasks. The model in Figure 13.9 captures the **party** assigned to a particular effort, where parties can be **employees** of an organization or **contractors**. When effort is assigned to a party, it can have an associated **rate**. Alternatively, the rate (cost or charge) can be based on the **level** of an employee or the rate charged by a particular contractor. The actual `cost-rate` or `billed-rate` is captured in the rate class. Each rate can have an associated `rate-type` (or rate 'schedule'). Note that the rate schedule to use for a particular work order is also captured in the work order class, as shown earlier in Figure 13.8, so efforts against the work order can use the appropriate charging or costing rates.

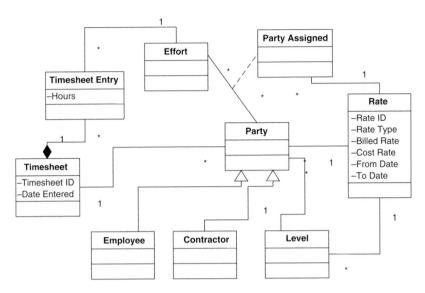

FIGURE 13.9. **Rates and timesheets**

Once parties complete some effort, they enter it into a **timesheet**, containing **timesheet items**. Each timesheet item corresponds to the time spent on a particular work effort. Timesheets are central to large parts of the services industry, as also to shop floor operations in manufacturing plants, and are critical for billing, costing and accounting.

## 13.6 BILLING

Once products have been delivered, customers must billed and payments received. Similarly, payments need to be disbursed for purchases made from suppliers. In either case payments need to be traced to invoices along with the billable goods or services against which an invoice was raised. Figure 13.10 illustrates a basic billing model. Billing involves raising an **invoice** on a partner (or receiving an invoice from a supplier); so invoices can be sales invoices or purchase invoices. Since there may be additional partners associated with an invoice, such as the 'ship to' or 'ordered by' partner which may differ from the 'bill to' partner, we include all of these via a class association **invoice role** between invoice and partner.

An invoice may comprise of many **invoice items** each capturing the amount being invoiced for some goods or services along with their

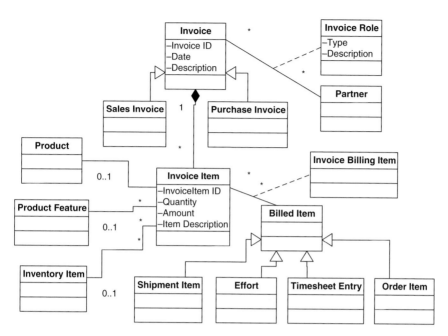

**FIGURE 13.10. Billing model**

description and quantity. Each invoice item can correspond to a **product**, a **product feature** or a specific **inventory item**; these are therefore shown as optional associations to the corresponding classes. Further, each invoice item is linked to actual delivery of some goods or services, i.e. one or more **billed items**: each billed item may be a **shipment item**, some **effort** or **timesheet entry**. Alternatively invoices may be billed on order, in which case a billed item may be an **order item**.

Once an invoice has been sent, payments are received against it. (For procurements, this is reversed, i.e. payments are disbursed against invoices received.) Figure 13.11 shows a payment model. Payments can be **receipts** or **disbursements** and are made by a partner. A payment captures the amount being paid, a reference-number, and the date when the payment becomes effective (as opposed to when it is physically received). A payment may be applied against one or more invoice items; likewise many payments may be made against a single invoice item. This many-to-many relationship is modeled as a **payment invoice** class association. Finally, each payment results in a **financial transaction** in some **bank account**; receipts result in deposits and disbursements result withdrawals. Note that financial transactions are

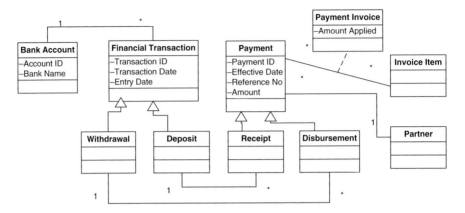

**FIGURE 13.11. Payment model**

real-world transactions between legal entities through a third-party financial institution (such as a bank).

## 13.7 ACCOUNTING

Financial transactions, such as payments, clearly affect the financial position of an enterprise. But so do invoices that are raised but not paid, as well as inventory build up, which represents a potential loss if it cannot be sold. The financial position of the enterprise is captured by its accounting model, wherein *accounting* transactions are created to reflect the impact of each *business* transaction (such as actual payments or mere invoices) on the financial position of the enterprise.

The financial structure of an enterprise is captured through its chart of accounts, comprising of a set of 'general ledger' (GL) accounts. Each GL account represents a bucket into which accounting transactions are posted. Figure 13.12 illustrates a simple accounting model. The **general ledger accounts** each have a GL-ID, name, and description: Examples are 'cash' account, 'accounts receivable,' 'payments owed' and 'travel expenses.' A GL account also has an account-type that captures its place in the organization's balance sheet, specifying whether the account tracks revenues, expenses, assets or liabilities.

The chart of accounts consisting of the set of GL accounts determines how the enterprise captures financial information. However, in a large organization financial reporting is needed at the level of each **budget entity**, i.e. an

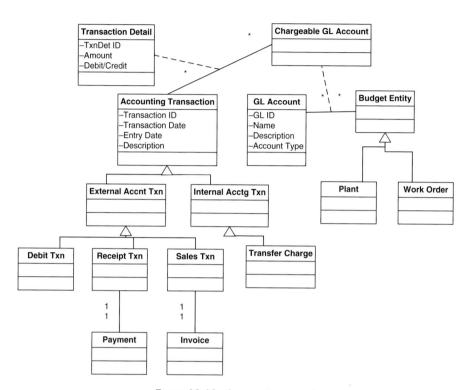

**FIGURE 13.12. Accounting model**

entity that has the ability to spend or receive money, such as a manufacturing plant, or project. GL accounts are related to such budget entities via
**chargeable accounts**, against which actual accounting transactions are posted.
Using chargeable accounts and relationships amongst them (not shown in the
figure), a profit and loss statement or complete balance sheet can be drawn up
for any chargeable account or collection thereof, including the organization
as a whole.

As mentioned earlier, accounting transactions are posted for certain business transactions. An **accounting transaction** may be an **internal transaction**,
such as a *transfer charge* between two parts of the organization, or an **external transaction**. Such external transactions can be real financial transactions,
such as payments, and so posted to a 'cash' GL account. Alternatively these
could be invoices, representing a future obligation by another party to pay,
and therefore posted to an 'asset' GL account. In case an invoice is not paid
it becomes a bad debt, and needs to be transferred to another 'liability' GL
account through matching credit and debit accounting transactions.

Accounting is a complex function as can be seen even from the highly simplified model above. It is also a core function of the IT systems of any enterprise. Accounting functions are very similar across enterprises, and almost all enterprises use packaged software providing generalized accounting systems. Original ERP systems grew out of such accounting packages as a means to automate the capture of business transactions and relate them to accounting transactions in a configurable manner so that a single system could serve the needs of an enterprise. As we discuss in the next section, this is both an advantage as well as a disadvantage of integrated ERP packages.

## 13.8 ENTERPRISE PROCESSES, BUILD VS. BUY AND SaaS

Original ERP systems were designed around the accounting function, seeking to expand it to cover different types of business transactions. Depending on their roles, users would have access to different types of business transactions. So, sales people would have access to order creation and invoice generation, but not effort tracking or shipments. In such a scenario, the ability to easily track an order from inception to collection of payments was missing. Tracking such an 'order to cash' process is critical to organizational efficiency. Similar end-to-end processes are involved in managing inventory or procurements. Each such 'horizontal' (see Chapter 4) process usually cuts across different parts of the enterprise data model.

If an organization were to build its systems from ground up, it should ideally implement end-to-end processes on a unified underlying data model. However the situation gets complicated when packaged software is used. For example, suppose a core ERP package does not cover, say, shipments, and custom software is developed to track these. Shipments need to be linked to order items, as we have already seen. The order items must correspond to those maintained in the core ERP system. All this is still doable, using various APIs that a core ERP system usually provides. Now, consider the case where *two* major packages are used, say an SCM and a core ERP system. The SCM will also maintain order items and customer shipping details, which will have to be kept synchronized with those in the core ERP system. Add a CRM package and now customer information is being tracked in three systems, which all need to remain synchronized.

Further complications arise because of domain specific functionality, as opposed to the cross-industry functions we have covered so far: For example, financial services organizations may need to deal with trading and securities transactions. These require a complex partner model including brokers, customers, stock exchanges and banks. A standard CRM package would be unlikely to include these aspects. At the same time the core CRM functionality provided in a CRM package would be expensive to redevelop. Thus, the 'build vs. buy' decision needs to consider the challenges of integration between software packages, legacy systems, and custom applications need to be weighed against the high costs of developing and maintaining a single integrated application with a unified data model.

Additional considerations arise when deciding which enterprise applications are appropriate for software as a service (SaaS). Here, apart from data security considerations (or fears), it is important to consider not only the degree of replication of data but also the volume of data that would be need to be regularly transferred from the SaaS system to applications deployed on premise. From this point of view, CRM systems are well suited for SaaS, since the only point of replication is some customer data. New customers are added, or customer details updated, relatively slowly as compared to business transactions; so synchronizing customer data in the SaaS product with on-premise applications poses less of an overhead. Order management is another natural candidate for SaaS, especially in conjunction with web-based orders. Human resources is another such case where SaaS is a plausible option: A SaaS HR system can generate a monthly payroll and even broker direct debits and credits from bank accounts of the organization and employees. On the other hand, if one considers SCM or other parts of core ERP, the situation is different as the volume of data transfer involved may be significantly higher. Furthermore, the closer these systems are linked to physical assets such as manufacturing plants, inventories in warehouses, the less attractive they become as candidates for SaaS, or cloud-based deployment. We shall return to this thread of discussion towards the end of the book in Chapter 18.

# CHAPTER 14

# Custom enterprise applications and Dev 2.0

In the previous chapter we examined the myriad information needs of a typical enterprise. We saw that at a high level these needs can be distributed across CRM, SCM or core ERP systems, which can be implemented as enterprise systems using packaged products or SaaS offerings. At the same time certain horizontal business processes, or domain-specific functionality may necessitate custom application development.

In this chapter we shall explore *how* such enterprise systems are built, whether as part of a packaged product or a custom-built application. In the process we shall examine the technical architecture layers, abstractions and principles required to build modern scalable enterprise applications.

In Chapter 12 we described the emerging Dev 2.0 paradigm that enables application development to be done largely without custom programming. Our discussion of technical architecture principles, common practices and abstractions will also enable us to understand how Dev 2.0 platforms are internally architected.

## 14.1 SOFTWARE ARCHITECTURE FOR ENTERPRISE COMPONENTS

As we saw in Figure 4.1 of Chapter 4, enterprise applications can be viewed as consisting of *application components*, each of which is responsible for a

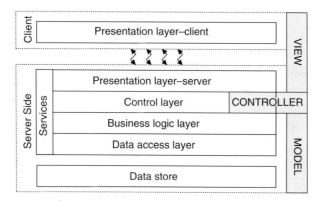

FIGURE 14.1. Architecture layers

collection of enterprise sub-processes that all access a cohesive set of data items, such as a 'partner,' or 'order' model as covered in the previous chapter.

At the technical level each application component can be viewed as an independent application, or a part ('module') of a larger enterprise application, such as a CRM package. What is important for the discussion below is that the application (component) performs the following tasks: It maintains some information in a **data store**, supports user interactions with this information through a **presentation layer**, and in the process executes some **business logic** computations. Figure 14.1 depicts such a *layered* architecture. These architecture layers correspond to those of a traditional 'model-view-controller' (or MVC) design, wherein the user interface and information model are separated by a control layer. The useful properties of such a design are well known [34], and we shall cover these in more detail in the next section.

To see how the layered architecture of Figure 14.1 is implemented in practice, consider, as an example, a typical 'application server' architecture (such as Apache Tomcat, or a J2EE platform, as discussed in Chapter 2): The 'client' is a browser that connects via HTTP to an application server. The application server could be deployed on a cloud platform such as Amazon EC2, on any server on the internet or a server within an internal enterprise network. The presentation layer comprises of client-side JavaScript code that runs in the browser as well as server-side JSPs. The business logic layer is Java code that executes in the appropriate application server container (i.e. servlet or EJB). The business logic layer accesses the data store (typically a relational database) via a data access layer. The controller layer is responsible for (a) regulating access from the presentation to the business logic and data layers as well as (b) implementing access control, i.e. application level security. Finally, in addition to these layers, the entire application can make some of its functionality available to other applications through services, such as web services or mashups as discussed in Chapter 7.

## 14.2 USER INTERFACE PATTERNS AND BASIC TRANSACTIONS

### 14.2.1 Layered MVC and the AJAX Paradigm

Functions performed by typical transaction-processing applications, such as capturing orders, or maintaining inventory data, involve users viewing, entering and modifying information stored in the data store through data-entry and manipulation screens, such as the 'order entry' screen illustrated in Figure 14.2. Let us consider the sequence of steps that take place while entering a new order using this screen. We assume a layered architecture such as in Figure 14.1; in particular a browser-based J2EE architecture: The user accesses a URL that returns an HTML page and enters data. This data needs to be *validated*, ensuring for example that numeric data is entered into numeric

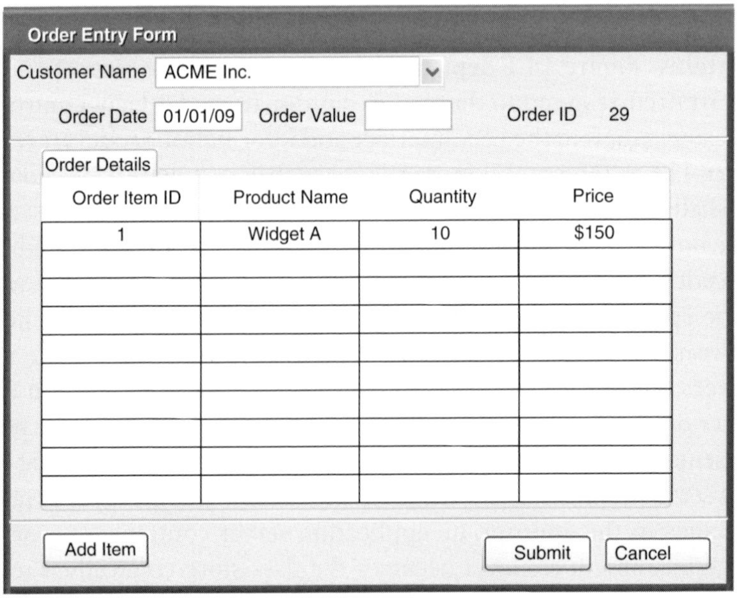

FIGURE 14.2. An order entry Form

fields. Such validations are usually done through JavaScript functions embedded in the HTML page. Next the data is sent across the network, as an HTTP POST request (or an AJAX request, see Chapter 7) to the *server side* of the presentation layer. The server-side presentation layer is implemented using a servlet container[1] in the J2EE architecture. The server-side presentation layer manages user-interface *state*, i.e. data entered or modified by the user, before it is submitted to the remaining layers. For example, while entering a single object, such as an order and its associated order items, a fresh HTML page is invoked for each order item via the 'Add Item' button. Since the HTTP protocol is essentially memoryless and asynchronous, it is more efficient to maintain partially entered data in memory on the server rather than exchange this information repeatedly over the network. (In J2EE parlance, server-side memory constructs called 'form-beans' are used for such purposes.) However, we note that in a traditional client-server architecture, such server-side functionality was not needed, since state could be maintained within the 'fat-client' application itself. Similarly, in the emerging AJAX paradigm, user interface state can also be cached in the browser between different asynchronous requests from the *same* HTML page. Thus, the server-side presentation layer is once again becoming partially redundant. (When the user navigates to a new HTML page, however, the JavaScript memory space is lost, so maintaining server-side presentation state can still be useful even in the AJAX paradigm.)

Now let us understand the motivation for the controller layer in more detail: Consider again a data entry task that spans multiple 'pages.' How does the user navigate from page to page? In a client-server architecture, as also with the AJAX paradigm, such navigation is implemented by the client application or JavaScript user interface respectively. However, in a traditional web architecture, each such page would be retrieved in response to a HTTP POST request, with the decision of which page to return being taken on the server. This architectural constraint led to the development of sophisticated controller frameworks, such as 'Struts,'[2] and 'Spring.'[3] Navigation rules defining which page follows another could be coded in the controller layer using such frameworks. The controller layer also decides which 'model' functions, either business logic or data access, to call, and in what order. It is also responsible for exchanging data between the model and presentation layers along

[1] See Chapter 2.
[2] http://struts.apache.org
[3] http://www.springsource.org

with data type transformations entailed by the fact that data received from the client over HTTP comprises of ASCII strings, while implementations of business logic and data access are expected to accept strongly typed parameters in binary representation.

Let us now examine the above layered web architecture from the perspective of the traditional MVC paradigm [34]: The controller layer as described above performs many of the functions required by MVC; for example it isolates the presentation layer from remaining layers, so that in cases where model functions change (e.g. new business logic is introduced) these can be easily introduced into the application code in a maintainable manner. However, an important feature of traditional MVC, which the layered web architecture does *not* fulfill, is that in case model information changes value, the controller is supposed to immediately reflect this change in the 'view' or presentation layer: Clearly if a user accesses a database record its latest value is shown. However, if the record changes *while* a user is viewing it, the user's view of the record is *not* immediately updated; since no new HTTP request has been made so no new data can received from the server! It is important to note that in the AJAX paradigm the client can, and usually does, make periodic *asynchronous* calls to the server so that a *true* MVC model is far easier to implement.

Now let us examine how the controller layer changes in an AJAX paradigm as compared to the traditional layered web architecture: Using AJAX, navigation from one page to another within the same logical database transaction is most often possible *without* requesting a new HTML page. Thus, some of the navigation functions of the controller move to the client side, much as in the traditional client-server architecture. The remaining functions of a controller, such as interfacing with other layers are implemented on the server side as before. The modified layered architecture in the AJAX paradigm is shown in Figure 14.3.

Finally, recall that modern AJAX-based user interfaces make use of *mashup* services, as described in Chapter 7. Note that each mashup service must also essentially replicate a layered architecture as in Figure 14.3. In addition the client-side controller of the *calling* application must also handle calls to different mashups, taking care of parameter passing between these.

## 14.2.2 Common UI patterns

We have covered in some detail *how* a browser user interface communicates with a server. It is just as important to focus on *what* functionality such an

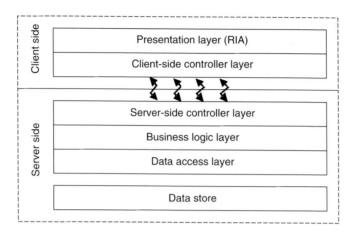

FIGURE 14.3. MVC layering with AJAX

interface should contain. As we have seen in the previous chapter, there are many data model patterns that are common across enterprises. These can form a basis for defining the information maintained by an enterprise application. Similarly, it is possible to elicit commonly occurring user-interaction patterns for a class of applications. For example, 'transaction-processing' applications, wherein users enter, modify and search for data records in the course of executing a business process, such as 'order management,' form one such class. In contrast, 'decision-support' applications involve complex visualizations of data based on different kinds of analytics, and we shall cover such applications in detail in Chapter 16.

Consider again the order-entry transaction of Figure 14.2, wherein a new order needs to be entered, either by an order-entry clerk or by an end customer via an online form. Referring to the order model of Figure 13.6 of Chapter 13, the order-entry transaction needs to ensure that a new order record along with all associated order item records are created. During this process information regarding the product or product features being ordered, for which customer, along with appropriate billing and shipping addresses need to be searched, chosen and linked to the order object being created. It should be clear that even such a simple process can potentially have many complex variations depending on the structure of the products and features being ordered, the way customers and their various addresses are stored, as well as intricacies of product pricing and shipping charges. Consequently the user interface of even a simple order-entry transaction can involve detailed design and custom development. Developing such user interfaces makes up a large component of application programming efforts.

## 14.2.3 Formal models and frameworks

Now let us see whether we can find some abstractions within the order entry transaction that might enable us to more formally model its behavior. Let us formally define a *form* as a set of *fields* corresponding to columns in the application database. These fields could correspond to columns of multiple tables, but for the moment we assume all fields in a form correspond to columns from a single table. For example, *fields* `customer_name`, `order_date`, and `order_id` comprise the 'order' *form*, and each corresponds to a column of the ORDER table. At the same time another 'customer' *form* might have fields `customer_name` and `customer_address`, corresponding to columns of the CUSTOMER table. Similarly `order_id`, `quantity`, etc., are fields in the 'order item' form. *Fields* with the same name in different *forms*, such as `customer_name` in the 'order' and 'customer' forms, or `order_id` in the 'order' and 'order item' forms, have a special significance, as we shall see below. Let us define the following primitive user interface patterns, or 'pages' for any *form F*:

$$\text{\textbf{Pages of a form:}} \hspace{4cm} (14.1)$$

1. A `Search` page retrieves a set of records matching any values entered into *F*'s fields and returns them as a result set *R*.
2. A `Result` page displays the result set *R* from a search operation and allows any one of the displayed records to be selected for editing or deletion.
3. An `Edit` page allows any fields of *F* for a particular record to be edited by the user and the changes submitted to the server.
4. A `Create` page allows a new record to be created via an entry screen displaying the fields of *F*.

The 'order entry' screen shown in Figure 14.2 is an example of a `Create` page for the 'order' form. Figure 14.4 depicts a 'search orders' screen, which is an example of the `Search` and `Result` 'pages' of the 'order' form: Here two 'pages,' i.e., `Search` and `Result`, albeit of the same form, 'order,' are included in the same screen. In general a 'page' of a form can include other

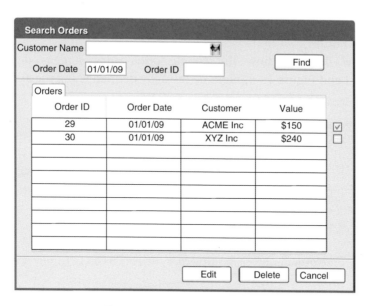

**FIGURE 14.4. Search orders form**

'pages,' possibly of different forms: For example, the `Create` 'page' of the 'order' form in Figure 14.2 includes the `Result` 'page' of the 'order item' form. Note that the two pages from different forms are linked through the common field `order_id`, so that the order items shown in the screen correspond to the particular order being entered.

Notice also that an entry field of F could be one whose value is directly entered by the user, chosen via a fixed set of choices presented as a drop-down list, or chosen from a 'list of values' (LOV) thrown up by *another* search form that opens in a pop-up window. For example, the `customer_name` field in the 'order' form may be defined in this manner as an LOV, taking values from the 'customer' form. Here the fact that the two forms share the same field is again important, with this field, `customer_name` being used to search the customer form.

A form can also have any number of buttons that enable a user to navigate from one form to another, or alternatively, to display other 'related' forms on the same page. For example, the 'Add Item' button in the order-entry screen of Figure 14.2 navigates to the `Create` page of the 'order items' form. Once again, the fact that the 'order' and 'order item' forms are related by the common field `order_id` is used to ensure that the `order_id` field is automatically populated with the correct value (i.e. the order_id of the order being entered) in the `Create` page of the 'order item' form each time it is invoked via the 'Add Item' button.

We now illustrate how the simple order-entry screens depicted in Figure 14.2 and Figure 14.4 might be formally defined using the abstractions (14.1):

$$order \xrightarrow{\text{has fields}} order\_date, \ customer\_name, \ order\_id$$

$$Create(order) \xrightarrow{\text{invokes}} Create(order\_item)$$

$$Edit(order) \xrightarrow{\text{invokes}} Create(order\_item)$$

$$Create(order) \xrightarrow{\text{includes}} Result(order\_item)$$

$$Edit(order) \xrightarrow{\text{includes}} Result(order\_item)$$

$$customer\_id \xrightarrow{\text{type}} LOV(customer, \ customer\_id)$$

$$menu \xrightarrow{\text{has items}} New \ Order, Search \ Orders$$

$$New \ Order \xrightarrow{\text{invokes}} Create(order)$$

$$Search \ Orders \xrightarrow{\text{invokes}} Search(order)$$

Here each line is generated using a production rule of a formal grammar based on the abstractions (14.1). Therefore the type of each token is defined implicitly, so *order* is a *form* and *customer_id* is a field. Using such a formalism one can define which fields the *order* form contains, their types, and which other forms are either included in or linked to from this form. For example both the `Create` and `Edit` page of the *order* form *include* a `Result` page of the *order_item* form, which displays the order items for the particular order being created or edited. In addition, both these forms also display a button to *invoke* the `Create` page of the *order_item* form, so that new order items can be entered for the order while creating or editing an order. As already mentioned above, the common field *order_id* between the *order* and *order_item* forms ensures that the `OrderItem` record being created or edited corresponds to the correct `Order` record in either case. Further, the main menu of the application is seen to 'have' items *New Order* and *Search Orders* that invoke the appropriate pages of the *order* form.

To see how such a formal approach can be useful, consider a web-based order-entry interface where the customer is first entering his own details and then placing an order, as opposed to the scenario above that was more suited to an order-entry clerk entering orders on behalf of already existing customers. All we need to add is a navigation rule:

$$Create(customer) \xrightarrow{invokes} Create(order)$$

Now the `Create` customer page will include a link to a `Create` order page. Further, as before, since these forms share a common field *customer_name*, this field will be automatically filled when the user navigates the link.

Clearly, our formalism does not include many aspects of what goes into programming a user interface, such as the color scheme, which widgets are used for entry fields and links, how results are displayed (tabular formats), or how data which is entered is validated (including complex cross validations across data fields). Covering all of these aspects through a similar formalism would be cumbersome to say the least, and these are best left for programming. So what use is a formalism such as ours? The important thing is that *once* this 'programming' has been done for an instance of each page type (i.e. `Search`, `Edit`, etc.) and for each production rule of the grammar, the same 'framework' can be simply reused for *all* the forms in the application, and in fact for other applications as well. This is in fact what is done while building large enterprise application suites, such as ERP packages (SAP, Oracle 11i, etc.). It is also the basis for Dev 2.0 platforms such as Salesforce.com and InstantApps, as we shall cover in detail later in this chapter.

The creation and maintenance of such technical architecture frameworks is widespread in the industry. It is tempting to hope that there could be a universal framework that could be reused more widely across organizations. Unfortunately, the advance of technology makes any such framework rapidly obsolete. For example, many such frameworks created using JSPs and Struts are now considered antiquated in the face of the AJAX paradigm for web interfaces. Many AJAX-based frameworks will emerge, and will in turn be replaced as technology advances further.

At the same time, it is in the face of such rapidly advancing technology that the value of formalisms becomes most evident: If one has captured the user-interface behavior of an application in a formal *model*, with the programming details of how exactly this behavior is rendered *left out*, one can reuse the model of the application by re-encoding the patterns underlying the formalism (i.e the *meta-model*) using new technology. As we shall see later, this process can be automated via code generators, or interpreters as in the Dev 2.0 paradigm.

However there is a small but important caveat; what if new technology enables a completely new pattern? In this case the formalism (i.e. meta-model) itself needs to be extended, so the *model* of the application will need to change as well. We shall return to this issue in Section 14.4 below.

## 14.3 BUSINESS LOGIC AND RULE-BASED COMPUTING

### 14.3.1 What does business logic do?

Clearly there is more to an application than the user interface. How data is retrieved, and what happens when data is entered, manipulated and submitted to the server is often referred to as 'business logic.' Once again we consider a J2EE web application server architecture to illustrate how business logic works.

Business logic is part of the 'model' layer in MVC parlance. Pure presentation-related aspects are strictly not part of this layer. The controller layer in a layered MVC architecture is responsible for passing data to the model layer after it has been stripped of presentation-related aspects. For example, when an HTML form is submitted via a POST request, it is parsed by the controller layer, field values are extracted from the received REQUEST object and converted to, say, Java classes, which are passed to appropriate class methods inside the servlet container. Alternatively, business logic code may execute in a separate container, such as an EJB container (as described in Chapter 2). In modern web architectures using the AJAX paradigm, apart from serving up new pages and handling page submissions, the server also needs to process asynchronous HTTP requests initiated by JavaScript code running in the browser.

The functionality handled by the business logic layer can vary widely even within the same application. However, as in the case of user interfaces, we can identify some common primitive abstractions here as well. Consider again our order entry transaction example: As data regarding a new order along with all its order items is entered by the user, many server-side requests are likely to be made to save intermediate data, such as each order item as it is entered. The job of storing this intermediate data, usually in memory, remains the responsibility of the server-side presentation layer, as mentioned earlier. When all the data pertaining to a single order has been entered, the user will perform some action, such as press the 'submit' button, which is recognized by the controller layer causing it to invoke the appropriate business logic method, say `Order.enterOrder()`, on an object `Order`. The attribute values of this object are populated by the controller using data captured during the entry process. Note that such an object may contain many nested `OrderItem` objects, i.e. it may represent many database records that need to be created.

What does `enterOrder()` do? It could for example (i) verify whether the order has been completely entered, such as whether a customer-id has been entered, and whether each order item has a product-id and quantity; (ii) it may compute the total value of the order after adding shipping charges (which may depend on where the order is being shipped to); (iii) it would then prepare and submit all the required data manipulation (SQL) statements to the database as part of a single database transaction. In the process it would also take care to (iv) retrieve the order-id that may have been assigned by the database after inserting the ORDER record for this order, and ensure that this order-id value is also included in each inserted ORDER ITEM record so as to link it to the parent order. In addition, it may be necessary to enter records in other tables, such as an accounting transaction for the order. This would usually be done by (v) calling methods on other objects (e.g. the `OrderAccountingTransaction` object). Clearly similar logic is required when modifying an existing order.

Similarly, while retrieving orders and their items against a search criterion, say 'all orders placed in the past ten days,' (vi) complex or possibly multiple SELECT statements may need to be executed; for example retrieving orders and items together in a complex join or fetching orders first and followed by related items for each order. (The method used will differ depending on whether one is using a traditional relational database, or a more object-oriented cloud database where, while there are no joins, traversing from an order to its items is fast and easy, as we have already seen in Chapter 10.) We can now summarize the tasks a business logic method needs to handle as follows:

$$\text{Functions of business logic:} \qquad (14.2)$$

1. Validations (e.g. verifying whether the order is complete)
2. Computations (e.g. computing a total)
3. Transaction Management (e.g. accomplishing all required operations in the scope of a single database transaction)
4. Data Manipulation (e.g. actually inserting the order and order item records) and Object Relational Mapping (e.g. ensuring that the order items have the correct order id)

5. Calling other Business Logic Methods (e.g. posting an accounting transaction)
6. Complex Search (e.g. retrieving a set of orders and their related items)

A number of design strategies and architecture frameworks attempt to ease the task of writing the large volume of business logic needed in a typical enterprise application. Object relational mapping (ORM) tools such as Hibernate[4] attempt to provide an abstraction that allows users to program using operations on nested objects such as `Order` and leave the job of translating such operations into multiple SQL statements for the framework to handle. The EJB container of J2EE makes a similar attempt; it also handles transaction management to a certain extent. Unfortunately all of these approaches are in one way or another lacking: For example, consider ensuring that orders and items are linked by the same foreign key value, which is set only when the order record is actually created in the database; even this simple task remains cumbersome using most ORM frameworks. Cloud databases, such as Google's Datastore, on the other hand, do better; one can link `Order` and `OrderItem` objects in memory before persisting them, and exactly the same references are persisted in the Datastore.

In the next two sections we consider formally modeling business logic using primitive abstractions such as (1)–(6) above. Rule-based computing uses models based on formal logic, whereas business 'logic maps' are an example of a more informal model loosely based on the MapReduce paradigm.

### 14.3.2 Rule-based computing

Rule-based computation is an abstraction based on formal logic. Rules are especially useful for modeling validation rules, as well as many other computations, such as evaluating risk or rating insurance policies. A *rule system* contains *logical statements*[5] (i.e. rules) that may or may not become true when evaluated against *facts*[6].

For example, a 'valid' order may be defined by the following rules:

$$R1 : \forall x \forall y \forall z \; Order(x) \wedge OrderItem(y) \wedge OrderOf(y,x)$$

$$\wedge \; ValidOrderItem(y) \wedge CustomerOf(x,z) \wedge Customer(z)$$

$$\Rightarrow ValidOrder(x)$$

---

[4] http://www.hibernate.org
[5] Typically in first-order predicate logic (FOPL).
[6] More formally, *facts* are true propositions on application data.

$$R2 : \forall x \forall y \forall z \forall p \; Order(x) \wedge OrderItem(y) \wedge \neg OrderOf(y,x)$$
$$\wedge \; CustomerOf(x,z) \wedge Customer(z)$$
$$\wedge \; ProductOf(x,p) \wedge Product(p)$$
$$\Rightarrow ValidOrder(x)$$

In the above example, predicates such as $Order(x)$ and $Customer(z)$ evaluate to true if $x$, $y$ and $z$ are `Order`, `OrderItem` and `Customer` objects respectively; similarly, $OrderOf(y,x)$ evaluates to true if $x$ is the `Order` object pointed to by $y$ (via a foreign key). There are many algorithms for evaluating rule systems given data, which in the above example would be an `Order` object passed to the business logic layer. Additionally, to evaluate predicates such as $Customer(z)$ one would need to access the application database to check for existence of such a record.

Note that there are two possible rules that could result in the predicate $ValidOrder(x)$ evaluating to true: In $R1$ we state first that that $x$ is an `Order` object. Next, we state that all `OrderItem` objects for this order are themselves all valid. Alternatively $R2$ may apply, which states that there are no such `OrderItem` objects and the `order` object $x$ itself contains a valid product (i.e. such a `Product` record exists in the database). Both rules also insist that the `Customer` for the order exists in the database. The rule system would also include rules stating similar conditions for an `OrderItem` object to be valid, i.e. for the predicate $ValidOrderItem(y)$ to evaluate to true.

The fact that there are alternative rules for the same predicate, such as $ValidOrder()$, is typical of rule systems and gives them their power. When there are many alternative ways a validation can be performed it can lead to messy nested if-then-else statements in code, which are difficult to maintain and extend. In contrast, adding additional rules is a simpler task.

*Rule engines* are used to evaluate rule systems. There are two varieties of rule engines: *Backward-chaining* engines evaluate whether a particular predicate, say $ValidOrder(x)$ is true or not, evaluating all possible rules that are required to verify this. *Forward-chaining* engines, on the other hand, take a set of available facts and determine the complete set of predicates that evaluate to true, including $ValidOrder(x)$, as well as any other predicates that may be implied by these facts. Traditionally, backward-chaining rule engines have been used in applications, as they are more attuned to procedural programming paradigms (i.e. a predicate needs to be explicitly checked). However forward-chaining engines are useful in specific contexts, such as user interfaces or other event-driven systems, since they support 'reactive' programming, i.e. any rules that 'fire' because of the current state of application data can trigger exception conditions that are handled in an event-oriented programming style. See [40] for a more detailed explanation of rule-based deduction systems.

An important advantage of the rule-based approach is that many rule engines allow rules to added and changed while the application is running. In this sense, the rule engine approach embodies the spirit of Dev 2.0, with the rule system being the model that is interpreted at runtime by the rule engine.

Commercial rule engines include products such as Blaze Advisor and iLog. Recently open source rule engines such as Drools have also emerged. Most of these rule engines use XML schemas, programming language constructs (such as Java's JSR-94), or 'structured English' for defining rules so as to ease development and avoid having to deal with formal logic. At the same time, none of these have become widely used in large enterprise application architectures, perhaps owing to the relative novelty of the rule-based approach as compared to the procedural style in which business logic is typically written.

### 14.3.3 Modeling business logic using MapReduce

In Section 14.3.1 we have seen that data access and transaction management functions of business could potentially be handled using architectural frameworks incorporating preferred patterns to resolve these problems in a repeatable manner. Similarly, as we have seen in the previous section, validation rules can be abstracted using rule-based computing. What remains from the list (14.2) are Computations, Data Manipulation, Calling other Business Methods and Complex Search. Some Dev 2.0 platforms discussed in Chapter 12 attempt to abstract these functions of business logic as well. For example, TCS InstantApps uses a visual formulation called Logic Map that is based on the MapReduce cloud programming paradigm, borrowing also from the Map-reduce-merge [10] model that extends MapReduce for relational processing.

A Logic Map is a graph with *create*, *search*, and *update* nodes, each corresponding to 'pages' (as defined in (14.1)) of some application *form*. These nodes manipulate relational records in the same manner as the corresponding pages of their associated forms, but without a user interface. Such nodes can also be viewed as *map* nodes in the MapReduce parlance; they take key/value pairs (relational records) as input and produce new pairs, while

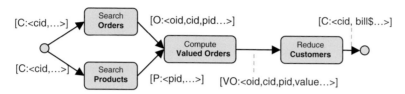

FIGURE **14.5. Logic map**

accessing/manipulating database tables in the process. In addition there are 'compute nodes' *merge* and *reduce* that perform computations on records obtained after joining (in the case of merge) or aggregating (in the case of reduce) records flowing along the edges of a logic map. (The *merge* abstraction, defined in [10], extends *reduce* by allowing inputs from independent *map* steps to be grouped together.)

For example, the logic map in Figure 14.5 performs a billing function for one or more customer records. Customer records flow into the logic map as instances of a customer form *C*, with fields < *cid,* ... > (where *cid* is the primary key of the customer table). This set of 'form instances' flows into a *search* node associated with the order form *O*. Because of the attribute *cid* is common between the order and customer forms, the *search* node retrieves all orders (from the order table) that were placed by any of the customers flowing into the node. Note that the output of the Search Orders node is now a set of instances of the order form. In parallel, the current prices of all products are retrieved using another search node on a product form *P*. These parallel record sets are then joined using a *merge* node on an intermediate 'valued order' form *VO*. The value of each order is computed in this merge operation using the product prices and quantities ordered, with the common attribute *pid* being used to associate records from the two incoming sets. Finally, instances of the *VO* form flow into a *reduce* node on the customer form *C* where valued orders are added to compute the billing amount *bill$* for each customer.

Logic maps also allow decision nodes that are similar to compute nodes but filter rather than manipulate records in the flow. Using decision nodes makes loops possible, thereby enabling a fairly general class of business logic functions to be modeled using logic maps. By leveraging the MapReduce paradigm, there is the possibility of parallel execution of logic maps in cloud environments, or efficiently using cloud data stores even though these do not explicitly support joins, since the join functionality is included in the *merge* abstraction.

## 14.4 INSIDE DEV 2.0: MODEL DRIVEN INTERPRETERS

Throughout our discussion so far, we have concentrated on finding patterns that could be formally modeled, such as user-interface patterns via the *form* abstraction, rules for business logic validations, and logic maps for the data manipulation, control flow and search functions of business logic. Our motivation has been two-fold: (a) Once application functionality has been modeled in terms of such patterns, migrating an application to another technical architecture (such as from a traditional web architecture to an AJAX paradigm) can be accomplished by first re-encoding the elementary patterns of the model using new technology and then reassembling the application from a higher level representation expressed in terms of patterns. We also saw that (b) in cases where the patterns can be directly interpreted, such as in the case of some rule engines, application functionality could be dynamically changed at runtime.

The Model Driven Architecture (MDA) approach popularized by OMG[7] generalizes the first approach (a) above. Modeling application functionality at different levels of abstraction is used as the basis for model transformations. Models at a higher level of abstraction are transformed to those at a lower level; at the lowest level actual code in a general purpose programming language is generated. The OMG view of MDA is shown in Figure 14.6. Each model transformation involves encoding higher-level abstractions in terms of patterns of lower-level constructs. At the lowest level, each encoding is nothing but an architecture framework for a particular behavior pattern, such as a *form*.

The Dev 2.0 platforms discussed in Chapter 12, on the other hand, generalize the second approach (b), i.e. runtime interpretation of higher-level abstractions. Thus, instead of generating code, a Dev 2.0 platform is in essence a model driven interpreter (MDI), as opposed to MDA that is traditionally associated with code generation. Figure 14.7 highlights the differences between the MDA and MDI (Dev 2.0) approaches.

In both MDA and MDI, patterns used to abstract application behavior are represented by a *meta-model* that describes the application model. For example, the user interface meta-model discussed in Section 14.2.2 consists of a formal model for the *form* abstraction that specify that forms can have fields, and can link to and include other forms. Similarly rule systems and the logic

---

[7] Object Management Group: www.omg.org

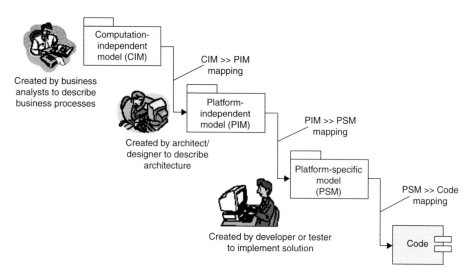

FIGURE **14.6. Model driven architecture paradigm**

map model of sections 14.3.2 and 14.3.3 are also specified by meta-models. Taken together these constitute the overall meta-model for the class of applications being considered. The meta-model merely *describes application models* that represent actual applications. For example, a specific set of forms, rules and logic maps that constitute say, the order management application, is an example of an application model. This is illustrated in Figure 14.7, where the meta-model captures the simple concept of an object and its attributes, while the application model captures actual instances of these, such as an Employee object and its attributes such as EID, Name, and Address.

The difference between MDA and MDI is in how these models are used. In the MDA approach, code generators associated with the meta-model use code templates to generate application code from a specific application model. For example, the code template for generating a class definition from the simple meta-model of an object and its attributes is illustrated in Figure 14.7. In MDI, on the other hand, the meta-model is interpreted directly at runtime: In the simple example of an object and its attributes forming a class, the MDI interpreter uses *one* generic class that creates its attributes dynamically when instantiated at runtime, by looking up the application model. It also sets its meta-properties in a similar manner, such as its name (e.g. 'Employee' in this case). For efficiency, the application model is cached in memory and kept synchronized with a persistent model repository, as in the InstantApps platform [53].

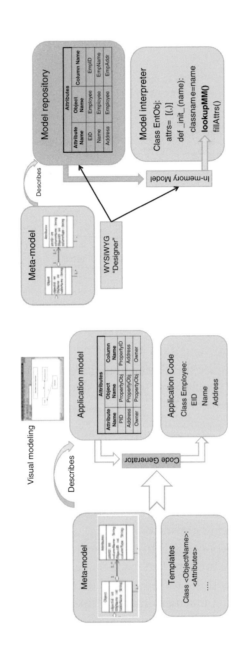

Model driven architecture

Model driven interpreter: Dev 2.0

**FIGURE 14.7.  Dev 2.0: MDA vs. MDI**

A second difference between MDA and Dev 2.0 platforms that use MDI is in how the application model is constructed and maintained. The traditional MDA approach usually involves visual modeling (using UML models) or specifications in higher-level languages, which are then translated into code using code generators. Dev 2.0 platforms, on the other hand, use a WYSIWIG ('what you see is what you get') approach: As soon as a change is made to the application model it is instantly reflected in the running platform. Thus the Dev 2.0 platform is 'always on,' and does not need to go through compile and build cycles. It is always running the application embodied in the application model. This model may be empty to start with; as functionality is incrementally added it can be immediately tested and even used. The potential for vastly improving development productivity because of this feature has already been discussed in Chapter 12.

## 14.4.1 Multi-tenant Dev 2.0: application virtualization

In Dev 2.0 platforms using MDI, application specifications are merely data in a model repository. Thus, in addition to interpreting and rendering any application model, a single instance of a Dev 2.0 interpreter can potentially interpret multiple application models *simultaneously*. Thus, a Dev 2.0 platform is also a *multi-tenant* platform. However, unlike the multi-tenancy of Chapter 9, where we considered a *single* application that needed to be used by multiple tenants, a Dev 2.0 platform can enable multiple tenants to use the same platform instance for *different* applications! In a multi-tenant Dev 2.0 platform, we usually use a single schema for all application models, but multiple schemas for each application database, so that conflicts between applications do not arise: So, for example, different applications can have their own definitions of an 'Employee' table, without any conflicts.

We now explore the relationship between hardware virtualization as covered in Chapter 8 and multi-tenant Dev 2.0: Just as a hypervisor implements an abstract *machine model*, on which different operating systems can run simultaneously, a Dev 2.0 platform implements an abstract *application model* on which many different applications run simultaneously. Thus, we can view multi-tenant Dev 2.0 as implementing **application virtualization** analogous to hardware virtualization provided by hypervisors. Consequently, just as hardware virtualization enables cost optimization in the face of dynamically changing hardware requirements, application virtualization can drive productivity improvements in the face of rapidly changing application functionality and needs. Therefore application virtualization should also be considered an integral element of cloud computing along with traditional virtualization.

## 14.5 SECURITY, ERROR HANDLING, TRANSACTIONS AND WORKFLOW

So far we have focused on developing abstractions for forms-based transaction-processing architectures so that application functionality could be modeled and interpreted by Dev 2.0 platforms. However, an enterprise application also needs architectural support for technical features that are not directly related to functional components. Figure 14.8 depicts such technical architecture components that perform the following functions:

1. Access to application functionality needs to be controlled via **application security** so that only authenticated users can access the application and perform only those functions that they are authorized to.
2. **Uniform error handling** is essential for informing users about errors, managing error messages, and handling different classes of errors appropriately.
3. **Transaction management** is needed to ensure that each logical user interaction is atomic from the perspective of concurrency control, over and above maintaining data integrity via underlying database transactions.
4. The flow of work from user to user in order to accomplish a business process needs to be handled through **workflow management**.

We cover the first three issues in the remainder of this section; workflow is covered in detail in the next chapter.

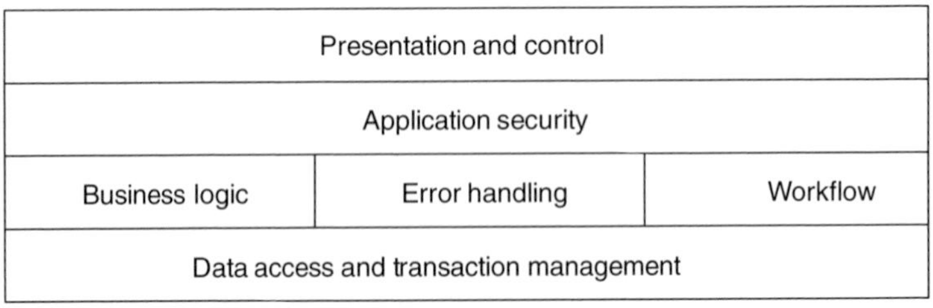

| Presentation and control | | |
|---|---|---|
| Application security | | |
| Business logic | Error handling | Workflow |
| Data access and transaction management | | |

FIGURE 14.8. Technical architecture layers

## 14.5.1 Application security

Secure user authentication in a distributed environment, whether a client-server or web-based architecture, is an involved subject. The Kerberos [39] protocol was developed to enable authentication over an unsecured network that would be still be safe from eavesdropping as well as replay attacks. Using such a protocol, a user's password is never transmitted on the network, even in encrypted or hashed form. Instead, a trusted server generates session keys used by client and server to communicate, as well as short-lived tickets that serve to authenticate clients to servers, and vice versa. Variants of Kerberos are now deployed as a core element of distributed security at the operating system level, in Windows as well as Linux operating systems, and in Windows Active Directory as well as LDAP-based identity-management servers.

A security framework for a web-based architecture needs to decide what level of secure authentication it will utilize and how. Simple security involves transmitting a hashed userid and password across the network which is then matched for authentication. The basic JAAS library of Java supports such authentication as well as more secure authentication (such as a Kerberos implementation) in a pluggable manner. Cloud computing platforms such as Google's App Engine or Microsoft Azure also provide the option for authentication using their public identity services, such as Google Accounts, or Microsoft's Live ID (earlier called Passport).

Once a user is logged in securely, each HTTP request contains a 'user context' that carries the security tokens or tickets required by the chosen authentication mechanism. The user context needs to be validated on the server by every application service before it is processed; this is usually ensured by the controller layer as it processes each request made to the server.

An authenticated user may be authorized to access all or only a subset of application *functions*, or *data*. We have already discussed data access control in some detail in Chapter 9. Function access control can be implemented using underlying features of the web application server, or as a part of the application architecture. Web application servers usually allow control access to application resources through access control lists (ACL) based on the URL or server-side code packages (e.g. a Java .jar file) being accessed. However this is often inadequate to support the fine-grained level of access control required by most enterprise applications. Further, rich internet interfaces (RIA) that

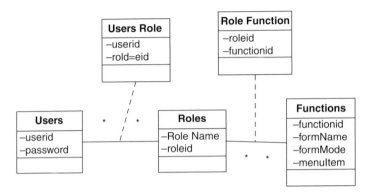

FIGURE **14.9. Function access control**

make heavy use of JavaScript cannot leverage these features easily. Thus, most often function access control, like data access control, is implemented at the application level.

Figure 14.9 illustrates a simple data model for function access control. Users have Roles, a many-to-many association through the User Role class. Roles have access to Functions, again a many-to-many association through the Role Function class, with each Function being either 'page' of a particular 'form' (e.g. Create, Edit, Search, etc.), or some menu item. The application security layer looks up the function access control model during login and adds the list of functions that the user can access to the user context. Thereafter, security needs to be checked in the presentation layer as well as controller layer to limit user access to only those forms and menus permitted by the function access control model. Note that application security is an example of a 'cross-cutting' concern in that its implementation spans multiple architecture layers.

## 14.5.2 Error handling

As users perform business transactions they will come across many different types of errors of which they will need to be informed. Apart from technical errors that could be due to bugs in the application, these also include business errors, such as when validation checks fail, or a warning that data being searched does not exist. Additionally alerts such as confirming success of a transaction need to be conveyed along with related information, such as the order-id automatically generated by the system. Mechanisms enabling an application to report such errors and allow the user to respond constitutes an error handling strategy; an error management framework implements such a strategy in a uniform manner across all user interactions in an application.

An important issue that needs to be handled is when to show an error. Clearly a fatal error such as a system fault needs to be shown to the user as soon as it occurs. Other errors, such as validations and warnings need not be sent to the user immediately, and can be bundled together until the application is no longer able to proceed from a business perspective. An error management framework should allow for such behavior to be included in business logic through suitable abstractions. Finally, as mentioned above, it should be possible to convey information to the user both during as well as after completion of a user transaction.

The implementation details of an error-handling framework are closely tied to the technology components and design strategies being used in the application architecture. Therefore, even more so than application security, error handling is also a cross-cutting concern: When an error or set of errors need to be communicated to the user, all architecture layers between the point where the error occurs to the presentation layer are involved.

### 14.5.3 Transaction management

Each user interaction in a transaction-processing application that involves creating, modifying or deleting data needs to be atomic from the perspective of concurrency control. It is important to note the difference between an atomic user interaction and an atomic database transaction as implemented by the controller layer. Recall that the controller gathers together all information that may have been sent by a user during the course of possibly multiple HTTP requests. It then submits all of these to the business logic layer to be executed as a single database transaction, thus guaranteeing database integrity. However, this may still not be sufficient to ensure concurrency control from the user's perspective in a multi-user scenario:

Consider a case where two users simultaneously access a database record, say to reserve a particular resource (e.g. a conference room), via an Edit form. Each makes their own modifications before submitting the changes, which are sent to the server via HTTP POST requests from these independent user sessions. Note that in the layered MVC architecture, reading a database record is deliberately *not* kept within the scope of a database transaction, to avoid long transactions and consequent timeouts and deadlocks. Therefore, both these user interactions appear to succeed, since each results in a separate database transaction being sent to the server. As a natural consequence, the final state of the database will be that sent by *one* of the two users; however, the other user will *not know* that his transaction has been overwritten, and that in fact he has *not* succeeded in booking the resource (conference room). The problem in this scenario is that users do not perceive a sufficiently high level of 'transaction isolation': one of them is reading and making decisions based on 'dirty' data. However, it is impossible to tell *which* until one of them succeeds!

The solution most commonly used in web-based architectures is 'optimistic' concurrency control using version numbers. Each table includes an additional field `ver` which is incremented by each update. When a record is read, its version number is also read. The update statement as executed by the data access layer has the following structure:

```
UPDATE <table> SET <col1>=:1, <col2>=:2, ver=ver+1
WHERE <key>=:key AND ver=:ver
```

Thus, in cases where the version number has changed between the time a record is read and the attempt to write it, the version number mismatch will result in no data being found (an error), which can be communicated to the user as a 'transaction failed' message. Thus, only one of the users will succeed in booking the conference room (i.e. the one that acts first!)

Transaction management via optimistic concurrency control is often called 'soft locking,' and is also a cross-cutting concern since each architecture layer needs to track the version number, which is also transported across HTTP requests, even though the actual check is only at the data access layer.

Note that we have emphasized that all the architectural issues discussed in this section are 'cross-cutting concerns'. Aspect-oriented programming (AOP) [19] is emerging as a mechanism to introduce and manage such cross-cutting concerns in complex applications, so that modifying the implementation strategies for such concerns can be conveniently done even after an application architecture has been deployed. For example, by incorporating AOP within Dev 2.0 architectures it becomes possible to efficiently modify cross-cutting functionality for the platform as a whole.

# Workflow and business processes

In the previous chapter we saw how basic forms-based transactions are assembled into an application. The resulting application resembles a 'playground' where each user can access available forms to create, modify or view data. In the process any business logic attached to the forms is also executed. In such a scenario, it is up to the user to decide what form to access and which transaction to perform. However, in real life users do not perform such tasks in a vacuum; rather they perform these tasks as part of an overall business process in which the user is participating. In this chapter we examine mechanisms by which an enterprise application can track such business processes and drive the 'flow of work' to users.

## 15.1 IMPLEMENTING WORKFLOW IN AN APPLICATION

We consider a simple 'leave approval' process. An employee places a leave request that goes to a supervisor. If approved it is forwarded to the HR department for their records; simultaneously the result, i.e. approval or rejection, is conveyed back to the employee. First let us design an application that implements this process, using a data model as shown in Figure 15.1. A

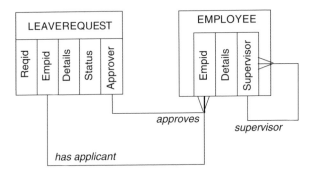

FIGURE **15.1. Leave request model**

LEAVEREQUEST table keeps track of the requests placed. The EMPLOYEE table captures each employee's supervisor as a self-referential foreign key. The application provides a *New-Leave-Request* form using which an employee can apply for leave. When a user submits a leave request using this form, a record is inserted in the LEAVEREQUEST table with the Status field set to 'pending approval,' and the Approver field containing the supervisor of the employee applying for leave. A *Pending-Requests-List* form lists all requests awaiting approval by a particular employee: The user can chose any particular request and navigate to an *Approve-Request* form that displays the chosen leave request with buttons to either approve or reject it. Each of these buttons in turn invokes business logic to update the Status field to 'Approved' or 'Rejected' respectively. Finally, an employee in the HR department accesses a *Completed-Requests-List* form listing all requests that have either been approved or rejected. Similarly the *My-Requests-List* and *My-Request-Status* forms enable each employee to view their individual requests and their status.

To approve a leave request, any employee who is also a supervisor needs to access the *Pending-Requests-List* form and approve or reject each pending request. But how does a supervisor come to know that there is something in this list that needs their attention? Similarly, how does an employee come to know that their request has been processed? One possibility is to augment the business logic attached to the *New-Leave-Request* and *Approve-Request* forms so as to send email to the next person who needs to pay attention to the request. The operation of this simple application is depicted pictorially in Figure 15.2.

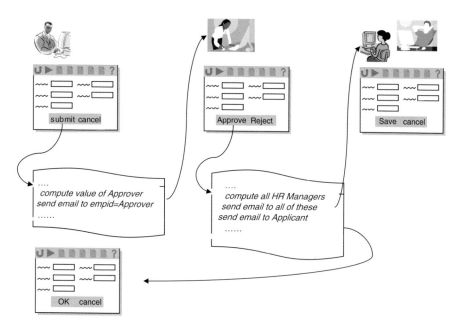

FIGURE 15.2. Operation of workflow

## 15.2 WORKFLOW META-MODEL USING ECA RULES

Let us now examine what abstractions can be derived from the above implementation of workflow: The process consists of a set of activities, such as
applying for leave, approving leave, recording and viewing the result. These
activities are performed by different actors (employees) each performing different roles, such as the applicant, supervisor and HR manager. Some of the
activities are performed in sequence, such as applying and approval, and
others can be in parallel, such as recording the request in HR and the applicant viewing the final result. For each activity there is a corresponding form
using which the actor performs the activity in the application. During each
execution (or 'instance') of this process, each of these forms is accessing the
same object, i.e. a particular record in the LEAVEREQUEST table. Further,
an activity can change the state of this object, in this case the Status field of
the record. We shall refer to this object as the *process object*.

Let us construct a meta-model using these abstractions to generalize the
workflow implementation. In particular, a key feature of the application is
the sending of email to the next participant in the process, also referred to

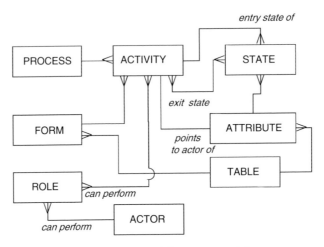

**FIGURE 15.3. Workflow meta-model**

as a workflow notification. This involves computing who is the next participant and which activity they need to perform. We now make the following
important observation: The 'Pending Approval' value of the Status field can
be considered as being the **entry state** for the **approval** activity. Similarly the
'Approved' or 'Rejected' values are **exit states** for **approval**, and entry states
for the next two activities, **recording** and **viewing** respectively. Thus, at any
point of time, the activities that are 'ready' to perform are those having all
their entry states true and exit states false, with states being computed using
attributes of the *process object*. As a second observation, note that the identities of the individual actors who play the role of applicant and approver can
be obtained from the Applicant Name and Approver attributes of the process object. Figure 15.3 depicts a possible workflow meta-model using these
abstractions.[1] The corresponding application model for the Leave Approval
process would have entries such as those shown in Figure 15.4. The InstantApps Dev 2.0 platform discussed in Chapter 12 includes a workflow engine
based on a similar model.

The meta-model of Figure 15.3 relies on state changes to model process
flow. This is a special case of a more general approach using *events, conditions
and actions to model processes*, also referred to as ECA-based workflow [30].
In the specific case above, *conditions* are entry and exit **states** defined on
database record values, *actions* are email notifications being sent to users to

---

[1] Figure 15.3 uses the 'logical data model' notation [55].

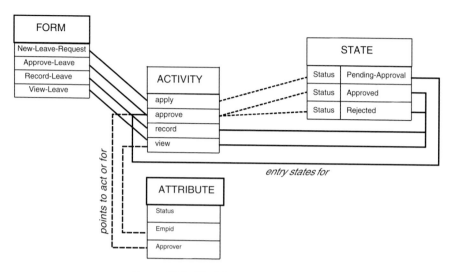

**FIGURE 15.4. Workflow model instance**

perform certain **activities**, and *events* are modifications to record values in any database columns that are part of state definitions for some activity.

## 15.3 ECA WORKFLOW ENGINE

A simple workflow engine using the ECA-based meta-model of Figure 15.3 can be implemented as follows: A process instance comes into existence as soon as the form corresponding to the first activity in the process is executed, for example when a record is created in the LEAVEREQUEST table through the *New-Leave-Request* form. This process instance is identified by the primary-key value of this record. We shall refer to this record as the 'object' on which the process instance is running.

After every transaction involving any form associated with a workflow activity, a generic function wf_update() is invoked to update the list of 'ready' activities, and send notifications as required. This function can be called either in course of transaction execution through business logic, by using database triggers or by polling the database for changes. The wf_update($p$) function takes as input the object $p$ on which the process instance is running: Entry and exit states of activities are computed using the attribute values of this object. Activities for which all entry states are true and all exit states false are added to a ready list. Next, for each entry in the ready list, a list actors who should be notified is computed using appropriate attribute values of $p$; for example the Approver field in the LEAVREQUEST

$L_A$ = [activities $a_i$]
initialize 'ready-list' r
for each $a_i$: all entry states and no exit state of p true:
        add $a_i$ to r
for each entry in r:
        R = list of roles that can perform $a_i$
        if pointer to actor defined for activity $a_i$:
                get actor u from p; if u can play any role in R:
                        send email to actor u
        else,
                send email to all actors that play any roles in R

**wf_update(object p)**

FIGURE **15.5. Workflow update**

object determines the supervisor who needs to be notified. If there is no such field specified in the model, such as for the 'recording by HR' activity, or if the field is empty, *all* actors who have roles that are empowered to perform the activity are notified. So, in the above example, all employees who have the HR manager role will be notified. The generic wf_update() function that drives our simple workflow engine is summarized in Figure 15.5.

We have used email notifications to inform participants that they need to perform an activity. Often a single user can participate in many process instances and activities at any point of time. In such a situation, having email notifications 'pushed' to the user may not be always desirable. Therefore most workflow implementations also include a 'pull' model via a *worklist*, i.e. a form where a user can see all items pending for action. The *worklist* form is similar to the *Pending-Requests-List* form in the above example, except that it contains items from a number of processes, so that a user can see all pending work at one place instead of navigating to separate lists for say leave requests, hardware requests etc. The worklist form enables the user to navigate directly to the corresponding application form for a chosen workitem. Email or other 'push' notification mechanisms can be used concurrently with a worklist-based engine for selected items or to escalate items that remain unattended for too long.

Note that our workflow engine does not keep any persistent state apart from the process definitions, i.e. all information for a process instance level remains in the business tables, e.g. LEAVEREQUEST. Many workflow engines my_worklist(user u)

R = roles played by user u
A = activities that can be performed by roles in R
for each a in A:
        compute entry states of a
        compute exit states of a
        let O be the list of objects containing 'state attributes' of a
        search for instances of objects in O where all entry states are
            ... satisfied and no exit states are satisfied
        for each such object o, add (a,o) to the worklist w for u

FIGURE 15.6. Worklist computation

do maintain persistent state at the process instance level and use it for generating and keeping track of worklists. However, in theory it is not necessary to maintain persistent state merely for generating a worklist, provided the activities in the process are driven by their entry and exit states. The algorithm my_worklist(user) computes the list of workitems for a given user at any point in time: First compute the set of activities that are available to the roles played by user, and of these which have ready instances, i.e. corresponding objects in the database with all entry states for the activity true and exit states false. Next check if any of these have 'points to actor' defined in the model, and if so whether the user is the actor indicated. This algorithm my_worklist to compute a user's worklist is outlined in Figure 15.6. Note that the step of searching all objects to see which activities are potentially ready is likely to be computationally expensive. In practice this step can be more efficiently carried out by maintaining a cache of each user's *potential* worklist that is updated during wf_update(); this can significantly reduce the overhead by limiting the search to a much smaller number of objects as contained in the cache.

Note that the ECA-based workflow implementation described above does not separately track each process instance. However, most commercial workflow engines do keep persistent state at the process instance level, using which it is possible to track which transitions have fired, which activities have taken place in an instance, when, and by which actors, or more generally at which step the process instance is at any point of time. Having process state information available enables more efficient worklist computations as well as more sophisticated analysis on process execution, such as which actors are more efficient than others and which steps in a process could be taking longer than others. 'Process analytics' is an emerging research area that investigates these issues in depth; and commercial workflow engines often include 'business activity monitoring' features that provide analysis of this nature. On the other hand, by not maintaining its own persistent state at the instance level, the workflow engine does not have to track every process instance to 'closure.' This makes it possible for large process diagrams to be modeled using the workflow meta-model even whilst the workflow engine operates on only one part of the flow.

## 15.4 USING AN EXTERNAL WORKFLOW ENGINE

In practice, when transactions from multiple applications including enterprise software such as ERP systems need to be directly invoked by users, using an external workflow engine becomes essential. The interaction between an application and a generic workflow implementation can be viewed as consisting of:

1. **Updating** [the flow]: determining what activities are next
2. **Notification**: signaling users that tasks are pending for them to do
3. **Worklist**: allowing users to view what tasks are pending for them to do
4. **Navigation**: enabling a user to navigate to the appropriate application form

Furthermore, in order to compute the next step in the flow, i.e. *updating*, as well as for other functions, a workflow engine needs access to application data and application events, such as completion of an activity. A fundamental difference between an internal implementation of workflow, such as our ECA-based workflow engine described above, and an external implementation, is how the workflow engine gets access to application events and data. An external workflow engine needs application data passed to it explicitly along with application events as they occur, whereas for an internal implementation 'state' information can be derived directly from application database tables.

Figure 15.7 depicts the typical interaction between an application and an external workflow engine. The application updates the workflow engine when a transaction is completed. The workflow engine (from its *worklist* interface) enables invocation of the appropriate application transaction (form). Alternatively the application may request worklist data for each user from the

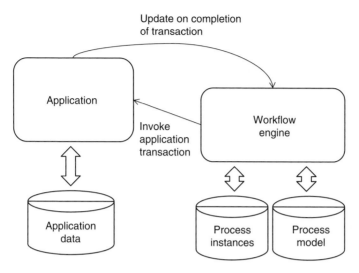

**FIGURE 15.7. Using an external workflow engine**

workflow engine and display its own *worklist* integrated with its user interface. Note also that the process model, as well as information about each process instance, needs to be tracked explicitly by an external workflow engine, since it cannot efficiently access application data internal to an application.

## 15.5 PROCESS MODELING AND BPMN

While ECA models of workflow are adequate to describe processes of signifi-cant complexity, process diagrams that explicitly depict the flow of activities are often found to be more intuitive than a set of rules that can be difficult to define and verify in practice. The Business Process Modeling Notation (BPMN[2]) is a graphical notation to capture process behavior. Consider the diagram in Figure 15.8 that depicts the example Leave Request process as an activity-transition graph. In fact Figure 15.8 is a also a simple example of a BPMN diagram. However, without ECA rules such as entry and exit con-ditions on activities, such a diagram is not adequate; further many process features require more sophisticated notation to describe them. For this reason the InstantApps platform includes the ability to draw BPMN diagrams while

---

[2] www.bpmn.org

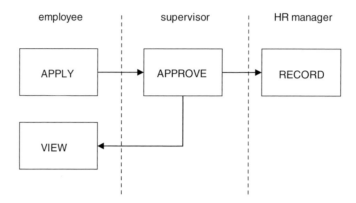

FIGURE **15.8. Leave request process**

still using the meta-model of Figure 15.3 to execute processes. To motivate BPMN we consider a few such features and how they can be represented using BPMN:

First, consider a case where two transitions point to an activity *a*. It is not clear from the activity-transition graph alone whether both these need to fire before activity *a* can be considered ready, or only one of them; entry and exit states are needed to define this. Similarly, it is normally assumed that if more than one transition emanates from an activity, both fire at the same time in parallel (e.g. so that the recording and view-result activities can take place in parallel). This need not be the case in all situations, and one may wish to have only one of these fire. Actual situations can be even significantly more complex with subsets of transitions behaving differently, e.g. two firing in parallel but only if a third does not.

The BPMN notation includes special nodes (i.e. other than activities) that capture flow behavior: Gateway nodes control the sequence of the process flow as transitions converge or diverge; decision nodes, and fork/join nodes are the most commonly used gateways. At the same time if the flow does not need to be controlled gateways are not required, and in their absence an activity becomes ready if any of its incoming transitions fire; also, all outgoing transitions fire on completion of the activity. A decision node (more precisely an 'exclusive OR' node) is used to ensure that only one outgoing transition fires, usually based on some decision criterion. (Note that such decision criteria would also be modeled as possible 'exit states' for decision nodes in our ECA-based workflow meta-model, with different states leading to different outgoing transitions firing.)

In our ECA-based workflow meta-model, we made an implicit assumption that a process instance was directly related to a particular object instance, and identified by its primary key value. The entry and exit states for the activities in the process were also assumed to be determined by attribute values of this object. In this sense, one could view this object as 'flowing' along a path directed by values of some of its attributes. The BPMN notation does not include the concepts of entry and exit states or ECA rules. Instead it allows information artifacts to be explicitly associated with transitions to define data flow and decisions based on data. In BPMN an activity can consume those artifacts associated with incoming transitions, and an activity is assumed to create or modify artifacts associated with its outgoing transitions. Further, decision criteria (for decision nodes) are assumed to use values that are contained in these artifacts.

The diagram in Figure 15.9 shows another BPMN diagram for the Leave Request process. The LEAVEREQUEST object is shown to explicitly flow along the transitions. A fork node explicitly captures parallel execution of the flow to the **record** and *view* activities. Participants, such a *employee, supervisor* and *HR manager* are depicted as horizontal 'swimlanes'; activities residing in a lane are performed by actors who play these roles.

The diagram in Figure 15.9 also explicitly depicts an 'exception' condition: Suppose during the approval activity it is determined that an employee requesting leave needs to be replaced for the duration of his leave. In this case the **approve** activity generates an exception that results in a transition

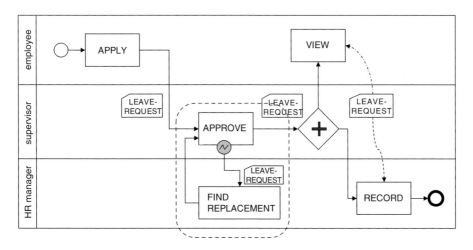

**FIGURE 15.9. BPMN model for leave process**

to the **find replacement** activity. Once this is completed, the flow returns to the **approve** activity, which resumes at the point after the exception was called. Thus, exceptions capture situations where normal processing needs to be interrupted and continue only after the exception has been 'handled.' The exception is an example of an event. Events include 'start' and 'end' events, which can trigger or be triggered by a process, as well as intermediate events, such as the exception above, which occur during a process execution. Note that **find replacement** is not part of the **approve** activity itself, rather the **approve** activity is suspended pending the execution of **find replacement**, which may not take place immediately, and may not be done by the same actor that performed in the **approve** step.

Exceptions represent elaborations of activities, i.e. an exception handler such as **find replacement** is an example of 'sub' activity. BPMN also allows elaboration of processes themselves. A process can have compound activities that represent sub-processes. In this manner a process can be defined hierarchically at increasing levels of detail.

Transactions are another important construct included in BPMN. An elaboration, i.e. compound activity (sub-process) can be designated as a transaction: This means it can be 'rolled back' during its execution, so that it behaves like an atomic activity even while representing a sub-process. Unlike the more commonly known concept of database transactions, workflow transactions can be long-running and involve many participants. Further, different activities within the transaction may be performed using possibly different software applications. So there may not be a single system, such as a database management system, to handle roll backs of data modifications. Instead, activities within the transaction have associated 'compensating' activities that are triggered by a compensation event that represents a roll back of the transaction. The workflow implementation needs to ensure that the appropriate compensating activities are performed, i.e. only those corresponding to activities that have already taken place at the time the transaction 'fails' and needs to be rolled back.

We illustrate some of these and other BPMN constructs in Figure 15.10, where the **approve** and **find replacement** activities are elaborated as sub-processes. The exception is raised in the **approve** process and results in the **find replacement** process being invoked. 'Link' events are used to return to the appropriate position in the **approve** process once the exception is handled, i.e. a replacement is found for the employee requesting leave. Note that the diagram includes decision gateways, as well as transitions having conditions attached to them (such as those outgoing from the **decide request** activity).

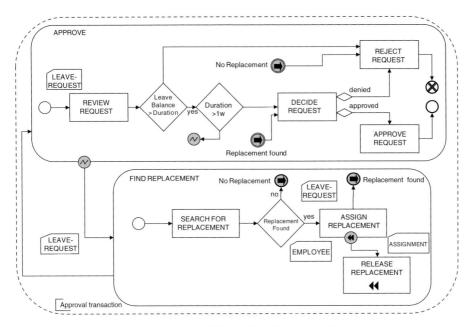

FIGURE **15.10. BPMN model with transactions**

Also note that in cases where the request is rejected, the **approve** process ends with a 'cancellation,' rather than a normal termination. This event causes a rollback of any long-running transactions that may be running. In this diagram, both the **approve** and **find replacement** processes are enclosed within a 'group' that has been labeled as a transaction. So, in case of a rollback, if the request is denied even after a replacement has been assigned, the assignment will be reversed by invoking the 'compensating' **release replacement** activity.

Automatic support for long-running transactions is usually not provided in generic workflow platforms, and is usually left to enterprise applications to incorporate into their implementation. If transactional behavior is required in large parts of a business process, implementing a generic mechanism for long-running transactions inside the application architecture may be called for.

In the above discussion we have described how some complex process features are covered in BPMN. There are also limitations to BPMN, many of which have been pointed out in [64]. For example, in BPMN we do not capture participant information beyond swim-lanes: So if we require a particular actor only to perform an activity, it is difficult to capture this using BPMN alone. Note however that the ECA-based workflow meta-model described earlier does enable this by capturing the attribute from where the actor value can be found in the application database.

BPMN-based process models are easy to capture and understand. At the same time modeling exception conditions using pictorial notation can become complex, as we have seen above; when the number of exceptions is large the difficulty is further compounded. ECA rules, on the other hand, are ideal for modeling even a large number of exception conditions. In practice therefore, a combination of both approaches can provide a happy compromise, as is followed in the InstantApps Dev 2.0 platform.

## 15.6 WORKFLOW IN THE CLOUD

As we have covered in Chapter 12, elements of service-oriented workflow are provided as a cloud service by Microsoft Azure's .NET services. Similarly, many Dev 2.0 platforms such as InstantApps and Force.com also include workflow in their meta-models. Workflow services are an ideal candidate for cloud deployment. It is through workflow and web-services orchestration that disparate applications can be made to behave as an integrated system. This need becomes even more important as applications are deployed on a mix of platforms, some on-premise and others in public clouds. While today there are few cloud-based inter-application workflow platforms, this is an area where more solutions are likely to emerge, and we reiterate this in Chapter 17 while discussing the evolving cloud computing ecosystem.

# Enterprise analytics
# and search

So far we have studied enterprise applications from the perspective of what data they typically need to store, and how business transactions can best be encoded into such applications so as to efficiently process and update such data. We have also seen how the execution of transactions can be orchestrated so as to drive the flow of work between users. Information captured by enterprise systems in this manner is used to drive the operational functions of an organization by maintaining accounts, tracking execution plans, receiving payments or disbursing a payroll.

However, another equally important motivation to maintain data about an enterprise's operations is to unearth hidden patterns and discover **knowledge** that can *improve* business strategy or optimize operational processes. Such knowledge discovery tasks are supported by *analytical* applications.

Additionally, with the advent of the web and the ubiquity of internet search, any knowledge discovery or creation exercise today includes web search as an integral supporting activity. This naturally leads to the question of whether similar search technologies can be applied to enterprise information retrieval. Interest in *enterprise search* has also been fueled by the increasing amounts of text (and other unstructured) information generated and maintained by large enterprises and the use of search technologies to index such data. There is also interest in exploring whether search techniques apply to structured data as well as combinations of structured and unstructured data.

In this chapter we study some motivations for and solutions to enterprise search and analytics problems. However, rather than an overview of a large number of standard techniques, we present a limited, and perhaps non-standard but unified view of enterprise search and analytics. This formulation has been chosen to illustrate techniques suited for *scalable* parallel implementation using MapReduce (see Chapter 11).

## 16.1 ENTERPRISE KNOWLEDGE: GOALS AND APPROACHES

Being able to search for and find information in a manner analogous to the web is an important knowledge discovery task that we shall explore in a subsequent section. Apart from search, other important knowledge discovery tasks include:

1. Segmenting customers, suppliers, markets or employees based on their behavior. Such analysis can be used to decide which customers to give a discount to, which suppliers to give more business to, which employees to retain and reward, as well as predict which segment new data might belong to.
2. Targeting advertising and marketing campaigns more effectively by determining what information needs to be pushed to which consumers, based on, for example, similarities in buying patterns.
3. Detecting anomalies and other rare events, such as credit card and insurance claim fraud, illegal duplication of mobile phone SIMs, and even terrorist activities.
4. Identifying problems and opinions, using data such as from customer feedback, blogs and emails.
5. Assessing overall situations and trends by fusing evidence from multiple sources to determine high-level explanations from large volumes of ground-level evidence.

A variety of techniques have been used for solving problems that arise in each task, some of which we explore in the rest of this chapter, motivating the discussion using the above examples.

We first cover traditional 'business intelligence' tasks involving aggregating, slicing and dicing data using OLAP ('online analytic processing') tools that allow users to view complex summaries of large volumes of data. OLAP-based analysis is the most popular approach to human-assisted *segmentation* of data towards optimizing business strategies, such as deciding which customers to target. In fact, segmentation remains the major goal of most of what is referred to as analytics in large enterprises.

Nevertheless, the other knowledge discovery tasks described above are equally important, and OLAP is often also used for these even though it may not be best suited for the task. Many traditional 'data mining' techniques proposed for solving these problems are less generalizable (unlike OLAP), and therefore less used. Text mining techniques have similar underlying roots but are applied on textual, or more generally, unstructured data. A unified approach that uses similar, possibly generalizable, formulations of mining techniques for unstructured as well as structured data is therefore desirable. There is also a close relationship between search technology and mining, beginning with text search, but also applicable to searching structured data.

## 16.2 BUSINESS INTELLIGENCE

An end-user's view of a business intelligence application is that of a variety of reports that *aggregate* operational details of the enterprise summarizing business performance. For example, sales analysis may require viewing quarterly sales of products from different categories (such as 'consumer' versus 'enterprise'), segregated by region, to arrive at a summary report as shown in Table 16.1. In the next two sections we describe the steps required to compute such a report from operational data.

### 16.2.1 Data warehousing

As discussed in Chapter 13, actual operational data maintained by the enterprise is in terms of orders placed by customers, shipments dispatched, invoices raised and payments made. Further, the number of such records can be very large. For example, a large global retail chain might generate a few million such records a day. Operational data needs to be transformed into a form on which a variety of reports, such as that in Table 16.1 can be computed. The process of extracting and transforming operational data into such a 'reporting database' is called **data warehousing**. This is not as simple a process as may appear at first glance; data warehousing usually involves steps

**TABLE 16.1 Quarterly product revenue by category and region**

| Category → | Consumer | | | | Enterprise | | | |
|---|---|---|---|---|---|---|---|---|
| Region ↓ | Q1 | Q2 | Q3 | Q4 | Q1 | Q2 | Q3 | Q4 |
| US | 100 | 130 | 120 | 150 | 90 | 100 | 110 | 120 |
| UK | 50 | 40 | 35 | 29 | 65 | 68 | 64 | 60 |
| EMEA | 80 | 95 | 100 | 120 | 80 | 75 | 70 | 65 |
| APAC | 10 | 20 | 15 | 18 | 45 | 50 | 55 | 60 |

such as:

1. Removing all purely operational data, such as remarks or shipping reference numbers.
2. Time stamping and related restructuring of data so that it represents historically valid snapshots: For example, the category of a product may change over time; therefore the product category at the time of sale needs to be stored along with a sales record instead of in a separate product category table, so that even if a product changes category, historically correct information is maintained.
3. Computing and inserting derived data, such as the location of a sale, which is possibly defined by the city and country specified in the customer's address, if available, or by the address of the retail store where the sale was made. Moreover, which rule to apply may differ from one sales record to another.
4. Aggregating measures by the lowest expected granularity required for reporting, such as aggregating sales figures at a weekly level rather than by date, if it is determined that this is the finest level to which reporting may be needed.
5. Computing any required aggregates based on the desired semantics. For example, is a 'sales record' an order, a payment, or an invoice? The period in which a sale may be counted may be different in each case. Moreover, some invoices may be unpaid or some orders rejected. Such facts would need to be accounted for while creating 'sales records' in the data warehouse.

Usually an enterprise data warehouse aggregates many different measures of enterprise performance. Thus, in addition to sales, other measures such

as income, costs, shipment delivery times and average manufacturing production throughput are also captured along with relevant dimensions. Such a
large data model becomes difficult to navigate and query; therefore purpose-
specific data is often extracted from the enterprise data warehouse into a **data
mart**. For example, a sales data mart would include only sales information
with relevant dimensions, leaving out dimensions such as manufacturing
location, or product cost.

## 16.2.2 OLAP on a star schema

Business intelligence tasks aggregate *measures* of business performance along
a set of *dimensions*: For example, in Table 16.1, the measure is *sales*, and
dimensions are *product category*, *region* and *time period* in quarters. At a data
mart level, the **star schema** is a popular data model for capturing multidimensional information, especially where dimensions are hierarchical. Figure 16.1
illustrates a simple star schema for sales data. The name 'star' comes from
its structure: A central *fact table* surrounded by associated *dimension tables*.
The dimension tables capture the hierarchical structure of each dimension,
such as time period in days, weeks and months, or product category in
terms of a hierarchy of categories (such as board games, toys, entertainment,

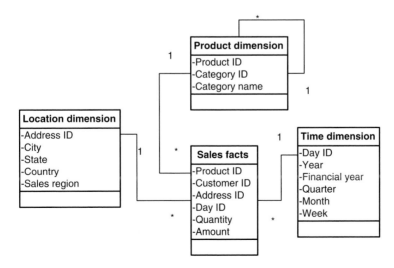

FIGURE **16.1. Star schema**

consumer). If the star schema is stored in a relational database, computing a sales analysis report as in Table 16.1 can be done via a SQL query as shown below:

```
SELECT SUM(AMOUNT), P.CATEGORY, L.SALES_REGION, T.QUARTER
 FROM SALES_FACTS S, PRODUCT P, LOCATION L, TIME T
 WHERE S.PID=P.PID AND S.AID=L.AID AND S.DID=T.DID
 GROUP BY P.CATEGORY, L.SALES_REGION, T.QUARTER
```

(Note that we have abbreviated attributes such as 'Product ID' to 'PID' etc.) The result is a set of tuples capturing sales for a each combination of category, region and quarter. Displaying the result in a format such as Table 16.1 can be easily handled through application logic since the number of records in the result will almost always be small (otherwise the report would be difficult for a human to comprehend).

Data marts are usually stored using specialized databases optimized for multidimensional queries, so that drilling down or rolling up through hierarchical dimensions becomes easy. For example, the next step in an analysis may be to investigate why consumer products are doing poorly in the APAC region as compared to enterprise products, unlike in other regions. For this the user may wish to view data at the next level of product hierarchy, and by months instead of quarters. However, handling recursive hierarchical dimensions, such as product, becomes cumbersome using SQL; notice that our SQL query above fails if for example, there is a nested hierarchy of categories.

To support iterative data analysis along a hierarchy of dimensions, many multidimensional databases support the MDX query language. For example the following MDX query computes the same results as the SQL query shown earlier:

```
SELECT { [PRODUCT].[CATEGORY].[Consumer],
         [PRODUCT].[CATEGORY].[Enterprise] },
       [TIME].[2009].Children ON COLUMNS
   [LOCATION].[SALES_REGION].Children ON ROWS
   FROM [SALES_FACTS]
```

Here the two-dimensional structure of the desired result is also encoded in the query. Complex dimension hierarchies can be encoded in MDX, and these may not be linear, e.g. computer games could be in both the 'toy' and 'software' categories. Lastly, multidimensional databases can optimize query execution better using MDX as it is a higher-level abstraction as compared to SQL.

## 16.2.3 OLAP using MapReduce

As we have already seen in earlier chapters, cloud databases, such as Google's Datastore or Amazon's SimpleDB, are not relational, do not support joins and grouping as in SQL, and certainly do not support MDX, at least as of now. We now examine how an OLAP query could be efficiently executed on a cloud database by exploiting parallel computing using the MapReduce paradigm covered in Chapter 11.

Say we are given a fact table with a very large number of records containing multiple measures and dimensions. The task is to compute the set of tuples aggregating the measures along a set of dimensions as chosen via an OLAP query. It is easy to see that such a query can be executed in parallel with each processor executing the query on a subset of records (the 'map' stage) followed by a 'reduce' stage in which these intermediate results are aggregated.

We illustrate this algorithm in more detail, primarily to introduce a matrix representation of data that will be used throughout the rest of this chapter: Suppose the fact table has $n$ data records (also referred to as data 'points'), each with $m$ features. We can represent these data points as an $m \times n$ matrix $A$. For example, considering a subset of the SALES_FACTS table of Figure 16.1, i.e., using only three dimensions (day, region and category) and one measure (sales):

$$n \text{ data points} \rightarrow$$

$$A = \begin{bmatrix} 01/01 & \ldots & 02/10 & \ldots & 04/13 & \ldots & 05/25 \\ UK & \ldots & UK & \ldots & US & \ldots & UK \\ ENT & \ldots & ENT & \ldots & CONS & \ldots & CONS \\ 10 & \ldots & 8 & \ldots & 5 & \ldots & 11 \end{bmatrix}. \qquad (16.1)$$

We shall use the above matrix representation of data repeatedly in the rest of this chapter, albeit with different interpretations of 'features' in different contexts. (Note that a relational table, such as SALES_FACTS, can be written in the form (16.1) by transposing columns and rows. For readers unfamiliar with matrix algebra concepts, a comprehensive treatment can be found in [27]. However, the discussion below does not require more than basic understanding of matrix notation and operations.)

The OLAP computation involves calculating $c$ aggregates, each an $m$-vector that aggregates a subset of features (i.e., the 'measures') corresponding to data records having a unique combination of dimension values. For the purposes of the discussion below we shall replace $A$ by a subset of rows consisting only of the rows representing measures. Thus, for our example above, $m = 1$, and we use only the last row of $A$, corresponding to the single measure 'sales.'

We can view the computation of $m$ aggregates as multiplying our new matrix $A$ with a $n \times c$ 'selection and summation matrix' $S$, where each column of $S$ has ones in rows corresponding to those data records (columns of $A$) corresponding to a particular unique combination of dimension values:

$$\underset{A}{\Sigma} = \underset{A}{\begin{bmatrix} 10 & \cdots & 8 & \cdots & 5 & \cdots & 11 \end{bmatrix}} \underset{S}{\begin{bmatrix} 1 & 0 & 0 & \cdots \\ \vdots & \vdots & \vdots & \cdots \\ 1 & 0 & 0 & \cdots \\ \vdots & \vdots & \vdots & \cdots \\ 0 & 1 & 0 & \cdots \\ \vdots & \vdots & \vdots & \cdots \\ 0 & 0 & 1 & \cdots \\ \vdots & \vdots & \vdots & \vdots \\ 0 & 0 & 0 & \end{bmatrix}}. \tag{16.2}$$

Each of the $c$ columns of $\Sigma$ yields a set of $m$ aggregate measures to be placed at the appropriate *cell* in the final OLAP matrix. Thus, the first two sales values shown contribute to the same cell of the output, i.e., Q1, UK and ENT, so the first column of $S$ has ones in two rows corresponding to these values. In contrast, the remaining values contribute to different cells of the output. Note that we assume that the aggregation function is 'summation' (as opposed to, say, 'average'). The algorithm we derive below also works for other measures, but is no longer easily represented in matrix form.

Consider $p = n/k$ 'mappers' working on arbitrary subsets of $k$ columns of $A$, multiplying each subset with a $k \times c$ matrix constructed as is $S$ above, i.e. whose columns have ones in positions based on dimension values of the columns of the sub-matrices $A_k$ (each sub-matrix $A_k$ consists of $k$ columns of $A$): Then (16.2) can be rewritten as follows:

$$\Sigma = \begin{bmatrix} A_1 \ldots A_p \end{bmatrix} \begin{bmatrix} S_1 \\ \vdots \\ S_p \end{bmatrix} = A_1 S_1 + \ldots A_p S_p. \tag{16.3}$$

Each of the $p$ partial sums $\Sigma_j = A_j S_j$ computed in the map phase is an $m \times c$ matrix, or equivalently a vector of length $mc$. The final result $\Sigma$ can be computed by $r$ reducers adding these $p$ vectors in a 'reduce' phase, with each reducer summing $p$ sub-vectors of length $mc/r$ each. Since the size of the result, $mc$, is usually small, $r$ has to be small as well, and often $r = 1$ suffices. If $r = 1$, the reduce phase involves $mcp$ computations.

## 16.2.4 Parallel efficiency of OLAP using MapReduce:

It is instructive to compute the parallel efficiency of OLAP using MapReduce, especially since in this case, unlike earlier in Chapter 11, the number of reducers is a small constant unrelated to the data size. Note first that each column of $A$ contributes to exactly one of the columns of $\Sigma$. Let us assume that the distribution of this contribution is uniform, so each of the $c$ aggregates in the final result is, on average, a sum of $n/c$ columns of $A$. With this assumption, each column of $S$ has approximately $n/c$ non-zeros and $T_1$, the time taken to compute (16.2) on one processor is approximately $m \times n/c \times c = mn$. (Here the unit of time is that required for a single addition.)

Similarly, the time to compute each product $\Sigma_j = A_j S_j$ in (16.3) is $m \times k/c \times c = mk$. Additionally, the reduce phase involves each mapper sending a vector of length $mc$ to the single reducer. So the time to compute $\Sigma$ using (16.3) with $p$ processors and one reducer is $T_p = mk + dpmc$, where $d$ is the time required for data transfer. Therefore the parallel efficiency of OLAP using MapReduce is:

$$\epsilon_{OLAP} = \frac{T_1}{pT_p} = \frac{mn}{pmk + p^2 dmc} = \frac{1}{1 + \dfrac{p^2 dc}{n}}. \qquad (16.4)$$

Thus efficiency is high if $p^2 \ll n/dc$. In practice this will be the case for large $n$, especially as the size of the output, $c$, is much smaller than, and independent of, the input size $n$. However, also note that $\epsilon_{OLAP}$ shrinks rapidly with $p$, which is to be expected since no parallelism has been used in the reduce phase ($r = 1$).

## 16.3 TEXT AND DATA MINING

Using OLAP, analysts can perform some of the knowledge discovery tasks mentioned in Section 16.1 by looking through reports that slice and dice data in different ways. For example, if one categorizes suppliers by their average prices, delivery schedules and number of products being supplied, one can gain some insight into an organization's supply chain to identify and evaluate dominant suppliers. A similar analysis could also evaluate customers, or employees. On the other hand, detecting fraud, finding patterns in product purchases or identifying trends and opinions, are more difficult, and are perhaps impossible to achieve solely through OLAP. Further, when the number of dimensions on which data needs to be analyzed becomes large, slicing and dicing becomes difficult to comprehend and results in a trial-and-error process of iteratively choosing dimensions to see if they yield insight.

Instead, the data mining approach mathematically models the analysis task. This results in a few broad categories of problems that can be solved (using a variety of computational techniques), rather than relying on human analysis alone:

1. **Classifying** data by manually assigning labels (e.g. 'valuable') to a known subset of data, and using this to construct a **classifier**, i.e. a mathematical model, which can then be used to automatically assign the labels for remaining data, or for new records as they arrive.
2. **Clustering** data into groups that are more 'similar' to each other than to other clusters, for example to determine which documents discuss the same set of topics, or which customers exhibit similar buying patterns.
3. Identifying **anomalies**, which are records very dissimilar from the vast majority of data, such as in fraud detection, or crime and intelligence investigations.
4. Analyzing **patterns** in subsets of data that have particularly strong connections to each other, especially in conjunction with other techniques, such as anomaly detection or clustering: For example, automatically characterizing anomalous behavior in terms of 'explanations' that yield deeper insight, or describing the actual behavior patterns of customers belonging to the same cluster.
5. Making **predictions** by choosing hypotheses that might *explain* data, by constructing probabilistic models, such as in tracking a moving target, modeling price movements or fault diagnosis.

In the next few sections we examine some of these tasks along with selected solution techniques. The choice of algorithms used is more to bring out a common matrix formulation of each of the problems, rather than cover the state of art in the field, which is too vast to accomplish here. As we shall see, the advantage of our common matrix formulation is that it brings out the close interrelation of different techniques, presents the opportunity to treat text and structured data using a unified approach, and highlights computational techniques that can exploit a distributed cloud computing environment using the MapReduce paradigm.

## 16.3.1 Data classification

Let us consider our data matrix as defined earlier in (16.1), with $n$ data points characterized by $m$ feature attributes. (Note that we no longer distinguish between 'measures' and 'dimensions.') These could be actual attributes of structured data records, or features derived from actual attributes. For example customers may be characterized by structured features such as the number of products they buy, their average spend, as well as features of unstructured data such as the words they use in their communications. If the data is unstructured text, columns are documents, and rows represent $m$ terms, or keywords, for which each column entry in the matrix indicates whether that term is present in the corresponding document, or counts the frequency of the term in the document.

In a classification problem we assume that each data point has already been labeled as belonging to one of a number of classes. As an example consider 8 documents characterized by the occurrence or absence of 11 possible keywords, represented by the data matrix:

$$
A = \begin{array}{c}
\\
program \\
string \\
gravity \\
code \\
graph \\
velocity \\
random \\
quantum \\
chip \\
protein \\
cell
\end{array}
\begin{array}{cccccccc}
p_1 & p_2 & p_3 & c_1 & c_2 & c_3 & b_1 & b_2 \\
\left[\begin{array}{cccccccc}
0 & 0 & 0 & 1 & 1 & 1 & 0 & 0 \\
1 & 0 & 0 & 0 & 1 & 0 & 0 & 1 \\
1 & 1 & 1 & 0 & 0 & 0 & 0 & 0 \\
0 & 0 & 0 & 1 & 0 & 1 & 0 & 0 \\
0 & 0 & 0 & 1 & 1 & 1 & 0 & 0 \\
1 & 1 & 1 & 0 & 0 & 0 & 0 & 0 \\
0 & 1 & 1 & 0 & 0 & 0 & 0 & 0 \\
0 & 1 & 1 & 0 & 0 & 1 & 0 & 0 \\
0 & 0 & 0 & 0 & 1 & 1 & 0 & 0 \\
0 & 0 & 0 & 0 & 0 & 0 & 1 & 1 \\
0 & 0 & 0 & 0 & 0 & 0 & 1 & 0
\end{array}\right]
\end{array}, \quad
d = \begin{bmatrix}
1 \\ 0 \\ 0 \\ 0 \\ 1 \\ 0 \\ 1 \\ 0 \\ 1 \\ 0 \\ 0
\end{bmatrix}. \tag{16.5}
$$

Here $a_{ij} = 1$ if the ith term occurs in document $j$, and $a_{ij} = 0$ otherwise. As can be observed from the words they contain, the documents $p_i$ are likely to be on physics, $c_i$ on computing and $b_i$ on biology. We assume we have already labeled each document as to which of these classes it belongs to. Given a new document $d$ as also shown in (16.5) above, we would like to automatically determine which class label to assign to it.

Note that in practice we usually consider the normalized frequency of each term across all documents, for example if $f_{ij}$ is the frequency of the $i$th term in document $j$, a common practice is to set $a_{ij} = \frac{f_{ij}}{\sum_i f_{ij}} \log n/n_i$ where $n$ is the total number of documents and $n_i$ the number of documents containing the term $i$. This particular normalization, often referred to as 'TF-IDF' (term-frequency times inverse document frequency) ensures that overly common terms do not dominate the rarer but more meaningful ones. However, for simplicity we have used a simpler representation in our example. Also, in practice the number of keywords will be large, and $A$ will be highly sparse and never actually computed in its entirety. For example, since a document naturally stores only the words it contains, each document is itself a compressed representation of a column of $A$.

Let us partition the data matrix as:

$$A = \left[\ A_P\ ,\ A_C,\ A_B\ \right].\tag{16.6}$$

Clearly, each class is characterized by a different set of words, or features, so the columns of $A_P$ will be, on the average, 'further away' from those in $A_C$ and $A_B$ than within themselves (and vice versa). A common measure of the distance between data points $a_i$ and $a_j$ is the 'cosine' distance between two vectors, defined as:[1]

$$< a_i, a_j > \equiv 1 - \frac{|a_i^T a_j|}{((a_i^T a_i)^{\frac{1}{2}}(a_j^T a_j)^{\frac{1}{2}})}.\tag{16.7}$$

A naive algorithm for classification then follows naturally, i.e. compare $d$ with each of the columns and determine which class it is closer to, on the average. For example, the cosine distances of $d$ with each of the columns of $A$ can easily be computed:

$$[< d^T a_i >] = \left[\ 1.0\quad 0.75\quad 0.75\quad 0.42\quad 0.25\quad 0.33\quad 1.0\quad 1.0\ \right].$$

The document $d$ is closer to the columns $c_i$, i.e. $A_C$ than to $A_P$ or $A_B$. Examining the words contained in $d$ it is clear that this classification is indeed correct, i.e. the words in document $d$ mostly relate to computing.

---

[1] $a_i^T$ is the 'transpose' of $a_i$; and $a_i^T a_j$ the 'dot product' [27].

The above approach of determining which class a new data point belongs to is highly inefficient if the number of columns of $A$ is large, which will usually be the case. The classification algorithm needs to use a more compact representation of the pre-classified sets $A_P$, $A_C$ and $A_B$. For example, one could represent each set, $P$, by its *centroid*, i.e. the (normalized) sum of all the columns in that class: $c_P = \sum_{i \in P} a_i / n$. Then we need only compare $d$ with the three centroids, or more generally with $k$ centroids if there are $k$ classes. Many such classification algorithms are possible, ranging from the simple centroid method to fairly sophisticated algorithms called 'support vector machines' [38].

We introduce an algorithm for classification using the 'singular value decomposition', not because it is superior, but because it brings out a unified understanding of the structure of data when viewed in matrix form. This formulation will also come in useful in later sections as a common basis for understanding various data mining tasks.

**Singular Value Decomposition:**

$$
A \;=\; \underbrace{\left[\begin{array}{ccc} u_1 & \cdots & u_m \\ \downarrow & \vdots & \downarrow \end{array}\right]}_{U_{m \times m}} \;\; \underbrace{\left[\; \Sigma^1_{m \times m} , \; 0 \;\right]}_{\Sigma_{m \times n}} \;\; \underbrace{\left[\begin{array}{ccc} v_1^T & \rightarrow \\ \vdots & \cdots \\ v_n^T & \rightarrow \end{array}\right]}_{V_{n \times n}^T} .
\tag{16.8}
$$

It turns out that *any* matrix can be written as a product of three matrices as in (16.8), which is called the singular value decomposition, or SVD of the matrix [27]. The matrices $U$ and $V$ are *orthogonal* matrices, i.e. $U^T U = I$ and $V^T V = I$ (where $I$ is a diagonal matrix of all ones). Another way of looking at this is that the columns of $U$ and $V$ are pairwise orthogonal, meaning that they are very 'far apart' from each other according to our earlier definition of cosine distance, i.e. $< u_i, u_j >$ and $< v_i, v_j >$ are 1 if $i \neq j$, and 0 if $i = j$.

The matrix $\Sigma$ is a diagonal matrix whose entries ($\sigma_i$) are called the 'singular values' of $A$. Note that since in general $A$ is an $m \times n$ matrix, $\Sigma$ will have a set of $n - m$ columns of zeros at the end if $n > m$ (if $n < m$, these would instead be rows of zeros at the bottom). It is important to note that the SVD of a square matrix (i.e., $m = n$) is essentially *unique*[2] if one orders the diagonal entries of $\Sigma$ in say descending order; we say 'essentially' because it is possible to change the sign of any column of $U$ and the corresponding column of $V$ and still

---

[2] Except in the special case of repeated singular values.

preserve the decomposition. (For a non-square matrix, say $m > n$, only the first $n$ singular vectors of $V$ are unique, since the remaining $n - m$ columns of $V$ can be *any* 'orthogonal complement' to the first $n$ columns. Similarly, if $m < n$, it is the last $n - m$ columns of $U$ that are not unique.)

To understand how the SVD provides insight into the structure of large data sets modeled as matrices, we make a few observations (proofs are available in any matrix algebra text, such as [27]):

1. Each column of $A$ is a *linear combination* of the columns of $U$ (which are called 'left singular vectors'; similarly the columns of $V$ are called 'right singular vectors').
2. If the columns of $A$ are very similar to each other, it is highly likely that it would be possible to express them as linear combinations of a small set of, say $k$, columns of $U$ where $k \ll n$.
3. In the above situation, there will be $k$ 'large' singular values $\sigma_1 \ldots \sigma_k$ with the rest being relatively much smaller. We will refer to these as the $k$ 'dominant' singular values and the corresponding $k$ columns of $U$ as the dominant singular vectors of $A$.

The matrix approach to data mining, including observations such as the above, are treated in more detail in [56].

Returning now to our classification problem with two classes: Let us compute the SVD each of the matrices $A_B$, $A_C$ and $A_B$ to yield dominant singular vectors $\tilde{U}_P \equiv U_P^{1\ldots k_p}$, $\tilde{U}_C \equiv U_C^{1\ldots k_n}$ and $\tilde{U}_B \equiv U_B^{1\ldots k_n}$ (as defined in 3 above). Since these smaller sets of vectors approximately represent *all* the columns of $A_P$, $A_C$ and $A_B$ respectively, we can classify any new data point $d$ by computing the average cosine distance of $d$ to each of these sets. Performing the above computation for our example data matrix $A$ and document $d$ of (16.5), and using only the largest singular vector of each matrix $A_B$, $A_C$ and $A_B$, i.e. $k = 1$, we find that $< d, u_P^1 > = 0.78$, $< d, u_C^1 > = 0.25$, and $< d, u_B^1 > = 1.0$, clearly indicating that $d$ belongs to the same class as the columns of $A_C$.[3]

Computing the SVD is expensive, so in practice other methods of choosing 'representative' points are often used. For example one could choose a random set of points from each set, or choose a set of points from each set that are as far apart from each other as possible [28].

Finally we note that in our matrix formulation of the classification we do not distinguish between structured data with features and unstructured text with keyword terms. In fact the same algorithm works for both cases, and

---

[3] The SVD can be computed using packages such as MATLAB or Octave (open source).

also for the *mixed* case, where a data point includes a lot of structured data as well as unstructured text: In this case some rows of $A$ represent features of structured data and others represent keyword terms for unstructured text associated with the each data point. Last but not least, it is very important to note that the actual performance of the algorithm in practice does depend significantly on how the features and keywords characterizing a data point are defined. In the next few sections we shall apply the matrix formulation and SVD to other problems of data mining. However, before this we first describe what is involved in computing a large SVD and how it could be done using cloud computing paradigms such as MapReduce.

## 16.3.2 Computing the SVD using MapReduce

There are many algorithms for computing the SVD of a matrix, each of which perform better or worse depending on the nature of the matrix. All techniques for computing the SVD are *iterative*, i.e. the number of steps is not deterministic, and the computation *converges* after some steps so that the results are accurate to the extent of machine precision. Details of SVD algorithms can be found in [27]. Here we focus on the nature of the computations involved and how these can be executed in parallel using MapReduce.

Many iterative SVD algorithms rely on repeated matrix-vector multiplications namely $Av_i$ and $A^T u_i$, where the $u_i$ and $v_i$ are approximations to the left and right singular vectors of $A$, which are continuously refined and ultimately converge to the actual values, with the singular values also being revealed in the process. Such methods are especially preferred when $A$ is large sparse, as they do not destroy the sparsity of $A$ during the computation. Further, the techniques work just as well when applied to computing only the $k$ largest singular values and vectors, in which case only $k$ vectors $u_1 \ldots u_k$ and $v_1 \ldots v_k$ have to be maintained during the computation.

Let $\bar{U}$ and $\bar{V}$ be $m \times k$ matrices with columns $u_1 \ldots u_k$ and $v_1 \ldots v_k$ respectively. To see how the multiplications $A\bar{V}$ and $A^T\bar{U}$ can be executed in parallel using MapReduce, we split the matrix $A$ into $p$ sets of columns, as we did earlier for OLAP in (16.3). Similarly $\bar{V}$ is also split, as it also has a large number of columns ($n$). We then rewrite these products as follows:

$$A\bar{V} = \begin{bmatrix} A_1 \ldots A_p \end{bmatrix} \begin{bmatrix} \bar{V}_1 \\ \vdots \\ \bar{V}_p \end{bmatrix} = A_1\bar{V}_1 + \cdots A_p\bar{V}_p. \qquad (16.9)$$

$$A^T \bar{U} = \begin{bmatrix} A_1^T \\ \vdots \\ A_p^T \end{bmatrix} \bar{U} = \begin{bmatrix} A_1^T \bar{U} \\ \vdots \\ A_p^T \bar{U} \end{bmatrix}. \tag{16.10}$$

To compute $A\bar{V}$, $p$ mappers compute each of the products $A_i \bar{V}_i$ and a reduce operation computes the sum. For computing $A^T \bar{U}$, no reduce is required since once the computations $A_i^T \bar{U}$ are done by $p$ mappers, the result is ready.

The parallel efficiency of computing (16.9) can be computed in a manner similar to (16.4); moreover its behavior with $p$ and $n$ is also similar. The parallel efficiency of computing (16.10), on the other hand, is *one*, if communications costs are ignored.

Finally, it is important to note that in practice the matrix $A$ will be large and sparse, and will be stored in a compressed manner: For example, if each column of $A$ represents a document, as in the example (16.5), only the words present in each document will be stored; i.e. the non-zero values of $A$ will be stored *by columns*. Therefore our parallel algorithm described above partitions $A$ by columns, thereby distributing documents to processors. On the other hand, we may use an alternative representation *by rows*, such as illustrated in Figure 16.3 of Section 16.4.2 below. Then we would need to partition $A$ by rows instead, and compute $A\bar{V}$ in the manner $A^T \bar{U}$ is computed above, and vice versa for $A^T \bar{U}$. The choice of which representation and corresponding technique to use depends on the relative size of $m$ and $n$. If $m \ll n$, we partition $A$ by columns, and if $m \gg n$ we partition by rows.

For example, if we consider $A$ to be a term-document matrix for a document repository, $m$ can be as large as the number of possible words, which (in English) is a few hundred thousand. If the repository in question is the entire web, at least as many proper nouns, if not more, will occur. Further documents can be in many different languages; so we could end up with $m$ of the order of a few million. Nevertheless, the total number of documents on the web is already over 50 billion, so in this case we find that $n \gg m$. However, for a typical enterprise document repository with at most tens of thousands of documents, we will usually find $m > n$. On the other hand, if we consider structured data, such as records in a database, the number of features (i.e., columns) of interest for, say classification purposes, is usually much smaller than the total number of records; so once again we find $n \gg m$.

### 16.3.3 Clustering data

Classification is an example of 'supervised learning', where we are provided a set of labeled data and we use it to classify further data. Clustering, on the other hand, is when we attempt to learn what classes there are in an 'unsupervised' manner. For example, we may wish to determine which customers have similar buying patterns, or which products are bought by the same sets of customers, without any pre-existing knowledge apart from the data at hand.

Once again we examine what insight the matrix formulation and SVD can bring: The $n$ columns of $A$ (i.e. data points) are linear combinations of the columns of $U$ (singular vectors). In terms of these new axes, which we call '$U$-space,' the 'coordinates' of each data point is given by the columns of $\Sigma V^T$. It is observed in practice that the maximal variation in the data set is captured by the first few singular vectors $U^{1 \dots k}$ [57]. Thus the first few coordinates of each data point in $U$-space, which are the first few rows of $\Sigma V^T$, reveal the clusters. Using our example (16.5) we find that the first two coordinates of each data point in $U$-space, i.e. the first two *rows* of $\Sigma V^T$ are:

$$
\begin{array}{cccccccc}
p_1 & p_2 & p_3 & c_1 & c_2 & c_3 & b_1 & b_2 \\
-0.94 & -1.40 & -1.40 & -1.03 & -1.29 & -1.74 & -0.03 & -0.26 \\
-0.81 & -1.38 & -1.38 & 1.08 & 1.14 & 1.17 & 0.01 & 0.05
\end{array}
$$

Viewing each column as a point in two-dimensional space, as shown in Figure 16.2, we see that the clusters are revealed. In this manner, using

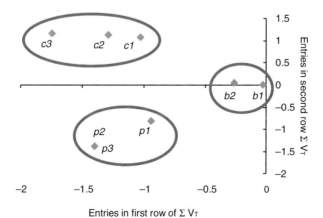

FIGURE 16.2. **Clustering using the first two rows of $\Sigma V^T$**

the SVD one can cluster high-dimensional data by reducing the problem to a simpler clustering problem in a low-dimensional space.

There are many related clustering algorithms, and the one we have presented is far from optimal; it does however bring out the close connection between classification and clustering through the insight offered by the SVD.

## 16.3.4 Anomaly detection

Often we are concerned with detecting if there are a few data points that stand out from the vast majority of data, i.e. 'outliers,' which could represent some form of anomalous behavior, either suspicious, fraudulent or eccentric. Once again our matrix formulation together with the SVD provides some insight: In practice we often find that the vast majority of data points are well represented by a smaller (than $m$) subset of singular vectors corresponding to the largest $k$ singular values. In such a situation, if there is a small set of data points that are different from the vast majority, they will *not* be well represented by these $k$ singular vectors. Instead they will be closer to some of the latter singular vectors, most often to $u_m$, corresponding to the smallest singular value: This is because the singular values also have an intuitive meaning; the larger values and corresponding singular vectors represent the dominant feature combinations in the data set. Similarly, the smaller ones represent those combinations that are rare. A clustering perspective provides another view: outliers are clusters having very few data points.

So, outliers can often be identified by those columns of $V^T$ in which the first $k$ values (corresponding to the dominant singular vectors) are *all* small. The corresponding columns of $A$ are likely to be outliers representing some kind of anomalous behavior. For example, using the matrix in (16.5), we find that the columns of $V_k^T$ (with $k = 2$) are:

$$\begin{bmatrix} -0.29 & -0.43 & -0.43 & -0.31 & -0.39 & -0.53 & -0.01 & -0.08 \\ -0.29 & -0.48 & -0.48 & 0.38 & 0.39 & 0.40 & 0.00 & 0.02 \end{bmatrix}.$$

The fact that the entries in the last two columns are much smaller than the rest indicate that the cluster $A_B$ is smaller than the other two clusters. As before, there are many mechanisms for outlier detection, the SVD-based technique is only one. However it clearly illustrates the relationship between outliers, clustering and classification.

## 16.4 TEXT AND DATABASE SEARCH

### 16.4.1 Enterprise search

The ubiquity of access to web search naturally raises the question of whether searching for information within an enterprise can be made as simple as it appears to be on the web. At the same time, the apparent simplicity of web search belies the tremendous complexity of what is taking place in the background behind every query, with the scale of information on the web being orders of magnitude larger than the data stored in even the largest enterprises. So it may appear at first glance that applying the same search technology within an organization should be relatively simple. Unfortunately, there are also many differences between web search and 'enterprise search,' such as:

1. Ranking search results is more difficult for enterprise data: On the web more 'popular' results are assumed to be better. However, in an enterprise, one is usually more interested in 'correct' results, rather than merely popular ones. At the same time, more information is often available about the user, such as their role, or the context in which a search is being performed. Further, it is easier to track user behavior in response to search results as compared to the web.

2. The structure of the web provides explicit information on how pieces of information are linked to each other, i.e hyperlinks; such links are far less explicit for enterprise data. For example, documents may contain names of the same important customer, but these are unlikely to be explicitly linked, and any such relationship would have to be derived. For structured data, such as in databases, some explicit linkages in the form of foreign keys are present; equally often however, it is the *absence* of such information that drives the need to 'search' structured data.

3. Information on the web is public, whereas enterprise data can have security restrictions that need to be enforced while deciding whether and how much access a particular user has to some piece of information.

4. The vast majority of information on the web is textual, and uniformly located via URIs. Enterprise data, on the other hand, is a mixed bag of textual information linked to structured records in databases, which in turn are linked to others via often circuitous foreign key relationships. Further, enterprise data exists in a greater variety of document and database formats, as well as sometimes being available only through calls to application services.

## 16.4.2 Indexing and search using MapReduce

The search problem can also be studied using the matrix formulation as in (16.1). For text search, as in (16.5), the columns of $A$ are documents and rows (features) are keyword terms. For database records the columns correspond to tuples (possibly from many different tables), and features are distinct values that can occur in field of a record, or may instead represent meta-data.

In practice the matrix $A$ will always be highly sparse, and also there may be a huge number of features, both terms and 'key' values as in the above example. So the issue of how such a matrix is actually formed and stored is also important. An example of such a sparse storage scheme is a 'postings list' [38] as shown in Figure 16.3: Along with each keyword we store a list of documents in which the word occurs; this can also be viewed as a sparsity preserving *row-wise* storage of the matrix $A$. In the parlance of search technology, this is also referred to as an 'inverted index' on the documents: Just as each document is a list of words, each entry in this 'inverted' index is a list of documents. As we have already seen in Chapter 11, index computation can be efficiently carried out in parallel using MapReduce.

We now examine how keyword search can be carried out using our matrix formulation. For simplicity we assume that data points are all documents (i.e. no database records). Recall that we could measure the closeness of any two documents $a_i$ and $a_j$ (columns of $A$) by the cosine distance (16.7) $< a_i, a_j >$. To model search, we view any *query* also as a (very short) document, defined by a vector $q$. Then, the search problem reduces to finding documents $a_i$ that have small $d_i = < q, a_i >$.

Clearly it is inefficient to compute the product of $q$ with all documents. Instead, we exploit the sparse storage mechanism shown in Figure 16.3 to access only the entries (rows of $A$) of terms present in $q$. As we traverse

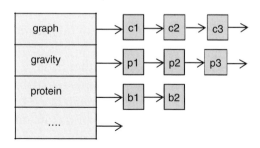

**FIGURE 16.3. Inverted index**

each of these lists sequentially, we accumulate the distances $d_i$ for only those documents encountered along the way (as for all other documents that do not contain any query term, $d_i$ will be 1). A detailed explanation of 'vector-space' based retrieval using the 'postings-list' structure can be found in [38].

It is also easy to see how this search can be performed in parallel using MapReduce: Each mapper accesses an index on a small subset of documents and computes a partial set of products, i.e. for those documents that it encounters. Each map operation returns a set of documents with small query distances $d_i$. Note that this may still be a large set. The reduce operation then computes (in parallel) the $k$ smallest of these products to determine the search result.

### 16.4.3 Latent semantic indexing

The search model described above is that of simple keyword search, i.e. the result set contains only those documents that contain some or all of the query terms, ranked by how closely they match the query in this sense. Simple keyword search ignores two aspects of natural language that may be important in certain kinds of search, *synonymy* and *polysymy*. Consider our example of (16.5): Two terms, such as 'code' and 'program,' could have the same meaning. We would like to discover this synonymy and exploit it, so that a search on 'code' also yields documents containing to 'program.' The cosine distance distance $< q, a_i >$ ignores such synonyms and underestimates similarity. Polysymy, on the other hand, is when the same term, such as 'string' is used in multiple contexts (e.g. 'string theory' in physics, text strings in computing, and nucleotide strings in biology); in this case simple search overestimates similarity.

It turns out that using the SVD one can automatically take into account both synonymy and polysymy to a certain extent. The technique that achieves this is called Latent Semantic Indexing [15] (or LSI). In LSI one computes the SVD of the document matrix $A$, and truncates it to the first $k$ singular vectors and values, to obtain an approximation $A_k$:

$$A = \begin{bmatrix} U_k & U_{m-k} \end{bmatrix} \begin{bmatrix} \Sigma_k & 0 & 0 \\ 0 & \Sigma_{m-k} & 0 \end{bmatrix} \begin{bmatrix} V_k & V_{n-k} \end{bmatrix}^T \approx A_k = U_k \Sigma_k V_k^T. \quad (16.11)$$

(Note that $A_k$ is still an $m \times n$ matrix, just like $A$.) Now, a query $q$ is compared with $A_k$ instead of $A$. Consider the data matrix (16.5) and a single term query 'code,' whose corresponding query vector will have $q_i = 0, i \neq 4$ and $q_4 = 1$. The cosine distances between $q$ and columns of $A_k$, for $k = 3$, are:

$$0.88 \quad 0.97 \quad 0.97 \quad 0.59 \quad 0.74 \quad 0.59 \quad 0.80 \quad 0.85.$$

We see that using LSI the query vector $q$ is found to be close to $c_2$ that contains the term 'program' in addition to $c_1$ and $c_3$ that contain the exact query term 'code.'

Note that unlike earlier, $A_k$ is no longer likely to be a sparse matrix; furthermore the number of rows (all possible query terms) $m$ is likely to be large. However, because of its structure, and the fact that $k \ll n, m$ computing the distance of $q$ to the columns of $A_k$ also lends itself to efficient parallel implementation.

The LSI algorithm is computationally more intensive than simple keyword search. However, it is found in practice that LSI captures synonymy and polysymy to a certain extent; theoretical as well as experimental research continues into understanding this phenomenon better [43]. Nevertheless, if the volume of records $n$, or number of features $m$, is very large the computational requirement of LSI can become prohibitive.

Recent results have shown that we can use a much smaller *random* sample of columns of $A$ to approximate $A_k$ to a high degree of accuracy [23]; further the random sample can also be efficiently computed in parallel. Nevertheless, even if we are able to compute $A_k$ using only a fraction of the columns of $A$, the fact remains that $U_k$ and $V_k$ are no longer sparse matrices. In this regard the *CUR* decomposition [18] provides an alternative approximation, where $C$ and $R$ are $k$ columns and rows of $A$ respectively, thereby maintaining sparsity. It is shown in [18] how to choose $C$ and $R$ such that the product $CUR$ is a close approximation to $A_k$.

### 16.4.4 Searching structured data

Searching structured data has traditionally been through query languages, such as SQL. However, for a variety of reasons, there is renewed interest in applying search technology, such as used for text, to structured data:

1. Applications that issue SQL queries are limited in the extent to which they enable search using keywords. Moreover, often many different screens need to be accessed to find all occurrences of a keyword as each screen accesses only a particular set of tables.

2. Enterprises often have a large number of applications that maintain their own interrelated but independent databases. Searching all these simultaneously can be looked upon as a cheap and user friendly way to provide integrated access to information across applications.

3. Related to the above case, often information about the same 'objects,' say a product, is present in a number of systems that are not well integrated. Search-based technologies could 'discover' data relationships by automatically traversing common foreign key *values*, thereby possibly retrieving related data from multiple systems.

4. SQL queries rely heavily on *joins* between tables; however, as we have seen earlier, cloud databases (such as Google's Datastore or Amazon SimpleDB) do not support joins. Therefore it is likely that while using cloud platforms, search-based access to databases, even from within an application, may become increasingly important.

5. It is often important to examine linkages between data items that are not explicitly maintained as joins, such as while trying to determine if two sets of information (objects) actually represent the same real-world entity (such as the same person).

6. Increasingly, structured data is augmented with unstructured information and it may be desirable to search both kinds of data at once.

A number of techniques for each of the above problems are the subject of much current research, such as [3]. For structured data (i.e. tuples from one or more tables, in one or more databases), the matrix $A$ is once again large and sparse, as before. The entries of $A$ are 0 or 1 depending on whether a term is present in a particular tuple or not. Exactly the same indexing scheme and search technique works as before, returning a set of disjoint tuples that contain the keywords in the query. For such an application, the terms included in $A$ should ideally be limited to text fields or data with categorical values, rather than continuous data such as amounts. Just as earlier, MapReduce-based parallel implementations are possible. Note however that using simple keyword search, we completely ignore joins and other interrelationships between tuples. Mechanisms to incorporate such linkages, without using joins, are currently the subject of research, as are techniques for exploiting joins when available, and ranking the results of such searches. The relevance of techniques such as LSI when used on structured data is also a topic that remains to be investigated.

# Enterprise cloud computing

The ecosystem of technologies related to the enterprise adoption of cloud computing is constantly evolving. In addition to the three major cloud providers, new ones are emerging from amongst those already in the data center hosting business. Apart from cloud providers, there are also tools to manage combinations of in-house and cloud resources. Similarly, there are frameworks to assist enterprises in creating 'private' clouds within their own data centers. As cloud computing matures, many of the concerns surrounding its use for enterprise applications are likely to be addressed. In the meantime, there are a few quick-wins that can result in immediate benefits by leveraging available cloud platforms. In the longer term, cloud computing will itself evolve in hereto unknown directions, and we speculate on a few of these: In particular, the convergence of public and private clouds, and the emergence of 'cloud-services.'

# Enterprise cloud computing ecosystem

So far we have covered a number of cloud computing technologies as well as explored their impact on the software needs of enterprises. In the process we have limited our discussion to the major cloud computing providers, viz. Amazon, Google and Microsoft, with most of our examples taken from the first two, given that Microsoft's offering is still in its nascent stages at the time of writing.

However, the cloud computing ecosystem includes other cloud providers, albeit smaller than the three major ones. Additionally, there are a range of emerging technologies that complement public clouds, enable interoperability between private data centers and public clouds, or facilitate the creation of private clouds within enterprises.

Figure 17.1 depicts our classification of the cloud ecosystem from an enterprise perspective, also indicating the organizations involved in creating and bringing these technologies to market. Needless to say this list of organizations is incomplete and evolving; moreover, given the rate of innovation in the cloud space, it is possible that additional technology categories may emerge in the future. (Note: there are other similar classifications, such as the OpenCrowd taxonomy[1], which includes a far broader range of technologies and applications.)

---

[1] www.opencrowd.com/views/cloud.php

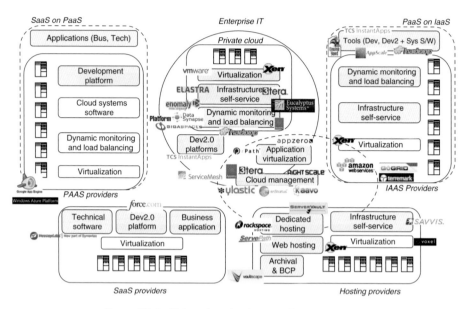

**FIGURE 17.1. Enterprise cloud computing ecosystem**

The enterprise cloud ecosystem comprises of three main categories; cloud service providers, tools for using and managing cloud deployments and tools for building private clouds. Each of these categories include a number of underlying technologies as illustrated in Figure 17.1 (some are shaded to indicate that they are directly available to enterprise while others are used internally by public cloud providers). We cover each of these categories in the next few sections. We also examine in detail some open source technologies that mimic public cloud implementations, which can therefore be used by enterprises embarking on creating private clouds.

## 17.1 PUBLIC CLOUD PROVIDERS

Let us recall the key elements of a public cloud platform, such as Amazon EC2, Google App Engine or Microsoft Azure. An infrastructure as a service (IaaS) cloud (such as Amazon EC2) offers self-service infrastructure (both compute and storage) provisioning built on an underlying large-scale data center based on virtualization. Dynamic monitoring and load balancing services are the latest addition to the Amazon cloud, i.e. CloudWatch, Auto Scaling and Elastic Load Balancing. Platform as a service (PaaS) clouds, such as Google App Engine and Microsoft Azure, offer a software development and deployment platform while hiding much of the underlying virtualization and dynamic resource management layers. The common feature of these offerings is the *ability of users to pay only for the resources they actually consume, at a very fine granularity*. **From a business perspective this is the essence of classifying any offering as a public cloud service.**

Data center hosting services are not new to the IT industry and have been around for decades. The traditional service offering from such providers has been 'dedicated server' hosting, where a set of physical servers and storage were provisioned and dedicated for use by a particular enterprise customer. In recent years, these providers have also begun to offer virtual servers, based initially on process virtual machines such as user-mode Linux and virtual private servers (see Chapter 8), but now almost universally based on native hardware virtualization, typically using the open source Xen VMM. Similarly, web-hosting services have been mainstream for a number of years as well. Many websites today, especially of small and medium enterprises, are hosted and managed by web-hosting providers. These providers have offered hosted storage and database space as part of their web-hosting services, and are now offering additional services based on virtual servers.

Hosting services (dedicated server as well as web) have traditionally charged on a monthly basis depending on the resources, dedicated or virtual, deployed for a user. Many traditional hosting providers are now offering additional features similar to cloud providers, such as self-service provisioning, while continuing to offer their traditional hosting offerings: Rackspace, Savvis, Voxel, ServerVault and ServePath fall into this category, as shown in Figure 17.1. However, only some, such as Terremark and GoGrid (which is operated by ServePath) have also begun to offer true cloud pricing, i.e. charging only for resources that users actually consume on an *hourly* basis. Therefore we have classified GoGrid and Terremark as an IaaS cloud along with Amazon EC2, but not the other hosting providers even though they are also 'cloud providers' in the more general sense of the term. It is likely, however, that many of these will enter the IaaS space in the near future, resulting in a rapid expansion of the number of public IaaS clouds. Still others may evolve towards niche infrastructure services with cloud pricing models, such as Vaultscape for storage backup.

The platform as a service (PaaS) space, as compared to IaaS, is still sparse, with very few entrants apart from Google and Microsoft. An example of a niche PaaS offering is Engine Yard, which provides a development platform using Ruby on Rails, based on underlying infrastructure running on Amazon

EC2; i.e. an example of 'PaaS over IaaS.' In a similar vein AppScale is an open source implementation of the Google App Engine interface on Amazon EC2. AppScale also leverages the Hadoop project's open source versions of Google's BigTable and GFS (covered in Chapter 10). We describe AppScale in more detail in Section 17.3.2 below.

Finally, recall our extensive treatment of the Dev 2.0 paradigm (end-user-driven application development tools) exemplified by Salesforce.com's Force.com platform, TCS's InstantApps, as well many others as mentioned in Chapter 12. We classify most Dev 2.0 platforms, including Force.com, in the software as a service category, since they limit application features as compared to a PaaS platform where access to a full programming language is provided. InstantApps on Amazon EC2, however, can be considered to be a PaaS (on IaaS) offering, since this tool allows users to write native client and server-side code (in JavaScript as well as Java), thereby in principle allowing any web application feature to be developed on it, just as for a full PaaS platform such as Google App Engine or Azure. (Additionally, InstantApps is also deployable on-premise as a traditional software development tool.)

## 17.2 CLOUD MANAGEMENT PLATFORMS AND TOOLS

Configuring and managing a small set of servers on an IaaS cloud can be accomplished easily using an IaaS offering's own infrastructure self-service APIs and tools. Managing a larger and more complex deployment requires more tools support and automation, just as it does within an enterprise data center. Cloud management platforms such as 3tera, RightScale, Kaavo, EnStratus and Ylastic provide web-based graphical tools to configure and manage complex configurations of servers deployed in the cloud. Some of these tools work only with Amazon EC2, while others, such as RightScale, enable management of multi-cloud deployments; for example, spanning Amazon EC2 and GoGrid. Further, all these cloud management platforms are themselves deployed in the cloud, either on an IaaS platform such as Amazon EC2 (e.g. RightScale) or in partnership with smaller, hosting providers (e.g. 3tera).

In addition to graphical self-service infrastructure management, some cloud management tools also offer dynamic monitoring and load balancing. These capabilities were crucial in the initial stages of IaaS before Amazon EC2 itself introduced Elastic Load Balancing, CloudWatch and Auto Scaling. Though no longer required if one is only using Amazon EC2, in a multi-cloud scenario they may become increasingly important when the number of IaaS clouds grows.

From an enterprise IT perspective though, at least for the foreseeable future private data centers (including those managed by dedicated hosting providers) will remain part and parcel of enterprise IT. Cloud deployments will only complement this infrastructure. Therefore, the ability to manage complex IT environments that span local infrastructure as well as cloud deployments will be required. Traditional infrastructure management tools, such as from CA or IBM, will certainly respond to this need. In the meanwhile, some cloud management tools, such as 3tera, Appistry or ServiceMesh can also be deployed within the enterprise and used to manage a combination of local and public cloud infrastructure.

Recall how application software is made available on an IaaS cloud: Amazon EC2 packages a virtual server along with its software configuration as an AMI; GoGrid has its own similar format called GSI. However, creating such virtual images from scratch, say from a deployment of an enterprise application, is not simple, further the images so created are large. Niche, 'application virtualization' technology from rPath or AppZero makes such tasks simpler and also optimizes the application images in size. Such tools also promise to enable portability of application images across different clouds and private data centers.

Finally, there is another emerging trend related to infrastructure management: Hosted technical software for email security and virus scanning, such as MessageLabs (recently acquired by Symantec). We foresee that even more technical software, such as middleware for managing web services, workflows, or identity, moving to hosted models. Leading in this arena are the .NET services included in Microsoft's cloud platform, as we mentioned briefly in Chapter 5.

## 17.3 TOOLS FOR BUILDING PRIVATE CLOUDS

Automation of data center operations within the enterprise using technologies such as virtualization promises to improve efficiencies by increasing server utilization, as we have seen in Chapter 8. Self-service infrastructure provisioning together with dynamic monitoring and load balancing are equally critical elements in achieving such higher utilization levels as well as in reducing manpower requirements and costs of infrastructure management.

There is considerable interest amongst enterprises, especially within corporate IT, in creating 'private clouds.' For the most part, such private cloud projects involve a combination of virtualization, self-service infrastructure and dynamic monitoring and load balancing. Many are re-branded versions of already on-going data center automation projects. Others have been driven by the emergence of public clouds as an attractive option for enterprise application deployments, motivating efforts to achieve similar efficiencies within the enterprise.

Tools for self-service infrastructure as well as some dynamic resource control capabilities are now being provided by products from virtualization tool vendors such as VMware. Cloud management tools that are deployed within the enterprise such as 3tera and Appistry (which are also available in the cloud), as well as others such as Elastra and Enomaly also provide such features. In high-performance computing environments, such as trading floors of investment banks or for scientific computing, Grid computing technologies such as from GigaSpaces, Platform Computing and DataSynapse (now acquired by TIBCO) offer similar features tuned for applications exhibiting large real-time demand fluctuations.

The question remains as to what extent data center automation using such technologies constitutes a 'private cloud,' and if so whether it can achieve efficiencies nearing those of public clouds. We shall return to this question in the next chapter. In the meantime, we examine the design of two open source projects that implement systems resembling Amazon EC2's IaaS platform and Google App Engine. One of these, Eucalyptus, is already available as a commercial open source offering: While data center automation technology aims to improve the efficiency of the entire data center, including a variety of platforms, legacy systems and hardware configurations, these open source projects (as well as some cloud management tools such as Enomaly) can be used to create private-cloud-like islands within enterprise data centers, but without promising to include all legacy platforms in their ambit. Deploying applications on these platforms involves similar steps as deploying on a public cloud, only that the hardware resources may be located in-house. It is also possible that hosting providers may leverage such platforms in the future to offer cloud-like services that mimic the larger cloud platforms, and in the process also offering interoperability and competing on price, location and personalized service. For this reason both these platforms, Eucalyptus and AppScale, merit a more detailed study.

## 17.3.1 IaaS using Eucalyptus

Eucalyptus [41] is an open source framework (developed at the University of California, Santa Barbara) that implements infrastructure as a service (IaaS) on a collection of server clusters. Eucalyptus Systems is a commercial offering based on this open source project, targeted at enterprises interested in building private clouds. The design of Eucalyptus also provides insights into the issues that need to be handled while creating an IaaS cloud, and serves as a platform for research in this emerging area. Since Eucalyptus implements external APIs identical to Amazon EC2, it also provides clues as to the possible internal architectures of such public clouds. For the same reason, Eucalyptus deployments can also be controlled by cloud management tools, such as RightScale (which in fact offers management of the experimental Eucalyptus cloud at UCSB).

Figure 17.2 illustrates the Eucalyptus architecture. Eucalyptus can run on a collection of one or more server clusters. Servers within each cluster are connected via a fast local Ethernet, while clusters can be connected to each other via possibly slower networks, such as private wide area networks or even the internet. Each server node runs the Xen hypervisor on which user virtual machines are provisioned on demand. Each cluster node also runs a Eucalyptus Instance Manager (IM) process on the XenLinux host operating system (provisioned automatically when Xen boots). One node in each cluster

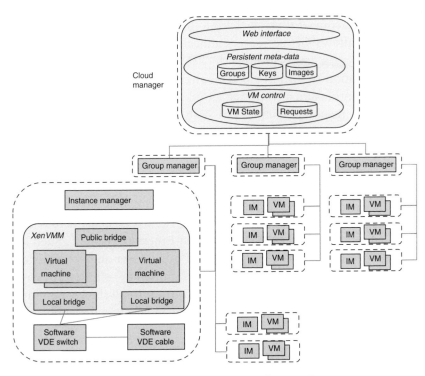

**FIGURE 17.2. Eucalyptus IaaS framework**

runs a Eucalyptus group manager (GM) process, and a single cloud manager (CM) process server is responsible for overall control of the Eucalyptus cloud, i.e. all clusters. The group managers and cloud manager run natively on specially designated servers rather than as virtual machines.

The cloud manager provides a web interface, including REST APIs identical to that of Amazon EC2, using which users can request for virtual servers and monitor their status. The cloud manager also maintains persistent meta-data describing the cloud, such as groups, their addresses, access keys given to users to connect to their assigned servers, as well as virtual machine images using which user virtual servers ma be provisioned. The cloud manager is responsible for controlling the entire cloud, and therefore also needs to track the dynamic state of all virtual machines in the cloud, the load, performance and utilizations of each cluster, as well as the status of all user requests.

Each instance manager on a cluster node is responsible for provisioning virtual machines as requested by its group manager, as well as communicating the status of the node, i.e. resource utilization and available capacity, to its group manager on request. Each group manager in turn monitors the status of its entire cluster and communicates that back to the cloud manager on request. The group manager also makes intra-cluster scheduling decisions in response to the requests it receives from the cloud manager.

Eucalyptus allows virtual servers allocated to a single cloud user (a virtual cluster) to span across groups; this feature ensures scalability as well as enable the creation of virtual clusters where some servers reside within an enterprise and others on an external cloud (akin to Amazon's virtual private cloud). Virtual machine instances in such virtual clusters need to be connected to each other, but must not be able to access any VMs belonging to another user. Vanilla virtualization does not cater to such isolation needs, i.e. a Xen VM that has access to the physical network of its server can in principle send packets to any server on that network. Therefore, to implement network isolation between users as well as provide transparent network connectivity within a user's virtual cluster, even if it spans across groups, Eucalyptus implements a virtual distributed Ethernet (VDE) [2]. Such a VDE is implemented using software switches on each server and software 'cables' between servers that hide the actual network topology, effectively providing a VLAN for each virtual cluster. Routing intra virtual cluster communication between groups via the VDE is therefore an additional responsibility of

---

[2] http://vde.sourceforge.net

Eucalyptus group managers. Finally, any virtual machine can additionally be connected to the 'public' network (via the local Ethernet), and publish a public IP address (via network address translation). Note that the 'public' network in this context could be the internet, a corporate wide area network or even a local LAN. At least one VM in a virtual cluster needs to be connected in this manner so as to enable users to access the virtual cluster from the public network.

## 17.3.2 PaaS on IaaS: AppScale

Recall (from Chapter 5) that the Google App Engine platform provides developers with an open source Python-based web-server (`dev_appserver.py`) that allows deployment of GAE applications on desktops, using which applications can be tested and debugged while being developed before they are uploaded to the Google PaaS cloud. The AppScale [11] open source project (also developed at the University of California, Santa Barbara) mimics the GAE platform through distributed deployment of the GAE development web-server on a cluster of virtual machines. Using AppScale, a GAE-like PaaS environment can be implemented in a scalable manner on an IaaS platform, such as EC2 or Eucalyptus.

Figure 17.3 illustrates the AppScale architecture. Instances of the GAE development web-server, `dev_appserver.py` are deployed on multiple virtual machines as an AppScale application server (AS) component. Since the datastore included with `dev_appserver.py` is a local file-based implementation that emulates the actual Google datastore APIs, this component is modified in AppScale so as to connect to a Hadoop HBase+HDFS deployment. (Recall that HBase and HDFS are open source implementations of Google's

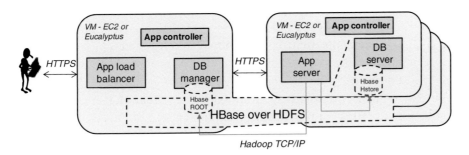

FIGURE 17.3. AppScale PaaS on IaaS architecture

BigTable and GFS architectures.) Therefore, AppScale also includes a collection of database server (DBS) components on a number of virtual machines on which HBase and HDFS run (these virtual machines can be the same ones on which AS components are deployed). Each AppScale node also runs an application controller (AC) that controls the AppScale components deployed on it.

An AppScale cluster includes one head node that implements a database manager (DBM) component that functions as the master node for the HBase and HDFS deployment. When an AS node needs to access the datastore, they communicate (via HTTPS) with the DBM to retrieve HBase meta-data following which it can communicate with the files storing HBase tables directly. A user interacts with the AC on the AppScale head node upload application code, which is also stored in the distributed AppScale datastore. Through this AC users also configure a set of virtual machines running AS servers; these VMs are dedicated to serve that user. The head node also includes an application load balancer (ALB) component which is responsible for directing incoming HTTP requests to one of the AS nodes assigned to a user.

It is important to note that the user's view of AppScale differs from GAE in an important respect: In GAE users are oblivious of which web-servers are used to serve their applications, how many servers are running, and how many different applications (belonging to different users) are served by each web-server. On the other hand, while AppScale enables execution of GAE applications, the level of control given to users as regards the VMs dedicated to serve their applications more closely resembles Microsoft Azure. For example, by combining AppScale and Amazon's dynamic monitoring and load balancing tools, it should be possible, in principle, to allow the set of virtual machines actually serving a user's application to vary automatically within pre-defined limits, just as in Azure.

# Roadmap for enterprise cloud computing

We are nearing the conclusion of our exploration of cloud computing; along the way we have also covered many aspects of enterprise architecture. Certain aspects of enterprise architecture may need to adapt to or be replaced by emerging paradigms, such as PaaS or Dev 2.0. At the same time many enterprise applications can, technically, be easily deployed in an IaaS cloud. We have also examined the question of cloud economics and shown that in principle public cloud can be cheaper, due to elasticity, and also faster to use, due to automated provisioning. We have also noted the additional cost advantages of PaaS platforms that enable public facing applications to be made available at no cost, with charges accruing only once load increases.

So, where could, and should, an enterprise begin leveraging the cloud? There are valid concerns with using public clouds from an enterprise perspective, especially with respect to (a) data confidentiality, lock-in, and auditability as well as (b) software licensing. Enterprises are still wary of placing production or sensitive data in the cloud, since current cloud offerings are essentially public networks and hence exposed to more attacks. While there are no fundamental obstacles to making a cloud environment as secure as an in-house data center, this requires careful planning using encrypted storage, virtual LANs and network middleware. Some cloud providers have begun to take the first steps towards these levels of security, such as Amazon's VPC.

When it comes to software licensing, while a few software vendors have begun making tools available in the cloud as bundled cloud-based AMIs, most have yet to transition to a usage-based model. High up-front software licensing costs can obviate any advantages of usage-based pricing at the infrastructure level, and to that extent limits the number of enterprise applications that can advantageously leverage IaaS public clouds.

Finally, when it comes to PaaS or Dev 2.0 platforms, these usually involve application migration or fresh development, primarily because of the novel development paradigms involved or non-relational data models. To what extent this will change with Microsoft Azure's support for standard relational SQL remains to be seen.

## 18.1 QUICK WINS USING PUBLIC CLOUDS

While keeping the above concerns in mind, we believe that the following areas, some of which have been briefly mentioned earlier in Section 4.4.3, represent opportunities for leveraging public clouds in the near term, without compromising on security or data risk. Further, each of these use cases specifically exploits the *elasticity* properties of public clouds.

### 18.1.1 Development and testing

The infrastructure needs for developing and testing enterprise applications are different from those of a production environment, for example the requirements regarding data security are lower. At the same time, variability and volatility is high, with servers being required for each new project, many of which can be released once the application is rolled out. Further, the time for provisioning and configuring a development environment can often become a significant overhead in many large organizations due to procurement and infrastructure management procedures. Leveraging cloud services for development-and-testing servers is therefore a cost-effective and low-risk option, which can also improve business agility in terms of how rapidly new applications can be developed.

Performance testing of new applications on a production capacity hardware configuration is difficult, especially early in the development cycle, simply because of non-availability of such an environment. Using the cloud a production-class infrastructure can be provisioned on demand and disbanded once the performance testing is complete.

## 18.1.2  Analytics in the cloud

We have already discussed the MapReduce-based cloud programming paradigm that enables massively parallel computations while automatically compensating for inevitable hardware and software failures. Such analytical tasks need the cloud and would be next to impossible in traditional data centers. On the other hand, normal enterprise analytics may not share such scale, but can benefit greatly from elasticity. Often enterprises need to run regular analytics on customers, supply chains or manufacturing operations, say on a daily basis. Such jobs may run for a few hours on dedicated hardware, and occasionally require even larger capacity, thus leading to over provisioning of infrastructure. Using the cloud, the required infrastructure can be provisioned when needed and disbanded thereafter. (Note that especially in the case of analytics, large volumes of data may be involved; it is important to recognize that one can circumvent this constraint by physically shipping data and transferring only small volumes over the network.)

## 18.1.3  Disaster planning in the cloud

Maintaining a disaster-recovery site that can be rapidly brought into production when needed to ensure business continuity requires replicating hardware infrastructure at least partially, which in normal circumstances may remain unutilized. Instead, it is possible to store a virtual image of the production environment in the cloud so that actual backup servers can be provisioned only when required. Similarly production data backups can be physically shipped to a location near the cloud provider on a regular basis and loaded into the cloud only when needed. Alternatively, updates can be replicated regularly over the network and exported to disk remotely rather than locally. Such cloud-based disaster-recovery mechanisms can be orders of magnitude cheaper than replicating infrastructure, while offering similar levels of protection and business continuity.

## 18.1.4  Low/Variable volume 24×7 portals

As a common scenario in the case of small or medium enterprises, consider a web-based portal or application that needs to be made available 24×7, but it is not clear how much traffic will flow to this site. Using a PaaS platform such as GAE such an application can be deployed without incurring *any* running costs, while also ensuring that the site will scale automatically if load increases. In fact, this model can be combined with IaaS processing, by using the PaaS platform to queue requests that are actually processed by more traditional applications that run on an IaaS cloud. Virtual resources on the IaaS cloud can be provisioned *on demand* when queues build up.

## 18.1.5 Enterprise mashup portals

A number of useful applications and data are available on the web in the form of 'mashups,' such as the Google Map mashup, that run as JavaScript code within the browser on a user's desktop. Allowing such mashups to be deployed within the user interface of an enterprise application is a potential security risk, since it requires the user's browser to allow 'cross-site scripting,' thereby allowing the browser to *simultaneously* connect to a server on the internet as well as the application server on the corporate network.

Instead, those pieces (i.e., pages) of enterprise applications that include public mashup applications can be hosted on servers deployed in a public cloud. Access to application services within the corporate network can be re-directed through secure web services instead of direct access from the user's browser, which is likely to be safer due to the additional layer of security introduced within the cloud-based server.

Thus, just as web-server technology was first used to create enterprise 'portal' architectures so that users could experience a single entry point to different enterprise applications, cloud platforms can play a similar role by integrating publicly available mashups with enterprise applications at the user interface level.

## 18.1.6 Mobile enterprise applications

Users now expect access to enterprise applications from mobile devices. Providing a rich mobile experience requires a return to 'fatter' client applications, as well as supporting disconnected operation via intelligent asynchronous data replication. Moreover, the fact that mobile devices are *personal*, rather than enterprise owned and controlled, introduces the need for an added layer of security. Cloud-based applications serving mobile clients could potentially provide such a secure intermediate layer, in a manner similar to that described above for mashups: Mobile clients could connect to specific subsets of application functionality deployed in cloud-based servers. Support for asynchronous data replication as well as secure access to web services published by applications within the corporate network would be provided within the cloud-based server.

### 18.1.7 Situational applications using Dev 2.0

As we have seen in Chapters 12 and 14, it is possible to achieve order-of-magnitude improvements in software development productivity using Dev 2.0 platforms, such as Force.com or TCS InstantApps. If one were to take an inventory of all applications in a large enterprise, we would typically find a small number of complex, highly loaded, mission-critical applications, a moderate number of departmental applications of medium complexity and usage, and finally a large 'long tail' of small, lightly loaded, 'situational' applications. Examples includes custom workflow and mashup applications assembled to drive simple internal automation or pilot new business processes within individual business units. Dev 2.0 platforms deployed in public clouds are ideal for situational applications, since business units can rapidly provision, configure, use and then discard such applications.

### 18.2 FUTURE OF ENTERPRISE CLOUD COMPUTING

Moving beyond the immediate, let us now consider what technological and industry trends are likely to drive the cloud computing ecosystem in the future. In the process we may unearth some clues as to how cloud computing may eventually come to impact enterprise IT.

As has been well elucidated in the popular book *The Big Switch* [8], the evolution of industrial use of electricity from private generating plants to a public electricity grid can serve as an illuminating analogy for the possible evolution of enterprise IT and cloud computing. In such an analogy, privately run enterprise data centers are analogous to private electric plants whereas the public electricity grid illustrates a possible model towards which the public clouds of today may evolve.

As another analogy, let us consider data communications: In the initial days of digital networks, corporations owned their own data communication lines. Today all data communication lines are owned by operators who lease them out, not only to end-users, but also to each other. The physical resource (bandwidth) has become a commodity, and it is only in the mix of value added services where higher profits are to be made.

## 18.2.1 Commoditization of the data center

We are already seeing trends towards commoditization of computation and storage hardware. It is precisely by utilizing commodity hardware efficiently that the large cloud providers have been able to achieve their operational efficiencies of scale. The next stage of evolution is for larger collections of hardware to become standardized, starting with racks of servers, and eventually the data center itself. We are already seeing evidence of this in dedicated hosting providers who are now striving to move 'up' the value chain into cloud computing, as their core business comes under margin pressure. Eventually, it is possible that the highly virtualized, power efficient data center, offering on-demand resource provisioning, also becomes a commodity product, much like servers and storage today, as illustrated in Figure 18.1.

Apart from the natural process of standardization and commoditization, there are additional drivers leading data center commoditization: An

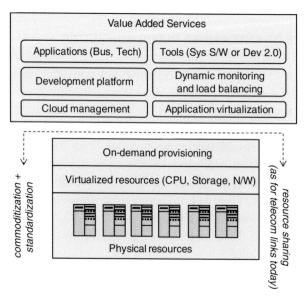

FIGURE 18.1. Commoditization of the data center

important concern for enterprise adoption of cloud computing is the physical location of data centers on which clouds operate. In certain industries, such as financial services and health-care, many governments regulate the location of physical storage of data to be within a specified geographical area, such as a country or continent. As a result, cloud providers such as Amazon maintain data centers in different geographical regions, and allow users to choose which 'regions' their virtual resources and data will be provisioned in. At the same time, a large number of enterprises already rely on managed hosting providers instead of housing their servers in-house, and as we have seen, many of these are already beginning to exploit virtualization and automated provisioning technologies. These data centers also need to be physically located so as to conform to the same regulations. The resulting possibility for evolution of the cloud ecosystem is outlined below:

## 18.2.2 Inter-operating Virtualized Data Centers

So far, data centers managed by different providers operate in isolation in the sense that while end-users can often provision resources on-demand in these facilities, trading of capacity between such facilities, such as is the case for electricity or even data communications bandwidth, does not take place.

The key technology elements that could enable on-demand exchange of capacity are already in place: It is possible to programmatically provision and access resources using web services, as demonstrated by IaaS providers and frameworks such as Eucalyptus. What is missing is standardization of such APIs so that business models and trading can be based on a non-proprietary mechanism of making requests and ensuring service levels. However, we believe this is not far away. What could become possible if and when such standardization does happen?

Recall that the larger data centers (such as maintained by cloud providers) are almost always located near cheap power sources, thereby significantly lowering their running costs. Now, we speculate whether a natural evolution of such an ecosystem might not see data center owners, be they providers of dedicated hosting or cloud computing, begin leasing data center resources to *each other* and not only to end-users. From an enterprise perspective this could, for example, enable a managed hosting provider to ensure that a customer's applications are run on a mix of servers, some physically nearby, while others are leased from a larger-scale provider who reaps economies of scale, while also ensuring that any geographical constraints on data storage are maintained.

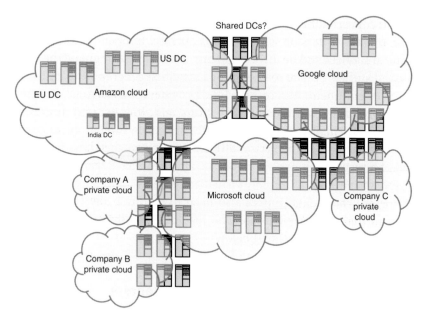

FIGURE 18.2. Future of enterprise cloud computing?

Further, with standardization of the virtualized data center and capacity exchange APIs, it should also become possible for different cloud providers to either co-locate or cross-lease their data centers, so that, for example a portal running on Google App Engine can communicate with a database running on an Amazon EC2 virtual server without having to traverse the public internet: In other words, while these services are managed by different providers, the servers they happen to use for a particular user reside in data centers that are 'near' each other from a network perspective, i.e. on a high-speed LAN rather than a WAN. Speculating even further, even some of the servers that an enterprise considers 'in-house' may also actually reside in the same or 'nearby' data centers, as part of a managed hosting service. Finally, of course, users connect to applications using VPNs over the internet, or through dedicated leased lines for better performance. Such a scenario is illustrated in Figure 18.2.

## 18.2.3 Convergence of private and public clouds

As we have mentioned earlier in Chapter 6, all but the largest enterprises are unlikely to enjoy economies of scale similar to public clouds, and those who do may end up becoming public cloud providers themselves in the future.

Further, the virtualized data center with on-demand provisioning may end up being a commodity that one can buy off the shelf, much like a basic server today. As we have discussed above, it may become the case that enterprises will use servers in managed data centers, be they based on dedicated hosting or clouds, with many of these servers naturally being co-located or at least 'near' each other from a network perspective. Moreover, whether or not servers are dedicated to an enterprise, or are virtual servers on shared resources, they can all be connected on the same virtual private network so that from both a performance as well as network address space perspective, they are essentially indistinguishable.

What this means is that the distinction between public and private clouds becomes blurred, just as it is today for communications: Users are essentially oblivious as to exactly which physical cables their data traffic travels on, even on an *internal* corporate WAN, and whether or not at the lowest levels it is multiplexed with traffic from other users.

So, what technologies should an enterprise focus on when exploring how their data centers will be managed? Virtualization and on-demand provisioning, we believe, will become available off the shelf. The areas to focus on when exploring private clouds are the higher layers of Figure 18.1, i.e. cloud management, dynamic load balancing, application virtualization and software tools. These are more complex features, where there is likely to be more competition and value addition, and where standardization is unlikely, at least in the near future. At the same time, it is also precisely these areas where the cloud ecosystem will provide many alternative solutions to choose from. Finally, the cloud ecosystem itself will become far more usable once such services deployed 'in the cloud' *appear*, for all practical purposes, to be 'inside' the enterprise, from either a network address or performance perspective.

## 18.2.4 Generalized 'cloud' services

As we conclude our exploration of cloud computing, it is natural to ask whether the efficiencies promised by the cloud computing model can, in any way, be generalized to other arenas of knowledge-based work. Recall the key elements of cloud computing, as we outlined at the outset of our journey in Section 1.1:

- Computing resources packaged as a **commodity** and made available over the internet.
- **Rapid provisioning** of resources by end-users.

- A **usage-based pricing** model that charges consumers only for those cloud resources they actually use.

In Chapter 12 and 14 we introduced and described Dev 2.0 platforms. In a sense, Dev 2.0 platforms offer similar 'cloud-like' features, but in the domain of software development:

- Application functionality packaged as re-usable templates; a **commodity** of sorts.
- **Rapid provisioning** of new applications using multi-tenant platforms.
- **Usage-based pricing**, on the basis of the number of users, transaction volume or application complexity.

Can such 'cloud-like' features be achieved in other arenas? We consider here the case of *services*, such as those often outsourced to a software development provider, a call-center or an insurance claims processor; more generally, any other knowledge-based task that can be outsourced using information technology.

The traditional outsourcing model has been that of 'time-and-materials' (T&M) billing. Using cloud vs. in-house resources as an analogy, T&M is the equivalent of deploying an 'in-house' data center, where the onus of making efficient use of the resources deployed lies entirely with the customer rather than the provider.

Another outsourcing model is that of fixed-price projects, where detailed specifications are drawn up by the customer and executed in by the services provider according to a pre-determined price and schedule. A fixed-price project is analogous to a data center managed by a dedicated infrastructure provider at a fixed price while adhering to stringent SLAs[1]. In the fixed-price model, all the risk lies with the supplier, be it a data-center provider or services contractor. Naturally, providers of fixed-price projects account for their risks within their pricing models. Further, the onus of providing detailed specifications or defining service levels falls on the customer. Thus, even the fixed-price model has inefficiencies built into it.

Is there something better, i.e., a model for outsourcing services that exhibits some of the 'cloud-like' features described above? For example, how can we define services as a composition of commodity tasks? How can end-users easily request for and 'provision' services once having broken up their project into such tasks? And finally, how can the price of such tasks be objectively

---

[1] Service-level agreements.

estimated, as unambiguously as, say, the price per cpu-hour in the domain of cloud-based resources?

Hopefully such questions can and will be answered. Perhaps the model-based abstractions used to architect Dev 2.0 platforms may also have a role to play in the process. Only time will tell how far and how rapidly the transition to 'cloud-like' infrastructure, development tools and services will take place in the complex world of enterprise IT.

# References

[1] A. Leff and J. Rayfield. WebRB: Evaluating a visual domain-specific language for building relational web-applications. In *Proceedings, OOPSLA,* 2007.

[2] Azza Abouzeid, Kamil BajdaPawlikowski, Daniel Abadi, Avi Silberschatz and Alexander Rasin. Hadoopdb: An architectural hybrid of MapReduce and dbms technologies for analytical workloads. In *International Conference on Very Large Databases (VLDB),* 2009.

[3] Sanjay Agrawal, Surajit Chaudhuri and Gautam Das. Dbxplorer: enabling keyword search over relational databases. In *Proceedings of the 2002 ACM SIGMOD International Conference on Management of Data,* 2002.

[4] M. Armbrust, A. Fox, R. Griffith, *et al.* Above the clouds: A Berkeley view of cloud computing. Technical report, UC Berkeley, 2009.

[5] M. M. Astrahan, M. W. Blasgen, D. D. Chamberlin, *et al.* System r: A relational approach to database management. *ACM Transactions on Database Systems,* **1–2**, 1976.

[6] K. Beck. *Extreme Programming Explained: Embrace Change.* Addison-Wesley Professional, 1999.

[7] Dimitri P. Bertsekas and Robert G. Gallagher. *Data Networks.* Prentice Hall, 1987.

[8] Nicholas Carr. *The Big Switch.* W.W. Norton, 2008.

[9] F. Chang, J. Dean, S. Ghemawat, *et al.* BigTable: A distributed storage system for structured data. In *Symposium on Operating Systems Design and Implementation (OSDI),* 2006.

[10] Hung chih Yang, Ali Dasdan, Ruey-Lung Hsiao, and D. Stott Parker. Map Reduce-merge: simplified relational data processing on large clusters. In *Proceedings of the ACM SIGMOD International Conference on Management of Data*, 2007.

[11] Navraj Chohan, Chris Bunch, Sydney Pang, *et al.* Appscale design and implementation. Technical report, Computer Science Department, University of California, Santa Barbara, 2009-02.

[12] Jeffrey Dean and Sanjay Ghemawat. MapReduce: Simplified data processing on large clusters. In *Proceedings of the 6th Symp. on Operating Systems Design and Implementation*, 2004.

[13] Jeffrey Dean and Sanjay Ghemawat. MapReduce: A flexible data processing tool, *Communication of the ACM*, **53**(1), 2010.

[14] Giuseppe DeCandia, Deniz Hastorun, Madan Jampani, *et al.* Dynamo: Amazon's highly available key-value store. In *Proceedings of SOSP*, 2007.

[15] S. Deerswster, S. Dumais, T. Landauer, G. Furnas and R. Harshman. Indexing by latent semantic analysis. *J. American Society for Information Science*, **41**, 1990.

[16] David J. DeWitt, Erik Paulson, Eric Robinson, *et al.* Clustera: an integrated computation and data management system. In *Proceedings of the VLDB Endowment*, August 2008.

[17] Jeff Dike. A user-mode port of the linux kernel. In *2000 Linux Showcase and Conference*, 2000.

[18] Petros Drineas, Michael W. Mahoney, and S. Muthukrishnan. Subspace sampling and relative-error matrix approximation: Column-row-based methods. In *Algorithms-ESA 2006*, Lecture Notes in Computer Science 4168, Springer, 2006.

[19] Robert Filman, Tzilla Elrad, Siobhán Clarke and Mehmet Aksit. *Aspect Oriented Software Development*. Addison-Wesley Professional, 2004.

[20] Martin Fowler. *UML Distilled: A Brief Guide to the Standard Object Modeling Language*. Addison-Wesley, 2004.

[21] G. C. Fox. *Solving Problems on Concurrent Processors*. Prentice Hall, 1988.

[22] Eric Friedman, Peter Pawlowski and John Cieslewicz. SQL/MapReduce: A practical approach to selfdescribing, polymorphic, and parallelizable userdefined functions. In *International Conference on Very Large Databases (VLDB)*, 2009.

[23] A. Frieze, R. Kannan and S. Vempala. Fast Monte Carlo algorithms for finding low-rank approximations. *Journal of the ACM*, **51**(6), 2004.

[24] T. Garfinkel, B. Pfaff, J. Chow, M. Rosenblum and D. Boneh. Terra: A virtual machine based platform for trusted computing. In *Proceedings of SOSP 2003*, 2003.

[25] T. Garfinkel and M. Rosenblum. A virtual machine introspection based architecture for intrusion detection. In *Network and Distributed Systems Security Symposium, February 2003*, 2003.

[26] S. Ghemawat, H. Gobioff and S.T. Leung. Google File System. In *Proceedings of the 19th ACM SOSP Conference*, Dec 2003.

[27] Gene H. Golub and Charles F. Van Loan. *Matrix Computations*. Johns Hopkins University Press, 1989.

[28] Sudipto Guha, Rajeev Rastogi and Kyuseok Shim. Cure: an efficient clustering algorithm for large databases. *Information Systems*, **26**(1), 2001.

[29] E. Huedo, R. S. Montero and I. M. Llorente. A framework for adaptive execution in grids. *Software Practice and Experience*, **34**, 631–651, 2004.

[30] Michael N. Huhns and Munindar P. Singh. *Service Oriented Computing*. John Wiley & Sons, 2005.

[31] J. Dobrowolski and J. Kolodziej. A method of building executable platform-independent application models. In *OMG's MDA Implementers' Workshop*, 2004.

[32] K. Kulkarni and S. Reddy. A model-driven approach for developing business applications: experience, lessons learnt and a way forward. In *1st India Software Engineering Conference ISEC 2008*, 2008.

[33] Pat Kennedy, Vivek Bapat and Paul Kurchina. *In Pursuit of the Perfect Plant*. Evolved Technologist, 2008.

[34] Glenn E. Krasner and Stephen T. Pope. A description of the model-view-controller user interface paradigm in the smalltalk-80 system. *Journal of Object-oriented Programming*, **1**(3), 26–49, 1988.

[35] L. Lamport. Time, clocks, and the ordering of events in a distributed system. *ACM Communications*, **21**(7), 1978.

[36] B. D. Ligneris. Virtualization of linux-based computers: The linux-vserver project. In *19th International Symposium on High Performance Computing Systems and Applications, HPCS 2005*, 40–346, 2005.

[37] Albert Lulushi. *Oracle Forms Developer's Handbook*. Prentice Hall, 2000.

[38] Christopher D. Manning, Prabhakar Raghavan and Hinrich Schutze. *An Introduction to Information Retrieval*. Cambridge University Press, 2008.

[39] B. C. Neuman and T. Ts'o. Kerberos: An authentication service for computer networks. *IEEE Communications*, **32**(9), 1994.

[40] Nils J. Nilsson. *Principles of Artificial Intelligence*. Springer, 1982.

[41] D. Nurmi, R. Wolski, C. Grzegorczyk, *et al*. The eucalyptus open-source cloud-computing system. In *Proceedings of the 9th IEEE/ACM International Symposium on Cluster Computing and the Grid*, 2009.

[42] Christopher Olston, Benjamin Reed, Utkarsh Srivastava, Ravi Kumar and Andrew Tomkins. Pig Latin: A not-so-foreign language for data processing. In *Proceedings of the 2008 ACM SIGMOD International Conference on Management of Data*, 2008.

[43] Christos H. Papadimitrou, Prabhakar Raghavan, Hisao Tamaki and Santosh Vemela. Latent semantic indexing: A probabilistic analysis. *Journal of Computer and System Sciences*, **61**(2), 217–235, 2000.

[44] Andrew Pavlo, Erik Paulson, Alexander Rasin, *et al*. A comparison of approaches to large-scale data analysis. In *Proceedings of the 2009 ACM SIGMOD International Conference on Management of Data*, 2009.

[45] G. Popek and R. Goldberg. Formal requirements for virtualizable third generation architectures. *Communications of the ACM*, **17**, 12–421, 1974.

[46] Raghu Ramakrishnan and Johanes Gehrke. *Database Management Systems*. McGraw-Hill, 2003.

[47] L. A. Rowe and K. A. Shoens. A form application development system. In *Proceedings of the ACM-SIGMOD International Conference on the Management of Data*, 1982.

[48] Lawrence A. Rowe, Joseph A. Konstan, Brian C. Smith, Steve Seitz, and Chung Liu. The Picasso application framework. In *Proceedings 4th Annual ACM Symposium on User Interface Software and Technology*, 1991.

[49] C. P. Sapuntzakis, R. Chandra, B. Pfaff, *et al*. Optimizing the migration of virtual computers. In *5th Symposium on Operating Systems Design and Implementation (OSDI), ACM Operating Systems Review*, 2002.

[50] Mary Shaw and David Garlan. *Software Architecture: Perspectives on and Emerging Discipline*. Prentice Hall, 1996.

[51] Gautam Shroff. Dev 2.0: Model driven development in the cloud. In *Proceedings of the 16th ACM SIGSOFT International Symposium on Foundations of Software Engineering (FSE)*, 2008.

[52] Gautam Shroff, Puneet Agarwal and Premkumar Devanbu. InstantApps: A wysiwyg model driven interpreter for web applications. In *31st International Conference on Software Engineering, ICSE Companion Volume*, 2009.

[53] Gautam Shroff, Puneet Agarwal and Premkumar Devanbu. Multi-tier web applications without tears. In *Proceeding of the 2nd Annual India Software Engineering Conference (ISEC)*, 2009.

[54] Gautam Shroff and S. Santhanakrishnan. Methodologies for software architecture definition: A component based view. In *International Conference on Software Systems and Applications, Paris*, 2001.

[55] Len Silverston. *The Data Model Resource Book, Vol. 1: A Library of Universal Data Models for All Enterprises*. John Wiley & Sons, 2008.

[56] David Skillicorn. *Understanding Complex Datasets*. Chapman & Hall/CRC, 2007.

[57] D. B. Skillicorn. Clusters within clusters: SVD and counter-terrorism. In *SIAM Data Mining Conference*, March 2003.

[58] Jim Smith and Ravi Nair. *Virtual Machines: Versatile Platforms for Systems and Processes*. Morgan Kaufmann, 2005.

[59] Michael Stonebraker, Daniel Abadi, David J. DeWitt, *et al*. MapReduce and parallel DBMSs: Friends or foes?, *Communications of the ACM*, 53(1), 2010.

[60] Michael Stonebraker, Gerald Held, Eugene Wong and Peter Kreps. The design and implementation of ingres. *ACM Transactions on Database Systems*, 1–3, 1976.

[61] Mike Stonebraker, Daniel J. Abadi, Adam Batkin, *et al*. '-store: a column-oriented dbms. In *Proceedings of the 31st International Conference on Very Large Databases, Trondheim, Norway*, 2005.

[62] Ashish Thusoo, Joydeep Sen Sarma, Namit Jain, *et al*. Hive a warehousing solution over a MapReduce framework. In *International Conference on Very Large Databases (VLDB)*, 2009.

[63] John A. Zachman. A framework for information systems architecture. *IBM Systems Journal*, 26(3), 1987.

[64] L. Zhu, L. Osterweil, M. Staples, U. Kannengiesser, and B. I. Simidchieva. Desiderata for languages to be used in the definition of reference business processes. *International Journal of Software and Informatics*, 1(1), 97–121, 2007.

# Index